Additional Praise for *Staging Politics and Gender*

"In *Staging Politics and Gender*, Cecilia Beach paints a vivid picture of the culture of radical politics in Paris during the period 1880 to 1923. Chapters on early feminists Louise Michel, Madeleine Pelletier, Nelly Roussel, Véra Starkoff, and Marie Lenéru describe and analyze long-forgotten dramatic works that were performed for popular audiences. What these agitprop, thesis plays, and plays of social protest have in common is the goal of creating a more egalitarian secular society in which women have control over their sexuality, reproductive and maternal rights, protection against domestic violence, and the right to divorce. The exhaustive and meticulous research that went into writing this illuminating study prepares Beach to place first-wave feminism in its historical context and to explain how militant activists used drama to fight for women's rights."
—Jane Moss, Robert E. Diamond Professor of French and Women's Studies, Colby College

"Through patient and original research, Cecilia Beach does an inspiring job of filling in the history of women in French theatre from the 1880s to just after World War I. Her broad-based study identifies five activists, often fiery, playwrights: Louise Michel, Nelly Roussel, Véra Starkoff, Dr. Madeleine Pelletier, and Marie Lenéru, shedding new light on anarchist and feminist cultural work and examining what forms politicized theatre and theatre for the 'people' have used to best effect."
—Judith Miller, Chair, Department of French, New York University

"Cecilia Beach has gone back to the heroic period of the battles for women's rights; to the time when universal secular education was available for the first time in France, when the new socialist ideas were being promoted through the Universités Populaires. She has demonstrated the key role played by women in the formulation of progressive thought at this time, and has written a meticulously researched study of the role of women dramatists in the most advanced political movements of the period. The names of Louise Michel, Nelly Roussel, Véra Starkoff,

Madeleine Pelletier and Marie Lenéru are almost unknown in the context of theatre history. This publication restores them to their rightful place and will be an essential volume in all libraries specialising in theatre studies. In the year when the Nobel prize went to Elfriede Jellinek, known partly for her play that portrays the struggles of Nora once she leaves her 'doll's house,' it is particularly good to see this study of Nora's contemporary sisters appearing."
—David Bradby, Professor of Drama and Theatre Studies, Royal Holloway, University of London

"The historical continuities highlighted by Beach are among the most valuable qualities of this book. It is now possible to contextualize properly Apollinaire's *Mamelles de Tiresias*—a nativist, antifeminist play on the burlesque mode—in the face of the feminists' early struggles for abortion and birth-control, and their works for the stage promoting women's issues. Madeleine Pelletier's tragic fate—a medical doctor, she was institutionalized as deranged—is only the best known case of the repression and censorship feminists were exposed to a century ago. The very history of feminist playwrights, journalists, and militants of the Belle Epoque has largely been ignored, so Beach's book brings both a sense of wonder and relief. Now we have new, fascinating, readable evidence of the debates on marriage and procreation women playwrights produced . . . The alliance of socialism and feminism—such as we have applauded it late in the century with Mnouchkine or Duras—is shown as another major phase in the dialectics of politics and art, one illustrated by an Olympe de Gouges, two centuries ago. This is a work of superb scholarship, sobriety of tone and style; it conveys admiration and respect for her "subjects," five women playwrights at the turn of the century. It opens a totally fresh, exciting window on the era: those struggles were stifled by WWI and Simone de Beauvoir grew up mostly sheltered from them, by circumstance and education. No doubt, the author of *The Second Sex*—who tried her own, modest sally on stage with *Les Bouches inutiles*—would have fully shared our enthusiasm for this compelling contribution to the writing of French women's cultural history."
—Christiane P. Makward, Professor of French, Francophone, and Women's Studies, Pennsylvania State University

Staging Politics and Gender

French Women's Drama, 1880–1923

Cecilia Beach

842.8099287
B36A

STAGING POLITICS AND GENDER
© Cecilia Beach, 2005.

First published in 2005 by
PALGRAVE MACMILLAN™
175 Fifth Avenue, New York, N.Y. 10010 and
Houndmills, Basingstoke, Hampshire, England RG21 6XS
Companies and representatives throughout the world.

PALGRAVE MACMILLAN is the global academic imprint of the Palgrave Macmillan division of St. Martin's Press, LLC and of Palgrave Macmillan Ltd. Macmillan® is a registered trademark in the United States, United Kingdom and other countries. Palgrave is a registered trademark in the European Union and other countries.

ISBN 1–4039–6585–4

Library of Congress Cataloging-in-Publication Data is available from the Library of Congress.

A catalogue record for this book is available from the British Library.

Design by Newgen Imaging Systems (P) Ltd., Chennai, India.

First edition: June 2005

10 9 8 7 6 5 4 3 2 1

Printed in the United States of America.

To Laurent

Contents

Acknowledgments

I am grateful to all the friends, family and colleagues who have given me support through the years while I have been working on this project. In particular, I would like to thank my chair, Sandra Singer, for her continual encouragement, as well as Kerry Kautzman, Ariana Huberman, Vicki Westacott, Carol Burdick, and Laurent Dappe for their help editing the manuscript in its various stages of development. This project would not have been possible without the help of the librarians at Herrick Library in Alfred; la Bibliothèque nationale de France, la Bibliothèque de l'Arsenal, and la Bibliothèque Marguerite Durand in Paris; the British Library; and the International Institute of Social History in Amsterdam. Special thanks to Yves Dappe, Francine Nguyen, Gilles Effront, Sonia Peterson, Anton Valdine, and Jim Yarin for their assistance uncovering the identity of Véra Starkoff and providing information about her family background. Finally, I would like to thank the Alfred University NEH Endowment Fund committee for awarding me two grants to conduct research in Europe.

CHAPTER ONE

Introduction: Theater, Politics, and Gender

Theater is a political practice. By this, I do not mean that all theater is self-consciously militant, but that all theater is influenced by the political systems at work in a society. It is impossible to separate any work of art from the social conditions of the time when it was created, whether it simply reflects the mainstream constructs of the day or challenges those constructs. Theater is no exception. The very public nature of most theatrical practice makes it all the more subject to the vicissitudes of society. Any given performance not only involves the collaboration of writers, directors, actors, designers, and technicians, but also depends on publishers, critics, spectators, financiers, and the government. A play that may appear harmlessly to depict the status quo in one time and place may be considered subversive in another. A work forbidden by the censors of one government may enjoy the moral and financial support of another. A performance that speaks to the social reforms at the turn of the century will most likely seem irrelevant 50 years later.

Similarly, the purported "quality" of a play depends greatly on the society and the time in which it was written, read, or performed. In his 1978 study of the relationship between aesthetics and ideology, George Szanto explains:

> the artwork has no intrinsic value. [. . .] Taste, like aesthetics, will be considered a product of ideological education. [. . .] It makes little sense to say, "Such a work is good." It becomes important to ask, "Good for whom as audience, or what organization or class or sponsor, and why is the specific result of such appreciation a good thing?" (11–12)

Szanto suggests that a more useful category would be "functioning art," based on whether the work of art has succeeded and whether it continues to be of interest. The fact that medieval mystery plays and the tragedies of Voltaire are no longer staged often does not mean that they are not "good plays," but rather that they have ceased to be "functioning art." They remain valuable for their place in literary history and may well function again for a future audience. The renewal of interest in the Paris Commune, for example, has led to a renewal of interest in the works of Louise Michel in the past decade. Her play *La Grève*, though rarely described as "good theater" since its original performance in 1890, was recently published in an anthology of political plays, and excerpts of the play were performed in a "Cabaret Anarchiste à la Belle Époque" in Paris.[1]

Szanto claims that all theater is a form of ideological propaganda. He distinguishes *agitation propaganda*, whose goal is to bring about change and to incite its audience to action, from *integration propaganda*, which, on the contrary, attempts to reinforce the status quo, to pacify its audience. Agitation propaganda is most often overt since it presents an obvious challenge to the authorities in place; integration propaganda is usually covert, unrecognized as propaganda by the members of mainstream society and often unintentional on the part of the author. A third, more complex form of propaganda, which Szanto calls *dialectical propaganda*, corresponds to the dramatic form of dialectical materialism:

> A theater of dialectical propaganda, as a theater of cognitive clarifi-
> cation, will present detailed and structured information through a
> dramatic medium in order to depict for its audience circumstances
> not previously understood. It will demystify relationships between
> individuals and institutions, so as to show, first, the nature of passions
> and of economic and social laws, and second, to demonstrate methods
> by which human beings can control themselves and their institutions.
> (Szanto 76)

Of these three types, integration propaganda is the most prevalent, though the least visible. Many more theatrical performances support mainstream ideologies rather than challenge them. This was certainly true in nineteenth-century France when the theater was heavily controlled by the state. Only three brief periods during the nineteenth century were free from censorship, each following a political revolution: for five years after 1830, for two and a half years after 1848, and for six months in 1870. Other than these periods, theater censorship always existed. Even without official censorship, the theater is dependent on the authority of those with socioeconomic privilege and power:

> Economic and social factors, indirectly or directly, determine *authority*—the production of texts and performances: who has the time and the status to write for the public, who publishes or performs the texts, which dramatists are deemed relevant and important, who is canonized as a "master," who attends the performances or reads the texts, and so forth. (Taylor 5)

On the other hand, theater as a live performance has the potential to undermine the authority in unpredictable and thus uncontrollable ways. A play that may appear to support the authority on paper may challenge it in performance thanks to a subversive mise en scène. The interpretation of a given performance by a bourgeois audience may differ entirely from its interpretation by a working-class audience. Those who are part of the hegemony may not recognize subtle criticisms that appear evident to less mainstream members of the audience.

Reaching a working-class audience has been a challenge in itself. The modern Western theater has attracted a primarily bourgeois, elite audience. As a commercial enterprise, theater was, according to Edouard Rothen in the *Encyclopédie Anarchiste*, "dévoué, pour la recette, au fumier bourgeois" (2768).[2] Moreover, the working and living conditions of the workers were hardly conducive to attending the theater on a regular basis:

> horaires, cadences, transports urbains pénibles et coûteux, niveau des salaires, insuffisances des équipements collectifs (crèches, garderies), autant d'éléments qui, conjugués aux inégalités d'accès à l'éducation, constituent des freins sociaux au développement culturel en général. (Poulet 31)[3]

Throughout the late nineteenth and twentieth centuries, partisans of social and political theater have attempted to develop alternative drama venues, aesthetics, and techniques in order to undermine the bourgeois monopoly on both theatrical production and consumption. Such endeavors have included community theater, the theater in the Université Populaire, decentralization, and the people's theater movement. According to Bradby and McCormick, "The most significant development in the theatre during [the twentieth] century has been the broadening of its social basis" (11).

The notion that the practice and reception of theater are influenced by the political systems of the society does not mean that all theater is political theater. Neither are all plays that represent the political arena necessarily political plays. In this study, I use the term political theater to refer to plays that are written and performed intentionally for political purposes. In this sense, nearly all the plays discussed in this book are political plays; their goal is to exert an influence on the political opinions and practices of their audience. With the exception of Marie Lenéru, all the authors we discuss were actively involved in political movements. Writing plays represented one form of activism for them along with public speaking and journalism.

Graham Holderness points out that modern political theater is most often inspired by left-wing ideology:

> What [the different types of political theatre] have in common is a clear and overt commitment to socialist ideas, which in turn colors the form and content of their cultural production. But where is there a political theatre of the right? It seems that political theatre can be progressive but not regressive; socialist but not conservative; subversive but not conformist or radically reactionary. (3)

Indeed, nearly all the plays analyzed in this book show an overt commitment to socialist, anarchist, or feminist ideas. The majority of conservative political theater by French women playwrights was produced by members of the religious Right. Much of the *théâtre de patronage* (theater for Church youth groups), in which women have traditionally been very active, could be considered political theater in that it overtly supports conservative, even reactionary, political and religious ideology and aims to exert an influence over the opinions and actions of its audience. Such would be the case, for example, of the natalist plays by Ève Baudouin and Henriette Charasson in the interwar period.[4]

In the second half of the nineteenth century, a tradition of socially significant drama developed throughout Europe; the theater for many playwrights like Ibsen, Shaw, Strindberg, and Zola became a means of making the audience think, of modifying their opinions, their habits and their behavior, and even of influencing political decisions. In *The Social Significance of Modern Drama*, anarchist revolutionary Emma Goldman applauds late-nineteenth-century European drama for its revolutionary potential. For Goldman, playwrights such as Ibsen, Strindberg, Hauptmann, and Tolstoy are the "social iconoclasts of our time":

> They know that society has gone beyond the stage of patching up, and that man must throw off the dead weight of the past, with all its

ghosts and spooks, if he is to go free to meet the future. This is the social significance which differentiates modern dramatic art from art for art's sake. It is the dynamite which undermines superstition, shakes social pillars, and prepares men and women for reconstruction. (3)

Goldman rejects the conservative distinction between artists and "the 'rabble' that makes revolutions":

any mode of creative work, which with true perception portrays social wrongs earnestly and boldly, may be a greater menace to our social fabric and a more powerful inspiration than the wildest harangue of the soapbox orator. (1–2)

German Marxists of the mid-nineteenth century had already understood the political potential of the theater. Freidrich Engels himself composed plays about revolution to be performed in political clubs, as did Ferdinand Lassalle. Jean Baptiste von Schweitzer wrote a play called *Der Schlingel* in 1867–1868 in which he hoped to introduce the audience to the concepts of Marx's *Capital* by way of an entertaining dialogue. In a second play, *Die Gans*, von Schweitzer clearly advocates economic equality for women. Drama flourished in the working-class educational clubs that multiplied in Germany in the 1860s and 1870s until the anti-socialist laws made it illegal to perform or publish political plays (Gray 5). This very prohibition is evidence of the perceived power of political theater.

Late-nineteenth-century anarchists, like the German Marxists earlier in the century, generally recognized the arts as a powerful mode of propaganda. Unlike other socialist factions, following the schism in 1881, anarchists refused to participate in the political system in its legal form. Having no unified political party or bureaucratic network to spread the message, they made use, instead, of a wide range of propagandistic media. These included not only the dramatic acts of violence that we associate with anarchism—propaganda by the deed—but also theater, cabaret songs, lectures, and the anarchist press—propaganda by the word. According to Richard Sonn, "[f]or every attention-getting deed there were dozens of anarchist schools, cafés, and cabarets, libraries and theater groups" (*Anarchism* 50). David Weir argues in *Anarchy and Culture* that "anarchism is as much a cultural as a political phenomenon" (12). He maintains "that anarchism succeeded culturally where it failed politically" (5).[5]

Theater was perhaps the anarchist art par excellence given that the culture was largely oral and the politics particularly dramatic. "Politics," explains Richard Sonn, "were prone to the fin de siècle love of stage settings and theatricality, in an era when personal acts acquired a highly visible and public character" (*Anarchism and Cultural Politics* 68). Furthermore, in the theater, a didactic message could be camouflaged within a cathartic experience like terrorist bombs or the death of a martyr. According to the *Encyclopédie anarchiste*, the theater is a more persuasive method of instruction than the novel "parce qu'il frappe plus vivement l'esprit, il y incruste son enseignement par le souvenir de l'image" (2757).[6] Thanks to the visual power of drama, the theater can inspire passions and new ideas better than other forms of literature. By combining propaganda by the word and propaganda by the deed, theater was therefore theoretically an effective means of, in the words of Kropotkin, "preaching by example" in order "to awaken audacity and the spirit of revolt" (Qtd. in Quail 9).

Anarchist theater could be staged anywhere, from cabarets to private homes to noncommercial theaters. Private venues were generally preferable, not for reasons of elitism but rather to protect the theater's intellectual and artistic freedom in a time when every play performed publicly in Paris was subjected to censorship. During the Third Republic, theater censorship was more repressive than prohibitive. Few plays were banned after a simple reading.[7] Most had to undergo the trial of the "censors' rehearsal" three days before the dress rehearsal. At this point, the play would either be approved, modified, or forbidden for performance. Finally, a play could pass both these tests and still be banned after the opening if it was judged politically or morally unsuitable for the stage.

Private theaters escaped the scrutiny of the "commission d'examen des œuvres dramatiques," as the censorship bureau was euphemistically called (Hemmings 222). These included amateur dramatic societies and *théâtres d'application* where aspiring actors and actresses could gain some experience, as well as private subscription theaters like Antoine's Théâtre-Libre and Lugné-Poe's Théâtre de l'Œuvre. Freedom of theatrical expression was contingent upon not selling tickets to the general public at a box office. Ironically, such restrictions actually worked in favor of anarchist artistic theory by excluding theatrical production from the marketplace of cultural consumption. Just as they strove to abolish professional politics and organized government, anarchist theorists wished ideally to do away with professional theater altogether. They objected to the fact that, in a capitalist society, theater depends on financing. What plays may be performed is governed in large part by the tastes and desires of those who have the money rather than by the artists themselves (playwrights, directors, actors, etc.). Anarchists held that, in the future society after the revolution, these financial constraints would ideally be removed, and the people would be free to participate in theatrical endeavors as they chose (Grave 364–365).

Anarchists scorned the myth of the "great artist" and the importance of masterpieces. For Proudhon, art must be produced by a community of potentially equally creative men and women:

> Ten thousand citizens who have learned to draw, represent a collective artistic power, a force of ideas, of energy and of ideals much superior to that of an individual, and who, having one day found their expression, will rise above the masterpiece. (Qtd. in Reszler 20)

Proudhon condemned museums and concerts as artistic tombs. He called for situational art (*art en situation*) in which creation would remain free, alive, ever moving. On the same lines, Tolstoy wrote: "the art of the future will not be the work of professional artists, being paid for, and only for their artistic activity. The art of the future will be the work of the people" (Qtd. in Reszler 28). Jean Grave, a militant anarchist, editor-in-chief of the journal *Le Révolté*, novelist, and playwright, adapted these principles specifically to his ideal of theater: a collective activity of, by, and for the people. Grave believed that even the audience should participate in the elaboration of the drama, taking on an active role in the creative process rather than the traditionally passive role of the spectator (Grave 265).

If most anarchist theorists agreed on the fact that artistic creation must be by and for the people, they differed greatly on the question of revolutionary art. One of the weaknesses of their aesthetic theory was, in fact, their failure to reconcile two very different, though not necessarily mutually exclusive forms of artistic practice: one a product of the revolution and the other a means of achieving the revolution, one which is revolutionary in form and the other revolutionary in content. Some late-nineteenth-century anarchists and artists saw a powerful connection between anarchism and symbolism, an avant-garde artistic and literary movement of the 1880s and 1890s that insisted on the primacy of form over function, style over subject matter. Many symbolists were affiliated with the anarchist movement, attracted by the revolt against a materialist and conformist society. *Les Entretiens Politiques et Littéraires*, a symbolist journal of the 1890s, "was permeated by anarchism" (Patsouras 56). Octave Mirbeau wrote in 1894:

> Moi, ce qui me séduit dans l'anarchie, c'est, avant tout, le côté intellectuel, le règne de l'individualisme [. . .]. Avec l'anarchie, plus d'Etat, plus de gouvernement malfaisant et dès lors, tout d'un coup, quel essor donné à l'art, quelle liberté offerte à la pensée, quel large champ ouvert à la libre initiative, au génie de chacun! (Qtd. in Asholt 351)[8]

Yet, most symbolists were partisans of art for art's sake and rejected any form of political engagement within the art work itself. Artistic anarchism for them involved a total freedom of expression. Some anarchists accepted their position in order to encourage the symbolists' allegiance to the anarchist movement. Elisée Reclus wrote, for example:

> It is necessary that you have the full and total liberty of comprehension and of personal expression and that you discard all dogmas, along with formulas and prosodies . . . Painters, engravers, musicians . . . it becomes you to remain yourselves, to reproduce freely that which you perceive in your interior mirror. (Qtd. in Sonn, *Anarchism and Cultural Politics* 191)

Other anarchists criticized the symbolists for their elitist and highly individualist tendencies, protesting that art for art's sake was a luxury that a society in need of a revolution could not afford. They welcomed the artists to their cause but invited them to use their creative capacities to serve the revolution. Kropotkin wrote, for example:

> You, poets, painters, sculptors, musicians, if you have understood your true mission and the interest of art itself, come put your pen, brush, engraving tool to the service of the revolution. Recount to us in your style of imagery or in your striking paintings the titanic struggle of peoples against their oppressors: enflame young hearts with the beautiful revolutionary breath that inspired our ancestors. (Qtd. in Sonn, *Anarchism and Cultural Politics* 190)

In the first issue of *L'Art Social*, a journal affiliated with the Club de l'Art Social that brought together anarchist and socialist militants including Louise Michel with members of the art world, the editors clearly state the group's position on this debate:

> [*L'Art Social*] sait qu'il est temps de substituer à une poésie crapuleuse et futile une poésie saine et vigoureuse. Il sait qu'à côté des lutteurs et des apôtres de la cause socialiste il y a une place à tenir. Il sait, enfin, que le moment est venu de rassembler et faire vivre les éléments épars du grand art de demain: l'Art socialiste. ("L'Art Social" 1)[9]

The journal claimed to be open to all forms of art—"*L'Art Social* ne répudie aucune forme littéraire ou artistique" (1)[10]—on the condition that the artists have the courage to put their talent to the service of the socialist ideal. In "Le Socialisme au théâtre," published in 1892 in *L'Art Social,* Auguste Linert strongly criticized art for art's sake:

> Ces intransigeants de *l'art pour l'art,* retranchés dans les extrêmes limites du mystère, finissent par produire en solitaire et pour leur usage intime, exclusivement [. . .]. Masturbateurs littéraires, ils se secouent la cervelle et après avoir palpité un instant dans l'éjaculation d'un symbole—peut-être d'un monstre sans sexe et sans chair; après avoir ressenti le léger spasme d'une joie non partagée, ils laissent tomber ça . . .—Dans le sable du désert. (62)[11]

Linert also criticized the realist thesis play for giving more importance to the thesis than to the drama, for confusing a rostrum with the stage. Yet, Linert defended the theater as the best form of social literature:

> Pour le peuple il faudra toujours de l'action physique. Le livre et le journal sont insuffisants. Indispensables sont la tribune et le théâtre, c'est-à-dire la communication directe, l'exemple frappant. Notre âme trésaille plus rapidement au contact direct d'une idée à laquelle la parole et l'action ont donné de la vie. (61)[12]

Linert specifically advocated the theater as a mode of socialist propaganda. He recognized, however, that the most effective form of social theater was yet to develop:

> Grâce à nos essais, nos tentatives, on trouvera la formule, la bonne. L'art social généralisera tous les genres, depuis ce drame dont on ne veut pas encore, de ce drame que l'on siffle aujourd'hui, jusqu'à la féerie pour laquelle il faudra une salle nouvelle, une qualification nouvelle aussi car la science aura remplacé par d'autres symboles les petites fées et les vilains diables. (61)[13]

One of the genres Linert most favored was comedy: "Il me semble que les farces, les sotties jouées jadis sur le tréteaux . . . ont fait autant pour le peuple que les grandes révolutions" (61).[14] The other was *le drame,* terrible and brutal: "L'art socialiste [. . .] est l'âme du peuple, cette âme faite de contrastes: émotions fortes, poignantes, terribles; joies larges, puissantes, bruyantes; notre misère, réalité trop cruelle; notre amour, source où nous puisons notre seul idéal" (61).[15]

Following Linert's advice, Octave Mirbeau wrote to Jean Grave in 1893 explaining that he was writing a *drame:* "une pièce sociale, et anarchiste, mais sans prêche, sans tirades. Je m'efforce à ne faire que de la vie, et de l'action directe" (*Correspondance* 60).[16] In his reply, Grave also insisted on the importance of action rather than speeches in social drama:

> La portée de votre pièce sera bien plus grande si la morale découle de l'action elle-même. Les tirades sont bonnes pour le livre de discussion, mais pour le roman, et le théâtre surtout, une situation bien décrite, une opposition de scènes bien dessinées, sont meilleures à mon avis. (62)[17]

Finding the balance between political discourse and dramatic action was one of the main difficulties that the political playwright faced. Another challenge was integrating both "notre misère" and "notre amour" (Linert 61). Anarchist dramatists had a tendency to favor a nihilist approach, staging the negative aspects of society without providing an alternative vision. Jean Grave criticizes Mirbeau's play, *Les Mauvais Bergers*, for its pessimist dénouement:

> J'ai vu *Les Mauvais Bergers* et j'ai applaudi aux éloges qui ont été faits. Il n'y a que la conclusion qui me paraît trop pessimiste. [. . .] Et l'idée de l'enfant de Jean Roule venant au monde, aurait été selon moi une allégorie plus vraie, plus vivante. En le faisant mourir avec la mère, c'est la négation de tout effort et toute critique. Il ne reste plus alors qu'à aller piquer une tête dans la Seine. (*Correspondance* 86–87)[18]

According to Grave, for the critique in anarchist drama to be productive, the play must give the audience a glimpse of what society could be like if the old world were destroyed. The playwright, like the anarchist militant, must not, however, tell the people what is best for them, but rather bring to the stage ideas that will lead the audience to find their own truths.

It was within this cultural and political climate of the nineteenth-century anarchist movement that Louise Michel, best known for her legendary role in the Paris Commune of 1871, wrote three full-length dramas that were performed on the Parisian stage between 1882 and 1890. After her amnesty in 1880, Michel was actively engaged in anarchist propaganda as both an orator and a playwright. The content, form, and conditions of performance of her plays, which I examine in chapter two, correspond to the principles of anarchist theater as described above. In *Nadine* (1882), directed by Maxime Lisbonne at the Bouffes-du-Nord, Michel stages an unsuccessful uprising in Krakow, Poland, in 1846. The political and dramatic intensity of the performance—with major crowd scenes, riots, fires, explosions, and obvious references to the Paris Commune— led to a violent confrontation between the bourgeois audience in the orchestra and the enthusiastic anarchists and former Communards in the balconies. Her second full-length play, *Le Coq rouge*, written at the time of the trial of anarchists in Lyons in 1883, brings to the stage issues of social and legal injustice, exploitation of workers, prostitution, the conditions in a women's prison, and a miners' strike. The play was an incitement to revolt and again led to a strong reaction from the audience. *La Grève* (1890), which was performed as part of a political event including anarchist speeches and revolutionary poetry and songs, involves a revolt fueled by social and economic injustice. Here, the insurrection is successful, though most of the protagonists have to sacrifice their lives for the revolution. I analyze the plays of Louise Michel as a form of what Robert Brustein calls "messianic revolt" and in relation to the "quasi-religious status of the [anarchist] movement" (Sonn, *Anarchism and Cultural Politics* 3).

Dr. Madeleine Pelletier (1874–1939), whose plays I discuss in chapter five, was also involved in the anarchist movement. Best known for her activities as a militant feminist and political activist, Pelletier wrote two plays: *In anima vili, ou un crime scientifique* (1920) and *Supérieur!* (1923), both published by the anarchist group L'Idée Libre. In her first play, Pelletier combines a commentary on war with a staging of a debate about the ethics of scientific research. While the main conflict in the play centers around the validity of vivisection and human experimentation, the overriding philosophical question concerns the meaning of life, reflecting Pelletier's despair and disillusionment during World War I when the majority of socialists and feminists had abandoned their pacifist ideals in favor of patriotic nationalism. In *Supérieur!*, Pelletier stages the making of an anarchist revolutionary. She weaves into the melodramatic and meteoric transformation of her protagonist, a serious critique of both the bourgeois society and the political arena in which she actively participated. Pelletier even braves the law in several scenes of the play, staging both an apology for propaganda by the deed and a discussion of abortion and contraception. Pelletier, as both a medical doctor and a feminist, had always been active in the fight for reproductive freedom. She both performed abortions and spoke on behalf of women's reproductive rights, in spite of the draconian measures passed after World War I forbidding all neo-Malthusian propaganda and increasing the severity of sentences for those convicted of performing abortions. Pelletier's 1923 play endorsing reproductive freedom was thus illegal and may have been one of the contributing factors that led to her arrest as an abortionist and her incarceration in an insane asylum. While the content of her play *Supérieur!* is favorable to anarchist practices and theories, its form does not correspond to the aesthetics of anarchist drama. Pelletier's plays, written several decades after Michel's, are closer in form to the type of social play that developed at the turn of the century in the effort to create a theater for the people. This social drama for the people was more educational than revolutionary and was part of a movement advocating socialist reform rather than anarchism.

The people's theater movement, which developed in France at the end of the nineteenth century and culminated in the creation of the Théâtre National Populaire, was another form of political theater. This movement was inspired by the writings of eighteenth-century philosophers and playwrights of the Revolutionary period. Rousseau, in his *Lettre à d'Alembert,* called for a theater with a more national and popular character. He underscored the importance of renewing the theatrical repertoire with plays written for the contemporary French stage and suggested creating people's festivals. Diderot wrote at length about reforms in the theater. He also had visions of large-scale national spectacles. Several decades later, Louis-Sébastien Mercier demanded the creation of a theater for the people that would draw its inspiration from the people in order to influence the morals and the behavior of the citizens (Rolland 72). Marie-Joseph Chénier would take up the latter theme in his *Discours de la liberté du théâtre* (1789) in which he claimed: "Le théâtre [. . .] est le moyen le plus actif et le plus prompt d'armer invinciblement les forces de la raison humaine, et de jeter tout à coup sur un peuple une grande masse de lumière" (Qtd. in Rolland 25).[19] Theater would, in a sense, replace religion in the secular republican society.

It is important to note that most people's theater in France was not really *by* the people, but rather *for* the people. The majority of initiatives were created either by the government or by well-intentioned members of the educated classes, usually from the Left of the political spectrum. One such project was conceived in 1794 by a decree of the Committee of Public Safety to replace the old Théâtre-Français. This new theater, called Théâtre du Peuple, was declared to be solely devoted to performances given by and for the people (Rolland 79), but the project certainly concentrated more on staging plays *for* the people than on encouraging those written or performed by the people. Ironically, the government had little confidence in the people they were purportedly serving since the plays performed at the Théâtre du Peuple had to be approved by the

Committee on Public Safety. In reality, censorship did not prove to be the major problem for the repertory, but a dearth of appropriate dramatic literature did. The committee made an appeal to theater professionals and writers to produce a new repertory to replace the debris and the chaos that encumbered the theater of the old régime:

> Il faut dégager la scène, afin que la raison y revienne parler le langage de la liberté, jeter des fleurs sur la tombe de ses martyrs, chanter l'héroïsme et la vertu, faire aimer les lois et la patrie. (Qtd. in Rolland 82)[20]

The contradiction between liberty and censorship may also have contributed to the difficulty the Théâtre du Peuple had in finding plays to perform in a time when freedom of speech often led directly to the guillotine.

In the mid-nineteenth century, Michelet again took up the cause of the people's theater. Once more, he did not call for a theater *created by* the people but rather a theater *inspired by* the people. Speaking not to workers or to peasants but to a group of students, Michelet encouraged them to take the lead in the creation of a theater for the people:

> Nul doute que le théâtre ne soit aussi dans l'avenir le plus puissant moyen d'éducation, du rapprochement des hommes; c'est le meilleur espoir peut-être de rénovation nationale. Je parle d'un théâtre immensément populaire, d'un théâtre répondant à la pensée du peuple, qui circulerait dans les moindres villages. (25)
> Ah! que je voie donc, avant de mourir, la fraternité nationale recommencer au théâtre! (268)[21]

Like Mercier and Chénier, Michelet stressed the educational potential of the theater. He spoke to the students as future leaders and teachers of the people; an educated young man should be a "médiateur dans la cité," "principal agent de rénovation sociale" (27).[22] It is his duty to bring the people to the theater and the theater to the people. This paternalistic attitude was common to the majority of advocates of people's theater.

One example of a theatrical endeavor in which the people were actively involved in the performance was Maurice Pottecher's Théâtre du Peuple at Bussang in the Vosges, inaugurated in 1895. This theater was a seasonal event involving the entire community. The actors were members of Pottecher's family along with workers and tradespeople from the village. Pottecher himself wrote a number of plays specifically for his

Théâtre du Peuple. The performances were very well attended. In order to make the plays affordable to all members of the community, Pottecher only charged admission at performances of new plays; revivals of plays from previous years were free.

The people's theater was most often inspired by socialist ideals, so much so in fact that the terms "théâtre du peuple" and "théâtre social" became virtually interchangeable in most cases. In the last decade of the nineteenth century, a number of ephemeral theaters were created to bring political issues and social protest to the stage. The Club de l'Art Social whose journal *L'Art Social* encouraged artists to put their talent to the service of socialism founded the Théâtre Social in 1894. The inaugural performance was a *grande soirée gala* at the Maison du Peuple in Montmartre. The program included Emile Veyrin's play *La Pâque socialiste* performed by Firmin Gémier[23] and Gina Barbieri, and a speech by author and politician, Maurice Barrès. A theater critic for *L'Illustration* described the scene:

> La salle? . . . un hangar dépourvu de vains ornements, semblables à une de ces granges où opérait la troupe du *Roman Comique*. A la lueur parcimonieuse de rares becs de gaz, imitant à s'y méprendre les quinquets de jadis, les spectateurs s'entassent pêle-mêle sur des bancs rustiques. (Qtd. in Ebstein et al., *Théâtre de contestation* 20–21)[24]

Having dressed down to attend this performance in a working-class district on the outskirts of Paris, the critic was equally surprised by the aspect of the public:

> De familles entières d'ouvriers congrûment endimanchées, avec une ribambelle d'enfants de tous âges [. . .], d'honnêtes commerçants et de paisibles bourgeois du quartier, d'employés de bureau très corrects, des commis de magasin bien cravatés [. . .]. (Qtd. in Ebstein et al., *Théâtre de contestation* 21)[25]

The same Maison du Peuple was the setting for a similar event in 1897. The program centered on the theme of *la justice*, beginning with a lecture by Laurent Tailhade on parliamentarianism and finishing with Octave Mirbeau's play *L'Epidémie* (Ebstein et al., *Théâtre de contestation* 21). Jean Jaurès, socialist philosopher and politician, future founder of *L'Humanité*, presided over the evening. Jaurès, like many socialist politicians, believed strongly in the power of theater to educate the masses. After seeing a production of Hauptmann's *Les Tisserands* at the Théâtre Antoine, Jaurès wrote to Antoine to ask him to perform the play for a working-class audience: "Une seule représentation de la pièce amènerait au socialisme plus d'adeptes que tous les discours" (Qtd. in Ebstein et al., *Théâtre de contestation* 26).[26]

In the same year (1897), Louis Lumet founded the Théâtre Civique with the collaboration of J.-G. Prud'homme, Philippe, Achard, Max, Lelong, and Basset. Performances of the Théâtre Civique were free "pour témoigner hautement de notre haine envers le grand corrupteur moderne, l'Argent" (Lumet 120).[27] Voluntary contributions were, however, welcome to help cover the costs. In order to avoid problems with the censorship bureau, performances of the Théâtre Civique were open only to those who had invitations, made available at a number of socialist clubs and journals. Local socialist government officials were given 400 invitations to distribute to the workers of Montmartre and Clignancourt. There were four performances in the first year, two at the Maison du Peuple in Montmartre, one at Mille-Colonnes in Montparnasse, and one at the Moulin de la Vierge at Plaisance. The opening performance featured a performance of *La Révolte* by Villiers de l'Isle Adam starring the popular actor Mévisto, along with readings by Michelet, Mirbeau, Vallès, and Clemenceau, and socialist songs (*Théâtre de contestation* 22). The plays at the Théâtre Civique were often followed by a lecture or debate. Speakers included politicians, writers, and theater professionals like J. Jaurès, Anatole France, F. Gémier, O. Mirbeau, and Lugné-Poe (Corvin 619).

Lumet claimed that his goal was neither to entertain the public nor to moralize, but rather to educate and to liberate the people:

> Non, nous n'avons jamais eu l'intention d'amuser ni de moraliser. Nous avons cherché parmi les pages des maîtres, parmi les œuvres des jeunes gens, celles propres à élever l'homme, à lui donner de la joie non de la gaieté, à susciter en lui des idées de justice et d'indépendance. Nous avons dit au peuple: écoute les paroles des philosophes, des poètes, des penseurs, écoute les paroles de Beauté et de Liberté. Ces génies qui ont pressenti l'harmonie finale de sociétés humaines, gémissent sur ton sort présent, ils découvrent à tes pauvres yeux éteints la lumière immortelle qui doit luire pour l'homme libre, prends conscience, peuple, de ta force, sois un peuple libre! (120–121)[28]

As opposed to the teaching methods used in schools, the theater educates not through reason but through emotion. For Lumet, the theater was not so much an intellectual endeavor as "une arme de combat" (120), a way of putting theory into action.

In 1903, E. Berny founded yet another theater called the Théâtre Populaire in Belleville, a working-class district of Paris. This was an ambitious undertaking. According to Rolland, during his first season alone Berny produced 61 plays from a wide variety of genres, employed 91 actors, and attracted 135,000 spectators (Rolland 101). At the first performance on September 19, 1903, the Théâtre Populaire performed *Monsieur Badin* by Courteline, *Le Portefeuille* by Mirbeau and Romain Rolland's *Danton*. In a preliminary address before the plays, Eugène Morel briefly introduced the audience to the history of the people's theater in general and to Berny's project in particular. Rather than simply entertain the spectators—"IL NE FAUT PAS ALLER AU THÉÂTRE POUR S'AMUSER" (Morel, *Discours* 283)[29]—Berny's ultimate goal was to stimulate the audience's intellect. Of his objectives,

1° *Procurer un délassement physique et morale;*
2° *Être une source d'énergie (soutenir et exalter l'âme);*
3° *Être une lumière pour l'intelligence (éveiller la pensée, apprendre à voir et à juger les choses, les hommes et soi-même).* (Morel, *Discours* 280)[30]

the third was the most important.

L'art est une fonction de l'intelligence qui veille. Ne laissons s'atrophier rien de notre capital d'homme, corps et cerveau. Que la joie des routes et de l'air refasse des muscles à ceux qu'anime une besogne assise! mais que l'art—et le théâtre est le plus puissant des arts—vienne forcer et muscler l'intelligence qui laissent sans emploi les travaux manuels qui assurent vos existences. Elles sont étroites, mais l'art va vous les agrandir. (Morel, *Discours* 283)[31]

Morel encouraged the audience moreover to come to the theater on a regular basis and to develop a critical judgment independent of reviews in bourgeois journals or the taste of the bourgeois public. The people must patronize, critique, and shape the future of the Théâtre Populaire themselves in order to truly make it *their* theater as Berny created it to be.

Shortly after the opening of Berny's Théâtre Populaire, Henri Beaulieu founded a Théâtre du Peuple in Clichy. Like Berny's, Beaulieu's theater offered inexpensive seats and an even cheaper subscription series giving the working-class audience an incentive to become regular theatergoers. Following the example of the Berlin Schiller Theater, the Théâtre du Peuple paid dividends to its actors, eliminated the ushers' tip, reduced the price of the coat check, and adjoined an exhibition space to the theater. The repertory consisted primarily of thesis plays. Unfortunately, the location of the theater in the Avenue de Clichy was not as favorable as that of the Théâtre Populaire. The bourgeois population of the neighborhood, equating cost with quality, was wary of the low price of the tickets. The working-class residents, who aspired to assimilate with the bourgeoisie, were insulted by the project's implication that they had not succeeded. Rolland attributed the failure of this theater to a regrettable loss of the sense of class distinction (105–106).

The theatrical activities of the Universités Populaires were arguably the most successful early attempts to create a widespread people's theater movement. These People's Universities were founded throughout the country between 1899 and 1914. Their goal was to educate the workers and to provide them with social services. Drama was one of the educational means chosen by many Universités Populaires. Though most did not have a theater as such, nearly all provided some form of theatrical activities, dramatic readings, or performances. Theater fulfilled various goals of the Université Populaire; it provided a healthy alternative to the cabaret and an occasion for the whole family to participate in an event that was both entertaining and educational. Whereas most of the plays performed were not written by the people, the members were encouraged to be active participants in all aspects of the productions to ensure that the theater of the Universités Populaires was indeed produced by the people.

The question of the appropriate repertory for the people's theater was a major subject of debate. In his articles on people's theater published between 1900 and 1903 in the *Revue d'Art Dramatique*, Romain Rolland takes inventory of the theater genres of the past analyzing whether they are appropriate for a people's theater. Beginning with the classical genres of the seventeenth century, he dismisses the tragedies of both Racine and Corneille as inappropriate. Racine is a "dilettante of genius" whose plays lack substance; the aristocratic language and subject matter, the dry tone and the rigid reason of Corneille's plays create too much distance from the people. Having seen Molière's comedies performed successfully in venues like the Université Populaire, he concludes that they may satisfy the initial needs of a people's theater though their usefulness is limited. Romantic drama has no redeeming qualities at all according to Rolland. The fact that it pleases the people is simply a sign of its "perniciousness":

C'est une peau de lion jetée sur la niaiserie. [. . .] Riche de bruit, d'éloquence, d'airs de bravoure, d'images éclatantes, de fausse science et de fausse pensée, ce théâtre est le capitan matamore de l'art français. Il ne se donne la peine, ni de penser, ni d'apprendre, ni d'observer; il n'a ni vérité, ni honnêteté; il *bluffe* avec maëstria. (29)[32]

Romantic drama is not only ineffectual as people's theater, it also exploits its audience and is detrimental to the cause. The bourgeois drama fares better in Rolland's analysis. Though he disdains modern bourgeois comedy as "fade, sentimentale et corrompue" (37), reflecting the lazy and degenerate bourgeoisie, Rolland approves of the bourgeois drama as a legitimate form for bourgeois audiences. These plays, which bring to the stage the social problems and preoccupations of the time, are useful to the class of society depicted, but they become irrelevant to people of another class or another time. Thanks to social reform, the issues discussed in these plays may quickly lose their relevancy. Rolland claims that if a similar form of theater were to be adopted by the people's theater, it would be necessary to have an entirely new repertoire that would be constantly changing. The works of foreign playwrights like Shakespeare, Calderón, and Schiller, though excellent, all fail to meet Rolland's criteria for the repertoire of a people's theater in France. As for more recent attempts to create people's theater, Rolland applauds Maurice Pottecher and Louis Lumet, but regrets that they were "isolés, épars, sans lien entre eux, sans cohésion, sans publicité suffisante, sans force capable de lutter contre la routine des artistes et l'indifférence publique" (92).[33] He praises the Universités Populaires for their efforts, but criticizes the "indiscriminate eclecticism" of their repertory.

For Rolland, the plays performed at the people's theater must be a source of joy, energy, and intelligence. They must achieve a balance of these elements so as to avoid either moral pedagogy or empty amusement. They must not be complicated or obscure, but monumental frescoes inspired by the people:

> De larges actions, des figures aux grandes lignes, vigoureusement tracées, des passions élémentaires, au rythme simple et puissant; des fresques, et non des tableaux de chevalet; des symphonies, et non de la musique de chambre. Un art monumental, fait pour un peuple, par un peuple.
>
> Par un peuple!—Oui, car il n'est de grande œuvre populaire que celle où l'âme du poète collabore avec l'âme de la nation, celle qui s'alimente aux passions collectives. (125–127)[34]

The theater and performance genres of which Rolland approves most for the people's theater are melodrama, historical drama, the social play, rustic drama, legends and tales, and the circus.

The feminists were one group of activists who made use of social protest theater to advocate their cause. The first specifically feminist theater organization was founded in 1897 by feminist playwright Marya Cheliga (1859–1927). Cheliga was born in Poland where, in reaction against her noble origins, she was involved in the socialist movement and *éducation populaire*. She also wrote comedies and *drames*. According to Cheliga, two of her plays, *Yvon Podkowa* and *Le Bonheur de Walus*, won a playwriting contest under the masculine pseudonym Georges Horwat, but their glory was short-lived as soon as the author revealed herself to be a woman (Cheliga 656). In the late 1880s, having been warned that she might be arrested for her political opinions, Cheliga moved to France. She quickly became involved in the French feminist movement, which she found disappointing, and founded the Union Universelle des Femmes in 1889 (Albert-Dulac 1–2). She would also become a vice president of the Ligue Française pour le Droit des Femmes; journalist for *La Fronde*, an all-woman run newspaper founded by Marguerite Durand in 1897; and in 1899, founding editor of *L'Almanach Féministe*, a yearly publication that covered a variety of topics related to the feminist movement.

Cheliga's first play published in French, *L'Ornière*, was performed in 1896 at the Théâtre Mondain. In *L'Ornière*, she criticized the law (article 324 of the Penal Code) that legally excused a husband for killing his wife for adultery: "Le meurtre commis par l'époux sur son épouse, ainsi que sur son complice, à l'instant où il les surprend en flagrant délit, dans la maison conjugale, est excusable" (Montmartre, n.p.).[35] The following year, Cheliga founded the Théâtre Féministe. She had noticed the exclusion of plays by women from the Parisian stage and wanted to give talented women playwrights an opportunity to have their works performed. Cheliga was, in fact, quite conservative in her evaluation of the quality of women's drama, but she felt that women's voices needed to be heard on the stage because they presented a different point of view:

Sans prétendre que les femmes puissent créer d'emblée des chefs-d'œuvre comparables à ceux dont les hommes ont d'ores et déjà doté la littérature dramatique, je suis certaine que l'esprit féminin apportera au théâtre un renouveau, dont le besoin se fait vraiment sentir. Il y a une foule de situations dans la vie, et par conséquent au théâtre, où la femme diffère absolument de l'homme dans ses opinions et dans son sentiment. Il serait intéressant et même instructif de l'entendre raconter elle-même ses impressions, ses joies, ses regrets, voire même ses griefs contre la société. (Cheliga 651)[36]

Cheliga suggested that women are also subjected to greater censorship on the part of theater directors who were afraid that this *difference* may not please the audience:

Même celles qui ont eu l'honneur, combien rare! d'être accueillies au Théâtre, toujours elles ont été obligées d'expurger leurs œuvres de toute idée nouvelle, de toute hardiesse, de toute originalité, de toute franchise. (652)[37]

In founding the Théâtre Féministe, Cheliga wanted to create a theater exclusively for women playwrights "afin qu'elles puissent librement donner la mesure de leur talent, exposer leurs idées, livrer le secret de leur âme réputée indéchiffrable" (652).[38] The Théâtre Féministe was meant to be "un Théâtre de combat [. . .] et surtout un Théâtre d'idées" (654).[39]

The first performance at the Théâtre des Menus-Plaisirs included *Hors du mariage* by Daniel Lesueur and a two-act play by the Danish playwright Emma Gad, preceded by a talk by Henry Fouquier. In 1897, Daniel Lesueur[40] was already well known as a novelist and poet having been awarded a prize from the Académie française for her novel, *Le Mariage de Gabrielle*, and for a collection of poems, *Fleurs d'avril*. She was also awarded the cross of the Legion of Honor and would eventually become vice president of the Société des Gens de Lettres, who had ironically refused to make her a member in 1890 because she was a woman (*Dictionnaire littéraire* 379). Her play *Hors du mariage* was "une franche révolte contre les mensonges conventionnels"[41] in which the author defended "[le] droit à l'amour" (the right to love) (Cheliga 652–653). According to Cheliga, the play received glowing reviews by theater critics. Indeed, Catulle Mendès wrote:

De fait, la pièce aurait pu être jouée soit au Vaudeville, soit au Gymnase, soit à l'Odéon; elle n'aurait pas manqué de plaire et même d'émouvoir. L'œuvre a été chaudement applaudie, et ce succès elle le mérite par la sincérité de l'émotion, et par de fiers surgissements d'idées, coulées dans le moule ferme de la phrase [. . .]. (Qtd. in Cheliga 653)[42]

The next performance of the Théâtre Féministe was at the Nouveau-Théâtre in January 1898. The program included *L'Enfant du mari*, a comedy in four acts by Jane Meyerheim and Serge Rello, and *A bon chat bon rat*, a one-act play by feminist Maria Deraismes. *L'Enfant du mari* is a sentimental comedy on the eternal theme of adultery but with a twist. When given an ultimatum by his wife, Jean de Ligny decides to break it off with his mistress. However, he forgot one thing: he had a child with her.

> CARMONA: Et ta fille? Que comptes-tu faire de ta fille? (*silence de Jean*) Tu ne réponds rien? Tu penses peut-être que je veux en supporter la charge toute seule? tu te trompes, mon cher, mes moyens ne le permettent pas. Quand on "fait" un enfant à une femme, on ne la laisse pas ainsi sans resources. (Qtd. in Marniè re "Théâtre Féministe")[43]

Carmona leaves the child with Jean who in turn abandons her. Thanks to the voice of reason, Jean's friend, Madame de Ligny, selflessly agrees to bring up her husband's illegitimate child as her own. In the final scene, Carmona, on her deathbed, requests to see her daughter one last time. She passes away just as the child has finished saying a prayer asking pardon for Marie-Magdeleine that her adopted mother has taught her (Marnière "Théâtre féministe"). Although this play denounces the vile actions of Jean, adultery and abandonment, its portrayal of women seems equally disturbing. Though it is Carmona who explains to Jean that he must take responsibility for the children he has fathered, she too abandons her daughter rashly without having sought a better solution for the child. Madame de Ligny, on the contrary, is a model of self-abnegation fueled by her love for her husband whom she forgives in spite of everything and by a Christian sense of moral duty. We are, indeed, far from a feminist representation of women in the contemporary sense.

Maria Deraismes (1828–1894), the author of the second play in the program entitled *A bon chat bon rat*, was one of the leading feminists of the nineteenth century. She wrote and published a number of plays in the early 1860s but became discouraged when she tried to have them performed. In the preface to *Le Père coupable*, she wrote:

> Le théâtre me présentait deux difficultés: la première comme femme, la seconde comme nouveau. Dans le premier cas, il me fallait me résigner à des démarches pénibles, dans le second je devais accepter des modifications qui dénaturaient mon manuscrit et lui étaient plus préjudiciables qu'avantageuses. Devant ces nécessités, j'ai cru devoir renoncer au prestige de la représentation et lui préférer une simple lecture, moins passionnée dans son appréciation, mais souvent plus impartiale. (1)[44]

Deraismes thus abandoned the theater and dedicated her talents to the feminist movement. She founded journals and feminist associations and organized the first international conference on women's rights (Krakovitch, "Préface" 24). In *A bon chat bon rat*, Deraismes stages a debate between a *bas-bleu* and misanthrope about whether women and men can be friends. These two aristocratic Parisians have each rented a room in a fisherman's cottage in a village on the Mediterranean seeking freedom and isolation from the urban society. Their plans are, however, thwarted as they discover they must share the cottage. As their discussion progresses, their relations gradually transform from open hostility to cold civility, intellectual adversity, and, finally, mutual respect and potential camaraderie.

A bon chat bon rat was also on the program at the next performance of the Théâtre Féministe at the Bodinière in February 1898 along with two other plays: *C'est la vie!* by actress Andrée Albert and *Libre!* by Jeanne Herter-Eymond. The evening, which was billed as the "premier spectacle d'avant-garde féministe," began with a lecture by Monsieur Jules Bois on "la chasteté de l'homme" (the chastity of man), judged much too long by J. Marnière, playwright and theater critic for *La Fronde* ("La Bodinière"). Both *C'est la vie* and *Libre!* were first plays, and neither is considered a chef-d'œuvre by Marnière. The first brings to the stage a young woman whose father is financially ruined and the parade of obnoxious suitors to which she is subjected. In *Libre!*, Herter-Eymond provides yet another outcome to the adultery plot. Here, the protagonist leaves her unfaithful and brutal husband to live chastely on her own. Though Marnière supports the efforts of the Théâtre Féministe, she does not hesitate to criticize their performances. For example, she justifiably reproaches the Théâtre Féministe for a sort of reverse sexism in representing all men as villains and all women as martyrs or saints:

> L'homme est toujours et constamment représenté sous un jour abominable; jamais encore on ne nous a montré un brave être de dévouement et d'amour. Cela c'est une faute. Tous les hommes ne sont pas des infects gredins, de sombres crapules; et toutes les femmes ne sont pas non plus, des martyres et des saintes. Il ne faut rien exagérer, de crainte de faire songer au proverbe: "Qui veut trop prouver, ne prouve rien!"[45]

The final performance of the Théâtre Féministe in May 1898 at the Salle du Journal was not a play but a concert of works by the Swedish composer Madame N. Lago and a talk by Madame Frédérick Hucher. In spite of encouraging reviews in the press and full houses, the Théâtre Féministe succumbed to financial difficulties after the first season. In retrospect, Cheliga claimed, however, in 1901 that the Théâtre Féministe had in fact successfully fulfilled its mission:

La carrière du Théâtre Féministe fut courte, trop courte, mais bonne. Il a, pendant la saison 1897–1898, tenu brillamment son rang parmi les théâtres d'à côté; il n'a subi d'autre échec que la perte matérielle. [. . .] il a contribué à la définitive conquête du théâtre par la femme. (654–655)[46]

She felt that an undergoing like the Théâtre Féministe *should* be short-lived and looked forward to a time when women would not have to create a separate theater in order to have their voices heard:

C'est au théâtre Mixte et Eclectique, accessible également aux jeunes dramaturges hommes ou femmes, ouvert à tous les efforts, ayant pour idéal la rénovation de l'art dramatique, et la rénovation sociale, c'est à ce théâtre—qui n'existe encore nulle part—qu'appartient l'avenir. (658)[47]

Both Nelly Roussel and Véra Starkoff were feminists who became involved in the theatrical activities of the Université Populaire in order to make their voices heard. Nelly Roussel (1878–1922) was a journalist and orator involved with the feminist, socialist, neo-Malthusian, and free-thinkers movements. In chapter three, I analyze three of Roussel's plays: *Par la révolte* (1903), *Pourquoi elles vont à l'église* (1910), and *La Faute d'Ève* (1913). *Par la révolte* was by far her most successful play. This *scène symbolique* was performed innumerable times at Universités Populaires and Maisons du Peuple throughout the country, as well as at meetings of a variety of different political and feminist organizations. *Par la révolte* is a short allegorical play advocating a radical neo-Malthusian doctrine: "la grève des ventres" (the strike of the wombs). According to this doctrine, women should refuse to have children until their work in childbearing and childcare is recognized and sufficiently remunerated. Both *Pourquoi elles vont à l'église* and *La Faute d'Ève* are stagings of another of Nelly Roussel's major spheres of activism: the freethinkers movement, whose goal was to secularize all sectors of French society. In *Pourquoi elles vont à l'église*, Roussel denounces the hypocrisy of the freethinkers who claim to promote a nonreligious moral code in which all men in all classes of the society would have equal access to truth, knowledge, and freedom, but who exclude women from their meetings and discussions. *La Faute d'Ève* is a revision of the story of Adam and Eve. In Roussel's play, Eve becomes a rebel who sees her banishment from paradise not as a punishment but as deliverance; freed from the boredom of a comfortable, sheltered, and passive existence, she is thrilled to discover life with all its action, struggles, and dreams.

In chapter four, I discuss the works of Véra Starkoff (1867–1923), a journalist, lecturer, and author of Russian origin, who emigrated to Paris in the late nineteenth century where she participated in the theatrical activities of Université Populaire. Of the five plays she wrote between 1902 and 1909, all were performed and three were published: *L'Amour libre, L'Issue,* and *Le Petit Verre.* Starkoff's plays were written for and about the Université Populaire. In *L'Amour libre* (1902), Starkoff stages the debate about *l'union libre,* a mutual agreement between consenting adults to be living partners free from the institution of marriage and the constraints of motherhood, and defends the rights of the unwed mothers and illegitimate children. In *L'Issue* (1903), she contrasts the bourgeois mentality of a tyrannical father with the enlightened ideas of his son's tutor, notably his condemnation of paternal authority and marriage as the only prospect for young women. In this play, Starkoff again advocates *union libre,* as well as shared parenting and women's work as a path to truth, social equality, and freedom. In *Le Petit Verre* (1904), Starkoff brings to the stage a theme popular among social reformers at the turn of the century: alcoholism in the working class. Her play is intended to enlighten her audience by making them aware of the dangers of excessive alcohol consumption, notably domestic violence, and by instructing them on how to improve the situation. In 1909, Starkoff founded the Théâtre d'Idées, which performed social protest plays in a variety of Parisian venues.

Though the socially conscious drama of Ibsen, Strindberg, Hauptmann, and Tolstoy was applauded by Goldman as revolutionary and shocked audiences at first, it was performed in mainstream theaters by the turn of the century. Authors such as Eugène Brieux and Paul Hervieu, who wrote thesis plays about social and political issues, were even elected to the Académie française during the first decade of the twentieth century. Many of these mainstream thesis plays defended feminist views.[48] However, few women were able to force their way into the old-boy network. Marie Lenéru (1874–1918), whose works I study in chapter six, was one exception. Lenéru is the only author studied in this book who was not a political activist and who was best known in her time as a playwright. She was also the only one to have her plays performed in mainstream theatrical venues. Lenéru's plays were directed by André Antoine, performed at the Comédie-Française, and acclaimed by such authors and theater critics as Catulle Mendès, Rachilde, and Léon Blum. Her preferred genre was the play of ideas, an intellectually challenging genre in which the author exposes a problem or an issue, showing all sides of the debate rather than giving a solution or developing a thesis, thus allowing each member of the audience to form his or her own conclusions. In *Les Affranchis* (1910), Lenéru examines the question of divorce, as well as the consequences of intellectual proximity between men and women. Divorce is again one of the central themes in her second play, *La Maison sur le roc* (1911), in which she explores the role of religious faith in a rapidly changing society. *La Triomphatrice* was accepted by the Comédie-Française in 1914, thanks to the efforts of Léon Blum, but was not performed until 1918 because of the war. Here, Lenéru revisits the role of the intellectual woman by staging the difficulties a successful woman author encounters in her personal life. In her last play, *La Paix*, written during World War I, Lenéru abandons the objectivity of the play of ideas in order to write a pacifist play that she hoped would prevent future wars.

Revolution and social reform, reproductive freedom, temperance, free love, pacifism, divorce, maternal rights, and domestic violence . . . women playwrights in France in the late nineteenth and early twentieth centuries brought to the stage a myriad of political and feminist issues in a variety of theatrical genres and venues. Yet all had a similar goal: to create plays that would change the world. Whether through emotional catharsis, educational drama, social critique, or philosophical enquiry, all these authors wished not only to entertain the audience but also to influence their opinions and actions. All braved the challenges of the male-dominated political and theatrical arenas in order to express their demands and to portray an alternate vision for the men, women, and children of the future.

CHAPTER TWO

Staging the Revolution: Louise Michel

Louise Michel, who is best known for her role in the Paris Commune, was the first major political woman playwright of the Third Republic. In her three full-length plays, which were published and performed in the years following the amnesty of the Communards in 1880, she staged grand spectacles of revolt and revolution. Her "messianic heroes," as Robert Brustein calls the protagonists of the nineteenth-century "theatre of revolt," aim to destroy the old world of injustice and corruption in order to form a new society based on freedom, social justice, and equality. Her protagonists, like the men and women with whom she had fought during the Commune, are willing to die for the cause. Louise Michel's plays function as a form of political proselytism combining the anarchist methods of propaganda by the word and propaganda by the deed.

Louise Michel was active in literary activities throughout her life. Born in 1830, Michel started writing poetry and short dramatic works as a child and corresponded regularly with Victor Hugo, sending him her poems, from her teenage years until his death in 1885. She came to Paris in 1856 to teach in a private girls' school, having been barred from the public school system for refusing to swear allegiance to the Second Empire. In Paris, Michel frequented a group of Republican intellectuals and freethinkers, a hotbed of antibonapartism, who organized semi-clandestine evening classes in the Latin Quarter, rue Hautefeuille. She also taught classes in literature, art, and geography at a free professional school, rue Thévenot.[1] Meanwhile, she continued her own literary activities, writing novels, plays, and poems. Michel was not the only woman involved in such endeavors; many young women, both writers and those in search of intellectual stimulation, frequented the rue Hautefeuille. She claimed in her *Mémoires* that rue Hautefeuille was a veritable breeding ground for blue stockings in the years preceding the Commune (110). By this point, Michel's literary works had become distinctly revolutionary in content, reflecting her growing interest in political activism.

> Ce que je envoyais [à Victor Hugo] maintenant sentait la poudre.
>> Entendez-vous tonner l'airain.
>> Arrière celui qui balance!
>> Le lâche trahira demain!
>> Sur les monts et sur la falaise,
>> Allons, semant la liberté.
>> Souffle par l'orage emporté
>> Passons, vivante Marseillaise. (*Mémoires* 75)[2]

Michel had become involved not only in the socialist movement, but also in feminist circles, joining both the International and the Société de la Revendication des Droits de la Femme. The latter was a feminist association founded by André Léo, Maria Deraismes, and Paule Minck that defended the political rights of women in reaction against a highly misogynist trend inspired by Proudhon within the socialist movement. Again, many of these feminist militants also wrote literature. André Léo (pseudonym of Léodile Champseix), for example, published a number of social novels and wrote at least one play, *Marianne*. Maria Deraismes also published a collection of plays. In retrospect though, Michel admitted that in the climate of political upheaval just prior to the Commune, their works went relatively unnoticed:

> La Révolution se levait! à quoi bon les drames? Le vrai drame était dans la rue; à quoi bon les orchestres? Nous avions les cuivres et les canons. [. . .] prose, vers et motifs s'en allaient au vent; nous sentions tout près le souffle du drame dans la rue, le vrai drame, celui de l'humanité; les bardits chantaient l'épopée nouvelle, il n'y avait plus de place pour autre chose. (*Mémoires* 81, 110)[3]

In reality, while this account may reflect Louise Michel's personal experience during the Siege and the Commune, the situation of the theater was more complex.

At the onset of the Franco-Prussian war, the majority of the theaters remained open with a carefully chosen repertoire. The actors and actresses sang or recited the *Marseillaise* and other patriotic songs and poems during intermissions. Gradually the theatergoing public decreased as the hostilities became more intense and the outlook grimmer. Some felt that the theater was an unnecessary frivolity in such tragic times. A number of theaters turned to patriotic benefit performances, while many actors abandoned the stage for active service. Others, like Francisque Sarcey, defended the civic role of the theater:

> Loin de blâmer leur persévérance [des directeurs de théâtre], il faut leur accorder l'estime dont ils sont dignes. Ils contribuent à tenir en haleine le moral des Parisiens; ils nous détachent un instant des idées de deuil qui, après nous avoir affligés, ne doivent pas finir non plus par nous abattre. (Qtd. in Labarthe 41)[4]

This attitude, however, would not prevail; on September 9, a declaration by the Prefect of Police officially closed all the theaters in Paris. Several days later, the Comédie-Française had found a way to make use of both its facilities and its unemployed personnel by transforming the theater into an ambulance unit. Other theaters followed suit. While many of the actors had joined the troupes, the actresses provided both bedding and care for the wounded. Even when the theaters reopened briefly in late October and November, they continued to serve the dual function of infirmary and stage.

The situation changed dramatically after March 18 during the Commune. Many theater professionals fled the city. Few were politically involved; they were for the most part primarily interested in continuing to practice their art and to earn their living. Eager to survive the deprivations but not wanting to choose between the governments of the Commune and Versailles, a group of actors formed a Federation of Independent Artists, which staged benefit performances for the wounded of both sides. The leaders of the Commune, recognizing the importance of theater as both an educational medium and a morale booster, also organized benefit performances for their troupes[5] and formed a commission of playwrights, composers, and actors to examine the role of theater in the new society (Labarthe 117). In May, the question was raised by Edouard Vaillant, Delegate for Education, in a session of the Commune Council. The debate that ensued only days before the defeat of the Commune reflects the ideological ambiguities of the government. Vaillant, an engineer and physician, member of the International, maintained that the theater should no longer be under the control of the Delegation for Security, but rather under the supervision of the Delegation for Education. While it was important to supervise the safety and the morality of playhouses, it was of even greater value to recognize the theater's role as an educational medium:

> Mais les théâtres doivent être considérés surtout comme un grand établissement d'instruction; et, dans une république, ils ne doivent être que cela. Nos ancêtres l'avaient ainsi compris, et la Convention, dans un décret de Germinal II, avait décidé qu'une commission, celle de l'Instruction publique, aurait la surveillance des théâtres. (Bourgin and Henriot Tome II, *Procès-verbaux* 413)[6]

Raoul Urbain, a teacher and political orator, concurred:

> Quant à ce qui touche à la représentation des pièces, on ne pourra jamais mieux faire que de rattacher les théâtres à l'Enseignement. C'est le plus grand et le meilleur enseignement pour le peuple. Les gouvernements qui nous ont précédés avaient fait du théâtre l'enseignement de tous les vices; nous en ferons l'enseignement de toutes les vertus civiques; et d'une nation de corrompus nous ferons une nation de citoyens! (Bourgin and Henriot Tome II, *Procès-verbaux* 414)[7]

Vaillant further argued that the theater should not be run as a commercial enterprise in which only the directors or owners made a profit, but rather as a self-managing association in which all involved would share equally in the profits:

> Nous devons chercher à créer partout des établissements socialistes. Le caractère principal de la Révolution du XIXe siècle est d'être une révolution sociale. Le produit du travailleur est un axiome d'une vérité générale et qui doit s'appliquer à l'artiste, comme à tout autre producteur. [. . .] L'administration générale des théâtres est chargée de transformer le régime propriétaire et privilégié actuel en un système d'association par l'exploitation entière des artistes. (Bourgin and Henriot Tome II, *Procès-verbaux* 427)[8]

Another member of the council, Felix Pyat, a journalist and playwright, while agreeing that a system of association was ideally better than commercialism, rejected Vaillant's proposal that the theater should be in any way controlled or supported by the state: "Pour ce qui est d'un patronage, d'une influence quelconque sur l'art, je trouve que ce serait empiéter sur la liberté de la pensée humaine" (427).[9] Unable to reconcile these conflicting ideological points of view within a reasonable timeframe given their imperative military concerns, the Council settled on an incongruous decree integrating both perspectives:

> Les théâtres relèvent de la délégation de l'enseignement. Toutes les subventions et monopoles des théâtres sont supprimés. La délégation se chargera de faire cesser pour les théâtres le régime de l'exploitation par un directeur ou une société, et y substituera dans le plus bref délai, le régime de l'association. (Qtd. in Labarthe 118)[10]

The Delegation for Education would, however, never have the opportunity to implement the law in practical terms. Two days later, on May 21, when the decree was published in the *Journal Officiel*, the Versailles army successfully entered Paris and thus ensued the *semaine sanglante* (bloody week).

Louise Michel was not yet writing for the stage during this period of theatrical instability. Her first play was not produced on stage until after the Commune and her exile in New Caledonia. She did, however, play a major role in the street theater of the Paris Commune. Louise Michel was among many women who actively participated in the revolution,[11] but no woman was involved in so many aspects of the fight or was so widely recognized as a leader in the struggle. No other woman, or man, has come to symbolically represent the Commune like Louise Michel. Indeed, in the mythology of the revolution, Louise Michel *is* the Commune. In order to understand Louise Michel's plays, it is important to be familiar with the events of the Paris Commune and her role in this revolution.

The events leading up to the Commune began during the Second Empire in 1870, three years after the spectacular World Fair in Paris, where exciting new inventions and discoveries were exhibited, such as dynamite, invented by Nobel, and petroleum, a product that would become symbolically inseparable from the history of the Commune. The emperor himself contributed a statue entitled "Peace" (Horne 4–5). By 1870, however, the excitement of the World Fair had long waned and peace was no longer on the agenda; in July, Napoleon III declared war on Prussia. Louise Michel, along with most opponents of the Empire, protested against the war. In August, Michel committed her first public political act of protestation. She and two other women, André Léo and Adèle Esquiros,[12] delivered a petition instigated by the exiled historian Michelet, to General Trochu, the governor of Paris, demanding the liberation of two members of a revolutionary faction who had been arrested after a failed coup d'état. As it turns out, the coup had been unnecessary since the defeat of the French army at Sedan led to the fall of the Empire and the declaration of the French Republic on September 4. Two weeks later, Paris came under siege by the Prussians; a siege that would last four months causing immense suffering owing to cold and hunger, in addition to losses in military action. During this time, Louise Michel organized ambulances and medical units, formed Le Comité de Vigilance des Femmes du 18e arrondissement to provide relief for the poor, and marched in a number of protest demonstrations. On October 2, she and André Léo led a group of women protesters to the Town Hall to demand that the government come to the aid of the town of Strasbourg, bombarded and under siege since mid-August: the two leaders were detained and interrogated, but released the same day. In late November, she again participated in a demonstration of women demanding to be allowed to enlist in the armed forces in order to defend Paris along with their male comrades. Though she was not a leader of this demonstration, she had by now gained a reputation as an opponent to the government and was arrested as an instigator. Thanks to the intervention of Victor Hugo and Théophile Ferré among others, she was released after only two days in prison, her first of many.

In January 1871, the government capitulated, and on January 22, Louise Michel marched once more to the Town Hall, dressed in men's clothes, with a battalion of National Guards, to protest against the capitulation. This time she was armed with a gun, which she allegedly used, according to witnesses of the event, when the army defending the Town Hall was given orders to fire on the crowd: "For the first time during the Siege, Frenchmen were firing at, and killing, other Frenchmen" (Horne 237). A new Assembly was elected in early February with a majority of conservatives; over half were monarchists and an overwhelming majority was for peace at nearly any cost. Their first act was to ratify the armistice treaty giving Prussia all of Alsace, most of Lorraine, an indemnity of five billion francs, and the humiliating right to a triumphal march of the Prussian army through Paris.

Many Parisians, however, were not ready to give in and thus began a civil war between the government, who had moved out to Versailles and was defended by the army, and la Commune de Paris, a government of the people (a third of the cabinet were from the working class), defended by the National Guard and innumerable civilian volunteers, both men and women, with a variety of political views. Contrary to propaganda by the opposition, they were not all "reds"; both "the leaders of the revolt (and their followers) espoused a variety of democratic and socialist philosophies" (Gullickson 61). Gullickson's narration of the events of March 18 in her book *Unruly Women of Paris* is an illustration of the important role that women played throughout what she describes as the drama of the revolution:

> The revolution known as the Paris Commune began with a day of high drama in the working-class neighborhoods of Paris, and women played leading parts. Street theater seemed to be their métier, and as we will see, they are often credited with the Parisians' success in defeating the army in the morning and blamed for the deaths of two generals in the late afternoon. (24)

During the Commune, Louise Michel was everywhere: building and defending barricades, organizing ambulance squads, giving speeches and writing placards to rally the people, and fighting in armed combat in the front lines. Michel survived *la semaine sanglante*, the final "bloody week" of the hostilities during which about 20,000 Communards were killed. She was arrested and sentenced to exile in New Caledonia where she spent seven years before the amnesty of the Communards in 1880. In New Caledonia, Michel spent a lot of time with the indigenous people, the Canaques; she gave them classes, teaching them enough French to challenge the authorities,[13] and she supported them in their revolt against the white colonizers. It was during her stay in New Caledonia that Louise Michel became an anarchist.[14]

Louise Michel returned to Paris on November 9, 1880. She was greeted by Henri Rochefort, Georges Clemenceau, and a crowd of 20,000 heavily controlled by the police (La Fournière 177). Two weeks later, Louise Michel spoke to an audience of some 4,000 at the Elysée-Montmartre, thus beginning her career as public speaker. She continued speaking to audiences not only in Paris, but throughout France, Belgium, Holland, and England until her death in 1905. In France, like all anarchists at the time, she was under heavy police surveillance. The Paris police had an army of informers who infiltrated political meetings, cafés, workshops, and even theaters—all the places that anarchists were known to frequent. Louise Michel was imprisoned a number of times: she spent two weeks at the St. Lazare prison in January 1882 for insulting police officers and was sentenced to six years the following year when several bakeries were pillaged during a demonstration march that she and Emile Pouget led. Amnestied in January 1886, she was again sentenced to four months in August of the same year for incitement to murder and once more in April 1890, when a demonstration at which she had spoken turned violent. Finally, two months after her release, threatened with internment at a psychiatric institution, Louise Michel left for England on July 29, 1890.

Three of Louise Michel's plays were performed in Paris during the decade after her return from New Caledonia: *Nadine* in 1882, *Le Coq rouge* in 1888, and *La Grève* in 1890. Only *Le Coq rouge* was published at the time, but all three were reprinted in *Au temps de l'anarchie, un théâtre de combat* in 2001.[15] The content, form, and conditions of performances of these plays correspond well to the anarchist principles of social theater outlined in the introduction. They were not performed reverently as great works to a silent, respectful audience, but, rather, were integrated as part of a political and artistic theatrical program including lectures, poems, and songs. Even the audience played an active role in the performance, not only reacting to what was being said and done on stage, but even becoming part of the play or reenacting the conflicts depicted in the play from their seats. The performances of Louise Michel's plays came all too close to Jean Grave's ideal of audience participation in anarchist drama.

Louise Michel's first full-length play, *Nadine*, was staged in 1882 by Maxime Lisbonne at the Théâtre des Bouffes-du-Nord, a theater in a working-class neighborhood on the outskirts of Paris that Lisbonne rebaptised le Théâtre Populaire—the Théâtre of the People. Lisbonne's career illustrates perfectly the blending of culture and politics in the anarchist movement. Like Louise Michel, he had fought in the front lines during the Commune and was exiled with her to New Caledonia. Pardoned in the amnesty of 1880, Maxime Lisbonne returned to Paris where, over the next 15 years, he set up a series of anarchist cabarets, mostly in Montmartre, a center of anarchist activity. His first cabaret, la Taverne du Bagne, was a staging of a penal colony: the doors were barred; the tables chained; and the waiters who were dressed as convicts, dragged chains and spoke in slang. Lisbonne also published an anarchist newspaper, la *Gazette du Bagne*, from his cabaret. In spite of strict and daily censorship, cabarets like Lisbonne's became very popular for their rabble rousing musical entertainment. They appealed to both the working class' and to the bourgeois' *nostalgie de la boue* (Sonn, *Anarchism and Cultural Politics* 66). Though music and songs were the most popular form of entertainment, Lisbonne also put on short revolutionary plays, such as *Le Sommeil de Danton* by bohemian socialist and former Communard, Clovis Hugues, which Lisbonne staged at his Brasserie des Frites Révolutionnaires in 1887 (Sonn, *Anarchism and Cultural Politics* 66).[16] Such cabarets were also used for no less theatrical political meetings. In July 1889, for example, for the centenary of the French Revolution, Lisbonne's cabaret housed a public anarchist meeting featuring none other than Louise Michel. Drawing a crowd of some 250 people, the heroine of the Commune proclaimed: "they must make more blood flow as their ancestors had done a century before" (Sonn, *Anarchism and Cultural Politics* 67).[17]

Lisbonne did everything in his power to turn Louise Michel's play into a media event. Contrary to current practice, on the posters advertising the play, Louise Michel's name was printed center page in gigantic capital letters, much larger than the name of the play. Several critics complained facetiously that they did not know at first if *Nadine* was by Louise Michel or if Louise Michel was by *Nadine*. The same posters, displayed before the opening, hyperbolically billed the play as "le plus grand succès du dix-neuvième siècle."[18] One journalist describes Lisbonne as one of the cleverest impresarios in Paris:

> Le citoyen Lisbonne, le nouveau directeur des Bouffes-du-Nord, va prendre rang parmi les impressari les plus habiles de Paris. Il sait que les exhibitions d'animaux exotiques et d'excentricités sont à la mode et font recette. [. . .] Le citoyen Lisbonne a voulu, du coup, dépasser tous ses confrères et il a trouvé le moyen de nous exhiber un des phénomènes de la Commune: la citoyenne Louise Michel. (*Figaro*, April 30, 1882)[19]

Though Lisbonne was the first to take advantage of Louise Michel's name in the theater, this was common practice in political meetings. Many posters advertising anarchist meetings in the 1880s had her name printed center page in large, bold capital letters. Her name was sure to draw a substantial crowd and bring in some revenue; many were willing to pay the 30 centimes just to see the famous Louise Michel. According to a police report, in one meeting, when a fellow anarchist complained publicly that the crowd had only come out of curiosity to see her, Michel answered "qu'elle s'en 'foutait' que l'on vient la voir comme une bête curieuse, car ils en restaient toujours quelque chose de ce qu'elle avait dit."[20] Michel herself, also known as *la bonne Louise*, generous, kind, and philanthropic, always gave away any money she earned in such events to those more in need.[21]

Though the action of *Nadine* takes place during the unsuccessful uprising in Krakow, Poland, in 1846, distant enough in time and place to get through the censorship bureau, the parallels to the Paris Commune and the internationalist message of the play are obvious. In the opening scene, for example, two bourgeois lament the fact that the government has allowed foreigners to invade the town and claim that they are ready to take up arms to defend their independence. Any member of the audience in 1882, only two years after the general amnesty of the

Communards, would hear echoes of the events leading up to the Commune. And echoes of *La Marseillaise* are obvious in the following lines at the end of Act I: "au nom de la Patrie expirante, au nom de la liberté et de l'humanité, au nom de nos morts, saisissons nos armes et affranchissons nos cités et nos campagnes! . . . Vive la liberté! . . . Délivrons nos frères martyrisés! Aux armes! Aux armes!" (I, 8).[22]

The internationalist message is stressed by the historically inaccurate presence of three well-known revolutionaries, whom Michel places in Krakow to help the patriots defend the republic. By integrating these characters into her play, Michel brings the events on stage closer to the audience, thus allowing them to become more involved in the action. Ludwig Mieroslawski, one of the leaders in the staged insurrection, was, in fact, one of the main instigators of the 1846 uprising. Yet, in reality, he and other leaders of the rebellion were arrested before the fighting actually began. Mieroslawski would have been a familiar figure to French anarchists since he lived in Paris at several intervals, most recently after the Polish insurrection of 1863, and died there in 1878. A more flagrant historical inaccuracy is the presence of two Russians who were not involved in this particular insurrection at all: anarchist Mikhail Bakunin and philosopher and writer Alexander Herzen. Though Bakunin was not in Krakow at the time of the insurrection, his presence in the play was not entirely anachronistic. Living in Paris at the time, he had been following the events in Poland carefully and had contact with the numerous Polish émigrés in Paris. The events in Krakow had attracted the attention of revolutionaries of all nationalities and intensified revolutionary excitement throughout Europe (Zimmerman 25). Bakunin welcomed the news from Krakow with enthusiasm. He claimed that the "heroic feats" of the Poles had:

> an unbelievable effect in Paris . . . This sudden awakening, this universal movement of passions and minds, engulfed me also . . . I awoke, as it were, and I decided, whatever happened, to drag myself out of my inertia and take an active part in the events that were maturing. (Qtd. in Kelly, *Mikhail Bakunin* 120)

Louise Michel gives him just such an active role on stage.

Another tactic that Louise Michel used to draw the audience into her play was language. Though the style is relatively varied, ranging from lyrical passages full of imagery, to the colloquial, slangy language of workers, marginals, or *déclassés*, the dominant language is that of the easily recognizable anarchist discourse, which was obviously meant to rally the

crowd and to provoke a reaction. The following words spoken by Herzen, for example:

> Nous ne bâtissons pas, nous démolissons. Nous n'annonçons pas de nouvelles révélations, nous écartons le vieux mensonge. Le monde où nous vivons se meurt et nos successeurs pour respirer librement doivent d'abord l'enterrer . . . En passant du vieux monde dans le nouveau on ne peut rien emporter avec soi. (III, 2)[23]

Michel even had the intention of including an excerpt from the Polish Declaration of 1846, spoken in her play by Mikhail Bakunin:

> Il faut que la Tyrranie toute entière s'écroule, dussions-nous périr avec elle. Oui frères, proclamons la République et après la victoire nous formerons une communauté où chacun prendra part au banquet de la vie, produisant suivant son mérite et ses capacités, consommant suivant ses besoins. Nous ne voulons plus de privilèges et d'oppression . . . (I, 7)[24]

Not surprisingly, this passage was cut by the censors. In spite of the censorship, the audience was obviously drawn in both by the discourse and by the play's parallels to the Paris Commune. As one critic wrote: "Il paraît que l'auteur a voulu tenter une petite réhabilitation de la Commune, mais prévoyant que la censure s'y opposerait, il a transporté l'action de sa pièce en Pologne. On n'a célébré que la Commune polonaise—et pas franchement encore, car au lieu de Commune on disait 'communauté' " ("La Soirée Théâtrale").[25]

From the detailed police reports on anarchist activities of the period and the numerous accounts in the press, we have a vivid description of the audience participation during the opening performance on April 29, 1882. The audience was split between the curious bourgeois in the orchestra and the enthusiastic anarchists and former Communards in the balconies. As the play progressed and the conflicts within the plot intensified, the level of audience participation also increased. The anarchists in the audience alternatively applauded the protagonists' efforts to overthrow an oppressive government, joined in the songs sung by the revolutionary factions within the play, and yelled angrily at the antagonists' betrayal of the revolution. Louise Michel's plays are grand spectacles with major crowd scenes, riots, cities burning, gun shots, and explosions. As the armed struggle became more and more intense and violent on stage, the commotion in the hall grew to a point where the theater administration hesitated to raise the curtain for the final act. The anarchists in the audience actually began attacking the bourgeois with various projectiles, crying "Vive le pétrole!" (Long live petrol!), thus making explicit the link to the Commune and its legendary *Petroleuses*—the name given to women, like Louise Michel, who had allegedly set fire to buildings during the insurrection. The judicious bourgeois, who had come prepared for such audience participation, protected themselves with umbrellas, crying "A bas le pétrole!" (Down with petrol!) in response. In the end it was necessary to turn off the lights in order to avoid a full-scale confrontation.

The reviews of the performance were, not surprisingly, as diverse as the political spectrum. Most described the event at length but dismissed the play itself. Some harshly criticized the audience for making so much noise, claiming that any play deserves to be heard. Others, such as Jean Richepin, gave Michel's play a backhanded compliment: "Eh bien! Il n'est pas plus mauvais qu'un autre, le drame de la grande citoyenne!"[26] Francisque Sarcey admitted to not liking political dramas as a genre, and a journalist of the *Revue Théâtrale* criticized the play on the grounds that politics had replaced the plot. On the contrary, in an article published in *L'Intransigeant* whose editor-in-chief was Henri Rochefort, a Communard and friend of Louise Michel, one drama critic defended the play for ideological reasons: "Une œuvre est toujours intéressante lorsqu'elle retrace avec sincérité les souffrances et les héroïsmes d'un peuple opprimé aux prises avec ses oppresseurs" (Fauchery, "Les Premières").[27]

Performances of *Nadine* continued for about a month at the Bouffes-du-Nord after which Lisbonne took the play on a short tour. The play was performed in Belgium but not in Switzerland where it had been officially banned (*Drapeau national*). As of June 7, when *Nadine* returned to the Bouffes-du-Nord, Louise Michel began giving a short speech before each performance of *Nadine*, most likely in order to attract a larger audience. The main theme of her speech on June 7 was censorship. Not only had her play been censored, but so were her speeches. Yet, in speaking about this censorship, she craftily makes allusions to the very subjects that had been forbidden:

Je me sens embarrassée, parce que je ne suis pas ici sur mon terrain: je dois me renfermer dans le domaine littéraire, et toutes les allusions me sont défendues. Peut-être m'en échappera-t-il? Tant pis? Ce ne sera pas de ma faute.

Nous aurions voulu laisser un souvenir de ce géant, Bakounine, devant la jeune génération: la censure a meurtri nos deux premiers actes. A quoi bon travailler pour voir massacrer son œuvre? (. . .)

Mais je m'arrête, car la censure—sous une autre étiquette—me surveille. Demain, je ne pourrai pas m'empêcher d'enfreindre cette loi qui m'oblige à ne parler que de littérature; demain je serai forcée de raconter la mort de la Pologne.

Demain, peut-être, je vous montrerai cette longue ligne de potence que j'avais élevée, au dernier acte, près des fenêtres du palais du prince, et que la censure m'a impitoyablement interdite. ("Spectacles et concerts")[28]

Evidently, even the presence of Louise Michel could not attract enough of a crowd to justify continuing. By June 12, the play was no longer on the bill at the Bouffes-du-Nord.

Louise Michel wrote her second full-length play, *Le Coq rouge*,[29] at the time of the trial of anarchists in Lyons in early 1883. She gave a reading of her play, which distinctly echoes recent events in Lyons, and donated the proceeds to the prisoners and to their families. Less than two years earlier, in May 1881, the anarchist movement had officially become autonomous from other socialist factions, and not long afterward France began to see the first examples of propaganda by the deed. In March 1882, during a long strike of weavers in Roanne, a young worker, who had been fired, shot and injured one of the bosses. The anarchists publicly defended his individual act of violent revolt. In August of the same year, in the poor mining region of Montceau-les-Mines, a secret revolutionary organization, la Bande Noire, carried out a series of violent attacks against the government and the Church, again lauded by the anarchists. Twenty-three people were arrested and were being tried when a bomb attack in a bourgeois bar shook up the town of Lyons.[30] By this point, the government had started to believe in an international conspiracy and began to arrest leading anarchist militants. The ensuing trial, "le Procès des 66," led to symbolically severe verdicts for leaders such as Kropotkin, Gautier, Bernard, and Bordat, for simply having participated in an international organization whose goal was allegedly to abolish private property, the family, the nation, and the Church. Though Louise Michel was not one of the accused, her destiny would coincide with theirs: Michel was arrested that same spring for her participation in a demonstration in Paris during which a number of bakeries were raided and was sentenced to six years in prison. Her liberation in 1886 coincided with the amnesty of the Lyons anarchists.

Her play, *Le Coq rouge*, was itself an incitement to revolt. Two innocent young peasants find themselves accused of a crime they did not commit and are sentenced to prison. When Rosalie gets out 20 years later, she meets

Paul by chance and finds out that he escaped from prison and has been working at a mine under an assumed name. He has become a rebel:

> PAUL: Il y a autre chose à faire que de se plaindre, c'est détruire le mal.
>
> ROSALIE: Comme vous êtes changé, Paul! vous qui étiez si timide et si doux!
>
> PAUL: La douceur est stérile, la haine sera plus féconde! (IV, 1)[31]

In the following scene, the miners go on strike in reaction to numerous layoffs. A growing confrontation between the strikers and soldiers literally explodes when Paul sets fire to the mine. The miners then strike up a song of revolt to the tune of *La Carmagnole* as the soldiers open fire on the crowd. Louise Michel explains in a published interview about *Le Coq rouge* that she wanted not only to expose social destitution and injustice, but also to illustrate the impossibility of reform, of a partial improvement of the society. For Michel, a new world could only arise from a cataclysm totally destroying the old society.[32]

Le Coq rouge was ill-fated from the start. It was originally to be staged by Lisbonne at the Théâtre d'Oran, which he was directing at the time. Unfortunately, he ceased to be director of the theater before the play was staged. He passed on the manuscript to Pascal Delagarde who was planning to stage it at the Théâtre Beaumarchais, but again the theater closed its doors before the play was staged. Finally, in 1888, five years after the initial reading, Delagarde was able to stage the play at the Théâtre des Batignolles. But even then the audience was not able to fully appreciate its revolutionary message. First, after the censors' rehearsal, the inspectors obliged Michel to make major changes: for example, she was forbidden to stage drunken policemen and had to change the words to *La Carmagnole*. More importantly, she had to cut an entire tableau that took place in a brothel. This was, at least in part, due to moral considerations. Though the "demi-monde" was a popular subject of nineteenth-century comedies, stagings of the "bas-monde" of prostitution in more serious drama were considered improper. In fact, it was the censorship bureau's decision to ban a play by Edmond Goncourt about prostitution entitled *La Fille Elisa* that triggered a new fight for theatrical freedom in 1891 (Krakovitch 252). However, there may also have been political justification for forbidding the brothel scene in Michel's play: the censored tableau in the manuscript housed at the International Institute of Social History in Amsterdam reveals a form of corruption in the prison system. The madam of a brothel bribed prison authorities to buy pardons for women prisoners in order to make them sex slaves. Jeanne, a young woman unjustly imprisoned for subversive political activities, burns down the brothel in order to escape. In the staged and published versions of the play, Michel substituted a scene among women inmates in the St. Lazare prison, a place she knew well, having been imprisoned there after the bakery incident in 1883. In comparing the manuscript with the published version, other important cuts appear in the final act eliminating much of the build up to the minors' revolt, most lines accusing the management of causing the strike and those that explain the protagonists' ideological stance. The censored version makes the revolt seem more precipitant and irrational. In a conversation with a drama critic from *Le Figaro*, Louise Michel underscores the absurdity of the censorship bureau:

> C'est idiot, cette censure. Ainsi, il y a des réunions. On ne sait pas ce que nous dirons. Nous pouvons tout y exposer et, parce que mes paroles s'appellent "pièce" au lieu de "discours," il faut qu'il y ait des messieurs qui taillent, qui rognent . . . (Chincholle, "Le Coq rouge")[33]

Evidently, in 1888, the censorship bureau would have agreed with Emma Goldman's statement that theater was a greater menace to society than public speaking.

As it turned out, these changes made little difference at the performance: the audience sang *La Carmagnole* with the original words before the play had even begun, and there was so much commotion during the play that it was impossible to hear the actors or to follow the rather complicated plot. In addition to the noise—political quips, animal noises, songs, and the firemen's *panpan, panpan*—the audience was seriously distracted by various projectiles: hats, scarves, sugar cubes, and the revolutionary *escargot*:

> Le Coq rouge—encore une invention pour armurerie dramatique. A *Juarès* nous devons la tomate crue. Au *Coq rouge* nous devons l'escargot cuit. Ce projectile a été expérimenté hier au Théâtre des Batignolles, à l'occasion de la pièce de Mlle Louise Michel avec un plein succès. Lancé des galléries supérieures d'une main sûre, il blesse légèrement avec sa coquille et salit à coup sûr avec son jus. De la vingtaine de redingotes sur lesquelles on l'a essayé, pas une n'en réchappera. Adopté comme le fusil Lebel, l'escargot sympathique servira désormais à toutes nos solennités théâtrales. (Martel)[34]

Though a number of papers printed a substantial article about the evening, few reviewers critiqued, in any way, the play itself. Only Fauchery, from *L'Intransigeant*, faithfully defended the play and its author: "un drame tel que la vaillante citoyenne pouvait et devait écrire, c'est-à-dire un chaleureux et vibrante plaidoyer en faveur des humbles et des déshérités" (Fauchery 1888).[35] He criticized the censorship bureau and the unruly audience, claiming, however, that the working-class members of the audience warmly applauded the play, which addressed their needs with such eloquence.

The audience participation at the performance of Louise Michel's *La Grève* in December 1890 was less violent than at *Nadine* and *Le Coq rouge*. One drama critic wrote that, anticipating some sort of incident, he came to the play wearing his "hat for places of ill repute," but that he was disappointed by the relatively calm performance as he had hoped for "a revolution" to relate to his readers (Larcher). The theater had distributed 300 tickets at reduced prices to the *compagnons* (term used by the anarchists to designate their own) in order to avoid having a dominantly bourgeois, elitist audience, as during the staging of *Nadine* and *Le Coq rouge*, where the tickets had sold for extravagant prices, much above the working-class budget. Considering there were an estimated 500 such *compagnons* in Paris, the movement was evidently well represented at the theater and a large part of the audience was a priori sympathetic to the political message of the performance. The censors nearly banned the play but finally approved it. It may have seemed less dangerous because the Théâtre de la Villette was not in the center of Paris, but in what was then a working-class suburb housing the stockyards. The fact that Louise Michel herself was exiled in London at the time may also have contributed to the censors' relative tolerance.

La Grève was not performed in isolation, but as part of a participatory cultural and political event. Between the prologue and the first act, Leboucher, an anarchist orator, gave a speech, first denouncing the censorship bureau for mutilating Michel's play. Then, making the link between artistic and political freedom, he went on to condemn economic exploitation and to call for the extermination of the propertied classes by means more violent than mere strikes: he declared, "il vaut mieux crever derrière un tas de pavés le fusil à la main que de mourir de faim dans un taudis."[36] He finished with the cries: "Mort aux gavés! Mort à la bourgeoisie! Vive les travailleurs! Vive l'anarchie! Vive la Révolution Sociale!"[37] The audience joined in enthusiastically. During the performance of the play itself, members of the audience continued to cry out "Vive l'anarchie!" each time the word "revolution" was pronounced.

Other forms of political-artistic entertainment were also integrated into the program. During the intermissions, a leading Montmartre anarchist recited a poem entitled "Germinal," and the audience sang revolutionary songs. At the end of the play, the audience left the theater singing *La Carmagnole*.[38]

Like *Nadine*, the Prologue of *La Grève* takes place in Poland, this time near Warsaw. A group of rebels has planned to assassinate the Grand Duke. Yet, once again, the assassination attempt fails due to a betrayal of one of the rebels. At the beginning of Act I, which takes place many years later, we find the traitor in Austria at the onset of another insurrection. She has become a rich and powerful baroness and is, in large part, responsible for the injustice, inequality, and poverty that have fueled the revolt. Though the insurrection is successful this time, few of the protagonists survive. Yet all die willingly, happy to have sacrificed their lives to the revolution, to the future republic. As in *Nadine*, the discourse of Michel's revolutionary characters, as well as their altruistic self-sacrifice, is a rally cry to the audience, and, in spite of major cuts by the censors, the universal message of the play is evident. Though actual reference to the rebels as "anarchists" was cut, there is no mistaking the ideology her characters are preaching.

In *La Grève*, Michel draws from her experience of the siege of Paris and the Commune. Like the Parisians of 1870, the rebels in Act III of the play are under siege in an abandoned mine, which has become their arsenal and refuge. A young mother holds a dying infant in her arms. They have no food left, and there is little hope of getting provisions past the soldiers surrounding the mine. By the time the rebels succeed in bringing provisions, the infant is dead. During the subsequent battle, as during the Commune, women and men fight and die side by side: "Il n'y a ni âge ni sexe dans les luttes comme la nôtre" (Prologue, sc. 2).[39]

In this play, Michel develops the metaphor of *les noces rouges*. Usually translated in English as "blood wedding," the French expression literally means "red wedding," which, while less poetic perhaps, is richer in meaning since it refers to both the revolution and blood. In *La Grève*, Marius, a young protagonist, is torn between his love for Marpha and the immense hate that drives his revolt. He resolves the conflict by seeing in Marpha not a fiancée but a comrade-in-arms. His sister Esther goes further. For her "Love would kill hate," and she thus refuses to allow herself to love her fellow rebel, Inrike, preferring instead to die with him for the cause. Just before battle, the four young protagonists and would-be couples exchange their vows:

INRIKE: C'est cette nuit, les vraies fiançailles—les rouges noces
de la mort.
ESTHER: Ce sont les plus belles. Je les avais choisies.

MARIUS: Et toi Marpha, veux-tu aussi les noces rouges—les noces des braves?

MARPHA: Oui. (III, 6)[40]

Louise Michel stayed single throughout her life, dedicating herself to the revolution. She was, in fact, known as the Red Virgin. Her relationship with the one man whom she allegedly loved, fellow Communard Théophile Ferré, was much like that of her protagonists: comrades-in-arms, fighting side by side, and willing to die for the revolution. Ferré was, in fact, executed for his role in the insurrection.

La Grève did not receive as much attention in the press as either Nadine or Le Coq rouge. There was, however, one unconditionally favorable review in Le Père Peinard, anarchist Emile Pouget's rabble-rousing newspaper, written largely in slang:

Foutre, ça lui arrive pas souvent au père Peinard d'aller au théâtre; pour une fois, y fait exception. Notez, que ça en valait la peine, nom de dieu! C'était une pièce de Louise Michel qui se jouait. Et le plus bath, mille tonnerres, c'est qu'elle se joue pas sur un grand théâtre, mais dans une piaule où le populo peut radiner facilement: *au théâtre de la Villette!* Là, au moins, c'est au milieu du populo, nom de dieu! Dans un autre théâtre y aurait eu de petites vaches bourgeoises, des petits crevés de la haute.[41]

In December 1890 when La Grève was performed, Louise Michel had taken refuge in London. Her first visit to London had been, in fact, in 1880. After her amnesty, Michel sailed from New Caledonia to London, where she was greeted by fellow Communards who had taken refuge there. She was taken to the Social Democratic Club on Rose Street (now Manette Street), a meeting place for English, German, and Russian revolutionaries, which had become a center for the defense and aid of political refugees (Quail 8). This community had accompanied Michel to Newhaven and paid the expenses for her return to Paris.

In July 1890, she once again found herself in London as a political exile. During her five years there,[42] Louise Michel frequented a group of European anarchists, that included the Italian Enrico Malatesta, the Russian Peter Kropotkin, and the French Charles Malato (Sonn, *Anarchism and Cultural Politics* 26). Here, anarchists exiled from less tolerant countries enjoyed relative freedom. Michel remembers in her memoirs:

Les anarchistes expulsés de France, de Belgique et d'Italie purent vivre en paix dans la grande cité londonnienne. Ils purent même continuer leurs travaux de propagande et tenir presque chaque jour des réunions . . . Et rien n'était curieux comme ces réunions. Elles débutaient par une conférence où une dizaine d'orateurs prenaient la parole et se terminaient par un bal ou un concert. (*Souvenirs* 179)[43]

Lousie Michel spoke regularly at such events and contributed articles to the anarchist press in England.[44] Drama also figured among the activities of these anarchists in exile. Michel says that she spent her time in London writing plays: "Je retouchais certaines comédies que j'avais ébauchées. Je mettais la main à certains drames qui ne verront probablement jamais les feux de la rampe" (*Souvenirs* 406).[45] At least one play that Michel wrote during this period, *L'Ogre*, was performed at the Autonomic Club in London. Michel gives a summary in *Souvenirs et aventures de ma vie*:

Un jeune homme, qui a toujours été honnête, qui a toujours travaillé, tombe soudain dans la misère. Il essaie de réagir, de se relever par tous les moyens possibles, mais il ne peut y parvenir. La société s'acharne après lui de plus en plus, jusqu'au jour où elle l'arrête pour avoir volé un pain. Alors, à sa sortie de prison, cet homme est devenu féroce. Il pose une bombe, fait sauter la maison du juge qui l'a condamné. Il est pris; il va être exécuté, quand la société, qui fermente depuis quelques années, est soudain victorieuse du vieux monde et remet en liberté le coupable. (412)[46]

According to Michel, the play enjoyed some success until the police banned it and sentenced the actors to eight days in prison (412). Even in London, then, anarchist theater was apparently seen as a threat to society.

In her *Souvenirs*, Louise Michel describes another play written during this period, *Prométhée*. She was so proud of this play that she sent it to Sarah Bernhardt in 1895 hoping the great actress would accept the role of the beautiful, young Prometheus. In Michel's version of the myth, written in verse, Prometheus is at the center of a Stone Age "groupe d'avant-garde," surrounded by artisans, poets, and musicians:

aux hommes qui se groupent autour de lui se réunissent de premiers forgerons, de premiers poètes; ils ont la flûte à trois trous, un premier luth; ils tracent sur les parois de leurs cavernes de premiers signes pour transmettre la pensée. Il y a des premiers essais de gravures sur os, de premiers essais de semences . . . (407)[47]

In the excerpts that follow, Prometheus, nailed to a rock in his final hour, dreams of a new world: "Il s'élève de la nature / Un chant magnifique et puissant, / Longtemps peut-être l'ombre dure / Mais le progrès va grandissant" (408).[48] As he dies, a Christ-like revolutionary martyr, the daughters of the ocean rise undulating toward him, announcing the coming of the revolution: "Tout s'agrandit et se transforme, / Resplendissant est l'avenir, / En le voyant il faut mourir" (409).[49] Sarah Bernhardt, wisely, declined the offer, but *Prométhée* may have been performed in London at Grafton Hall.[50]

During her exile in London, Louise Michel also opened a school, The International School, with such honorary members as Kropotkin, William Morris, and Malatesta. The prospectus for the school includes a quote about the anarchist theory of integral education by Mikhail Bakunin:

> The whole education of children and their instruction must be founded on the scientific development of reason, not on that of faith; on the development of personal dignity and independence, not on that of piety and obedience; on the worship of truth and justice at any cost, and above all on respect for humanity, which must replace always and everywhere the worship of divinity . . . All rational education is at the bottom nothing but this progressive immolation of authority for the benefit of liberty, the final object of education necessarily being the formation of free men full of respect and love for the liberty of others. ("The International School" prospectus)

Integral education was a combination of three principles: physical education; intellectual education, including professional training as of the age of 12; and moral education in which children were taught the importance of freedom, creativity, and solidarity. The children were taught to abhor authority, so that, in the words of anarchist educator Paul Robin, "l'esprit de révolte devienne à son tour la première des vertus" (Qtd. in Nataf 306).[51]

Theater could be used as a combination of these three educational principles, as both a physical and intellectual activity with a moral content. The archives at the International Institute of Social History in Amsterdam contain manuscripts of a number of plays that Louise Michel may have written for educational purposes. These plays are, in fact, very similar in genre to plays written for church-oriented youth groups, except that the moral message she was proselytizing was based on revolutionary rather than religious principles. In a notebook, also housed in Amsterdam, she wrote that theater should be a form of recreation in school: "Il offre un peu d'esprit, de gaieté et d'idéal."[52]

While gaiety may not be a word we would immediately associate with Louise Michel, it seems to have been a lesser known facet of her character. A journalist for *Le Gaulois*, for example, who was able to see beyond the stereotypes—"la Pétroleuse" or "la bonne Louise"—discovered her sense of humor and indeed her gaiety (La Fournière 262–263). Gaiety was present in many activities of the anarchist movement, notably in the theater. Maxime Lisbonne, for example, while taking the anarchist cause very seriously, was not averse to taking advantage of revolutionary themes for lighthearted entertainment, from his Taverne du Bagne to his Dynamite Polka, during which "revolver shots punctuated the music, and the odor of burnt powder filled the room" (Sonn, *Anarchism and Cultural Politics* 67). As one critic for *La Patrie* wrote, "One laughs at everything on the Butte" (Qtd. in Sonn, *Anarchism and Cultural Politics* 67). Albert Wolff, journalist for *Le Figaro*, was impressed by Lisbonne's gay attitude when he attended a rehearsal of *Nadine*:

> Au fond, Lisbonne, qui peut être terrible à son heure, est au repos, un bon enfant, qui parle de ses malheurs sans la moindre aigreur contre la société . . . Cela demeure pour moi un secret indéchiffrable de voir des hommes traverser les dures épreuves du bagne ou de l'exil et conserver néanmoins qui, tout son esprit, qui sa bonne humeur ou son insouciance. Il me pousse des cheveux blancs rien qu'en passant devant Mazas, et ce Lisbonne, qui a été dix ans au bagne, revient tout guilleret et avec une entière gaîté de Nouméa. En cette soirée mémorable, l'ex-colonel eut des accès de gaîté folle.[53]

Though it may not have been Louise Michel's intention, the performances of her plays seem to have inspired at least as much gaiety as thought or ideals.

The milieu of exiled anarchists in London in the 1890s seems to have been particularly gay:

> Louise a toujours fait preuve d'une gaieté aussi robuste que son sens de la tragédie. Mais il semble qu'à Londres cette disposition se soit trouvée tout spécialement favorisée. Contrairement à ce qu'on pourrait imaginer, son entourage immédiat, ce milieu d'exilés—pour la

plupart, comme elle, volontaires—n'engendre pas la mélancolie. Ces libertaires qui vivent comme l'oiseau sur la branche ont souvent autant de fantaisie dans l'esprit que d'anticonformisme dans les opinions. (La Fournière 278)[54]

In *Les Joyeusetés de l'exil*, Charles Malato describes the lighter side of life in London in the 1890s. Malato, anarchist militant and son of a Communard, got to know Louise Michel in New Caledonia, where he fled at age 17 after an *coup* against the French government—like father like son. He describes his "old friend" Louise Michel's life in London as divided between free schooling, the cult of philanthropy, and the Social Revolution (Malato 24). Malato claims, however, that the Autonomic Club was in fact a trompe-l'œil:"On criait beaucoup mais jamais une résolution sérieuse n'y fut prise" (Malato 103).[55] On the other hand, he describes a very gay evening at Grafton Hall, featuring his own one-act vaudeville entitled *Mariage par la dynamite* and a speech by Louise Michel on the subject of Art of the Future.[56] It would seem that the Autonomic Club was as much a social club as a political forum for anarchist exiles, whose militant activities were temporarily on hold while things cooled down in their respective countries.

In conclusion, it would seem that Louise Michel's involvement in the theater did indeed offer thought, ideals, and gaiety. Michel was, after all, a pedagogue, a political activist, and a performer. As a pedagogue, she sought to teach the truth about social injustice and the means of eradicating it. As a political activist, taking action was essential to her, and she was willing to use nearly any means to communicate her message or to reach her goals, whether it be taking up arms, demonstrating in the streets, haranguing to the crowds, or writing a play. Her various performances (on the barricades, in the streets, on the podium, or in the wings) had various outcomes (prison, exile, articles in the press, enthusiastic applause, laughter, and flying escargots) but always attracted attention to her crusade.

Indeed, like the mystery plays of the Middle Ages, which served to inspire the masses with religious fervor, Louise Michel's plays served her ideological crusade, her revolt against the bourgeois, capitalist society. Formally, Michel's was a theater of "messianic revolt," as described by Robert Brustein in his seminal book on modern drama, *The Theatre of Revolt*. Like the plays of Ibsen, Shaw, O'Neill, and others that Brustein categorizes as "messianic drama," Michel's plays are grand spectacles of epic proportions. They were certainly difficult to stage given their length, their large casts, and their numerous and challenging set changes. Like the messianic hero, Michel's protagonists are both malefactors and benefactors: "As a malefactor, the messianic hero desires to kill God and destroy the old order; as benefactor, he desires to build an order of his own" (Brustein 18–19). Similarly, though in Michel's plays God is already dead, her protagonists wish to destroy the old capitalist regime in order to create the possibility of a new postrevolutionary society. Yet, Michel's protagonists will not be able to build the new order themselves; in true messianic fashion, they sacrifice their lives for the cause.

I would suggest that the proselytizing tone of her dialogue, the self-sacrifice of her protagonists, and the apocalyptic climax of her plays most closely correspond to a theatrical version of what Richard Sonn describes as the "quasi-religious status of the [anarchist] movement" (Sonn, *Anarchism and Cultural Politics* 3). Sonn holds that, for the anarchists, "artistic images and powerful experiences such as a martyr's death were received as metaphoric wholes; they commanded an immediacy that engendered an essentially emotional rather than analytical response" (Sonn, *Anarchism and Cultural Politics* 3). Similarly, Michel's plays were not intended so much to instruct as to provoke an immediate experience, a social catharsis that would ideally make rebels. In her plays, as in her propaganda tours, which she carried on until her death in 1905, Louise Michel, the Red Virgin, spread the revolutionary gospel, "preaching what [she] thought to be the "good word" (Sizaire 94).[57] On stage, her prose-lytism reproduced the anarchist tactics of propaganda by the word and propaganda by the deed, discourse, and dynamite.

CHAPTER THREE

Feminism and the Freethinkers Movement: Nelly Roussel

In the last decade of the nineteenth century, following the performance of Louise Michel's *La Grève*, a number of ephemeral theaters were created to bring political issues and social protest to the stage. Both Nelly Roussel and Véra Starkoff were involved in this movement to create a theater for the people that would advocate the socialist ideal. They found a venue for their dramatic aspirations in the Université Populaire, a movement that began in the final year of the nineteenth century in which women were able to participate in theatrical activities as playwright, director, manager, critic, and actress. In 1899, Georges Deherme founded la Coopération des Idées, the first Université Populaire, in the Faubourg St. Antoine, a working-class district of Paris. Between 1899 and 1914, more than 200 such institutions were created throughout the country. Their goal was to educate the workers in order to produce new men and women for a new, freer society: to regenerate the individual to improve the social state. Deherme understood the notion of education in its broadest sense. Not content with organizing classes for adults, he wanted to provide a variety of medical, legal, and financial services, as well as recreational activities. The statutes of the Société des Universités Populaires in 1900 list a variety of such facilities and programs: a sports room, public baths, a library, a doctor's office and a pharmacy, legal and financial consultants, an alcohol-free restaurant, a system of mutual benefit insurance, and a theater (Qtd. in *Bulletin* 24).

The most active and well-equipped theater of any Université Populaire was the Théâtre du Peuple founded in 1899 by Henri Dargel at the Coopération des Idées.[1] It could seat an audience of 400 people, and though the stage itself was small (only about 18 square meters), it had heating and gas lighting, a variety of stage settings, wings, and dressing rooms. Some 200 plays were performed there between 1899 and 1901.[2] Though Dargel's troupe was not able to perform every week, they had no trouble finding other amateur acting groups to perform there.[3] Elocution teachers also occasionally used the theater to put on plays with their pupils (Bracco 317).

The facilities and the regular performance schedule of the Théâtre du Peuple were, however, exceptional. Due to financial constraints and the resulting logistic limitations, few Universités Populaires actually had a theater; most simply had one or two lecture rooms, a library, and a discussion room. Fortunately, the existence of an actual stage was by no means a prerequisite to organizing theatrical events. Many of the plays performed—like those we will be studying here—did not require any special facilities. Nearly every Université Populaire, no matter how ill-equipped, provided some form of theatrical activities and performances.

Theater fulfilled various goals of the Université Populaire. First, it was entertaining, and the recreational activities of the Université Populaire were considered essential to their mission. One of their goals was to provide an alternative to "l'homicide cabaret" and "l'ignoble café-concert," which were considered a plague by the organizers of the Université Populaire (Dargel 116). The Théâtre du Peuple literally replaced a café-concert when it found a permanent locale in the Faubourg Saint-Antoine: "[la Coopération des Idées] succède cette fois à un café-concert des bas-fonds parisiens, où la chanson ordurière et l'alcool à bas prix représentaient l'art et la vie" (Dargel 117).[4] Rather than spending their time drinking and watching shows with no redeeming social or artistic value, the workers were invited to the Université Populaire to participate in a variety of literary or musical evenings, parties, or excursions to museums or to the country. These events also provided an occasion for the whole family— men, women, and children—to get together for some wholesome fun.

No matter how entertaining, however, the theater at the Université Populaire was meant, above all, to be educational. Theater was an integral part of a program to develop the workers' artistic taste and to familiarize them with literary masterpieces. Theatrical performances were often preceded by a lecture about the author, the play, and the lesson to be learned from it, and followed by a discussion of the issues raised by the performance. Thus, the theater was an ideal setting to instruct the workers on social issues.

For the most part, three different types of plays were performed in the Université Populaire: major classics carefully chosen for their educational import; modern social drama by playwrights such as Eugène Brieux,

Lucien Descaves, and François de Curel; and finally, unpublished plays written for the Université Populaire, often by the activists themselves. This is the case for both Nelly Roussel and Véra Starkoff. Though these plays were less numerous, they were of considerable importance to the project itself. Henri Dargel wrote in 1903 that, in order to be a living enterprise, the Théâtre du Peuple had to create its own dramatic literature (Dargel 123–124). Organizers of the Université Populaire dreamed of a theater not only *for* the people but also *by* the people. The members of the Université Populaire were thus encouraged to be active participants in all aspects of the productions. They were even given classes in diction, music, and acting to prepare them.[5] A more practical reason for encouraging original plays written by activists was cost. In a report on entertainment given at the Congrès des Universités Populaires in 1904, Georges Baër, a lawyer by profession, pointed out that in order to perform plays publicly, the Université Populaire must pay royalties. The only way to avoid paying royalties was to make the performance private, open only to members of the Université Populaire. Baër suggested a temporary stratagem for avoiding this expense: "nos camarades sont en règle s'ils ont pris la précaution, avant l'audition, de faire adhérer leurs invités à l'Université Populaire où se donne un spectacle" (112).[6] In the long term though, he reported that he was currently negotiating on behalf of the Universités Populaires with the Société des auteurs dramatiques and the Société des auteurs, compositeurs et éditeurs de musique. He was confident a solution would be found given that Victor Meusy, who was attending the Congrès as the representative of the Université Populaire de Lagny, was also the secretary general of the Syndicat des auteurs, compositeurs et éditeurs de musique.

Baër also reported that, according to a recent survey of Universités Populaires, the most popular type of theatrical event involved performances of short plays in one or two acts by Courteline, Mirbeau, Villiers de l'Isle-Adam, Meilhac, Halévy, Pierre Veber, and Tristan Bernard. Dramatic readings of longer plays, classic or modern, had also been very successful. In fact, Baër claimed that prepared readings may be better adapted to the demands of the Université Populaire than full stagings when the members of the Université Populaire perform the plays themselves:

> Constatons à ce sujet que nos camarades n'ayant pas généralement le temps d'apprendre par cœur, le procédé de la lecture préparée, usité dans beaucoup d'Universités Populaires, est à la fois commode et très suffisant pour donner à nos soirées le relief qui leur est nécessaire. (114)[7]

In the discussion after Baër's report, playwright Maurice Bouchor concurred that a reading of a play with several voices could be more successful than performances staged with insufficient funds.

Eventually, the theater in the Université Populaire came to be recognized as legitimate by the theater community. Theater professionals regularly shared their talent either as actors, directors, or instructors of diction and acting. The Université Populaire also gave acting students from the Conservatoire and other aspiring actors and actresses the opportunity to gain some experience on the stage. In 1908, for example, while still a student, the well-known actor and director Louis Jouvet founded the Théâtre d'Action d'Art and performed plays at the Université Populaire du Faubourg Saint-Antoine (Corvin 461). In 1909, Jouvet and Gabrielle Fontan performed together there in Ibsen's *A Doll's House* (Ebstein et al., *Théâtre de contestation* 28).

In 1907, the theater journal *Comœdia* started listing performances at the Université Populaire:

> *Comœdia*, qui ne veut rester étranger à aucun mouvement théâtral, ouvre à ce titre, à partir d'aujourd'hui, une rubrique spécialement consacrée aux soirées des "Universités Populaires." On sait combien elles se sont développées en France, depuis quelques années; aussi, sommes-nous heureux de pouvoir leur consacrer, suivant les besoins de l'actualité, et sans aucun esprit de parti bien entendu, une place où nous enregistrons leurs manifestations musicales et théâtrales. (December 24, 1907)[8]

While being careful not to align themselves with the politics of the movement, *Comœdia* thus recognized the extent and legitimacy of theater in the Université Populaire.

Women did not play a central role in the administration of the Université Populaire; only five of the eighty some Universités Populaires in the Paris region had women among the founding members (Mercier, *Universités Populaires* 156). They were, however, relatively active as participants, organizers, authors, performers, and orators. Women made up a large part of the audience at many activities, and the organizers of the Universités Populaires applauded their participation. At La Fraternelle du IIIe, for example, "les femmes assistant aux séances sont en nombre à peu près égal à celui des hommes. C'est un grand point pour l'avenir de l'Université et le but qu'elle se propose d'atteindre" (Mercier, *Universités Populaires* 157).[9] At the 1904 Congress, one of the stated goals was to encourage women's participation by offering more lectures and discussions on feminist topics (134).

Nelly Roussel (1878–1922), a radical feminist, journalist, and orator, was involved in the Université Populaire from the start. In her early years, before dedicating herself to social activism, Roussel had aspired to have a career in the theater. It is unclear how seriously Roussel considered this career path or whether she actually had any training or professional experience on the stage. An article by Marbel, founder of L'Union Fraternelle des Femmes, makes Roussel's interest in acting sound like a childish occupation: "A l'âge où on joue encore à la poupée, elle est passionnée de littérature, de poésie, de théâtre. Elle écrit des histoires et joue avec ses petites amies des drames de sa composition dans lesquels elle révèle une véritable vocation de tragédienne" (Marbel, "L'Apothéose" 153).[10] Yet, in a biographical essay on Nelly Roussel, the same Marbel wrote, "Encouragée par tous ceux qui avaient pu apprécier ses dons de tragédienne, elle avait eu, après son mariage, l'idée de suivre sa vocation théâtrale" (Marbel, "Les femmes" 1).[11] In 1913, Roussel admitted that if it had been necessary for her to "work for a living," she would have pursued a career in the theater.[12] A number of factors were involved in this decision. Nelly was raised in a bourgeois Catholic family. As an adolescent, she had been both patriotic and religious.[13] By 1898, when she married artist and freethinker Henri Godet, though still very patriotic, she had already lost her faith in religion and rejected "l'étroitesse d'esprit et les préjugés."[14] Soon, she joined the freethinker movement herself. She and her husband also participated from the onset in the nascent Université Populaire. Many years later, Godet would write:

> Ensemble, nous prîmes bientôt part à la création d'Universités Populaires. Ce magnifique élan pour l'éducation du sens critique et du sens artistique des foules nous passionna. Nelly prodigua alors sans compter, organisant conférences, fêtes civiques, représentations classiques. (Godet 147)[15]

In 1900, Godet's sister married the neo-Malthusian militant Paul Robin who would have a great influence on Nelly Roussel's activism. Further, Nelly experienced three difficult pregnancies between 1898 and 1904, which reinforced her ideas about reproductive freedom and the rights of the mother. During her last pregnancy, she complained:

> Je croyais bien être à l'abri de ces redoutables épreuves qui ébranlent si profondément ma santé; et j'espérais pouvoir donner l'exemple de la "grève" que je préconise. Hélas! Malgré tous les progrès de la

science et de la conscience, la pauvre humanité n'est pas encore maîtresse de son destin; nous n'avons pas définitivement vaincu la fatalité! . . . Me voici donc condamnée au repos complet pour plusieurs mois. (Qtd. in Maignien and Safwan 9)[16]

By 1904, her favorite virtue was "l'indépendence de l'esprit"; her heroes and heroines were "tous ceux et celles qui osent affranchir des préjugés et conventions"; notably Louise Michel and the first feminists; her state of mind was "révoltée"; and her motto was "Ni dieu, ni maître!"[17] Roussel now considered her forte to be "l'art oratoire" as she subordinated her theatrical aspirations to her career in propaganda: "Son nouveau rôle de militante se révélait à elle comme plus noble et plus intéressant, et elle résolut de consacrer son talent à la défense de ses convictions" (Marbel, "Les femmes" 1).[18] Making use of her theatrical vocal training, she became "une oratrice géniale" with "une voix si belle, si prenante, si bien posée, ses gestes toujours justes et sobres" (Durand *Discours* 148):[19]

> Madame Nelly Roussel . . . la plus éloquente des féministes française, possède tous les dons d'une oratrice: une belle tête, un beau port, un beau geste, une belle voix, une diction irréprochable, une conviction et une émotivité chaleureuses et communicatives.[20]

Roussel also used her talents to help others develop such skills. She taught classes in diction, and, in 1920, she participated in the creation of an *École de Propagandiste*, a propaganda school to help teach other women public-speaking techniques. She taught not only vocal and body-language techniques related to giving speeches, but also how to answer people who interrupt and contradict them, and how to participate in a debate (Bodin).[21]

Having left the stage for the rostrum, Roussel did not, however, entirely abandon her involvement with the theater. In February 1903, for example, she performed in Racine's *Andromaque* for the Société Républicaine des Conférences Populaires in the Mairie du VIe arrondissement. The perform-ance was preceded by a talk on the theater of Racine by Monsieur Paul Peltier, a lawyer and a member of the Association de la Critique drama-tique. In June, Roussel organized another performance of the play at the Coopération des Idées in which she again played the role of Hermione.

Nelly Roussel wrote three short propaganda plays: *Par la Révolte* (1903), *Pourquoi elles vont à l'église* (1910), and *La Faute d'Eve* (1913). Roussel's first play, *Par la Révolte*, was her most successful. This *scène symbolique* premiered in Paris in April 1903 at L'Egalité, Université

Populaire of the 9th and 10th districts. Nelly Roussel played the leading role herself. *Par la Révolte* was performed as part of an artistic event along with songs, poetry readings, and other short forms of entertainment. During the following years, it was performed innumerable times at Universités Populaires and Maisons du Peuple throughout the country, as well as at meetings of a variety of different organizations including the unions of women writers, stenographers, and accountants, le Cercle de la Jeunesse laïque, le Groupe "Ni Dieu ni Maître" in Béziers, and le groupe de l'Union radicale-socialiste in Clargues. Most often the performance was preceded by a lecture by Nelly Roussel on related feminist topics like "feminism and socialism," "freedom and motherhood," and "woman: the eternal sacrificial victim."

Par la Révolte is a short allegorical play advocating "la grève des ventres." The protagonist of *Par la Révolte* is the rebellious Eve. Disassociated from her role in the Bible, Eve is an allegorical figure representing all women. Kneeling center stage, exhausted, dressed like a slave, her arms in chains, Eve laments her condition. On either side of her, we see the Church and the Society, seated immobile and cold like a statue raised on a sort of throne or podium. Eve turns first to the Church to ask for help. The Church has the aspect of a phantom covered in black veils, surrounded by flowers, candles, and altar boys holding censers. There is a large crucifix on the wall above her head, and she has one hand on the Bible. At the foot of the throne, a long succession of Church dignitaries and representatives stands immobile in hierarchical order from Bishops to simple nuns, each dressed according to his or her function. The Church, cold and severe, tells Eve that she has sinned and must suffer in consequence:

Femme, créature impure et maudite! tu nais pour la souffrance et l'humiliation. Enfanter dans les larmes et sans gloire; te soumettre en silence, et te courber toujours, c'est là ton châtiment! (8)[22]

The Church reminds Eve that life is not important, "l'éternité est tout!" (8). But Eve finds no solace in this: "l'espoir d'un paradis lointain est impuissant à calmer mes douleurs!" (9).[23]

Eve then hears phrases of the *Marseillaise*. She raises her head and turns slowly with confidence toward the figure of Society dressed as the Republic with the *bonnet phrygien* (the red bonnet, symbolic of the French Revolution) and draped in the French flag. One hand rests on the *Code*, the book of French laws, next to a *glaive*, a sword that symbolizes war, divine justice, and judicial power. At the foot of Society's throne, a succession of government officials from judges to jailors mirrors the Church dignitaries on the other side. Eve calls to the great republican Society, creator of liberty, to free her of her chains, but the Society, equally cold and severe as the Church, tells her that the French motto—Liberté, Egalité, Fraternité—was not written for her, that her duty in life is to produce children; the nation needs citizens. Eve counters that she has produced children, but with no reward, no recognition. At this moment, when Eve is at the height of despair, the character of Revolt arrives, much to the surprise and terror of the Church and the Society, accompanied by loud exclamations, chants, and phrases from the *Internationale*. Revolt, proud and superb, draped in scarlet, hair to the four winds, explains to Eve that she must not submit to her oppression; she must seize her rights in a superb and victorious élan. Eve is quickly inspired and turns against "perfidious Religion and the vile Society" who have erected the "monstrous barrier of prejudice and stupidity." The slave becomes a rebel whose weapon is her womb:

> Oh! n'attendez plus rien de moi! . . . Point de besogne sans salaire! . . . Trop longtemps l'Humanité, mon œuvre, a bafoué et renié son auteur! mes entrailles sont lasses de porter des ingrats! L'arbre de vie refuse des fruits à ses bourreaux! . . . Ferme-toi donc, flanc douloureux et trop fécond! . . . ferme-toi . . . jusqu'à l'heure du triomphe; l'heure glorieuse où crouleront les antiques forteresses sous mes clameurs exaspérées. (12–13)[24]

We can imagine the audience now standing up, cheering and applauding since accounts of performances in the press mention that the play was often interrupted by long bouts of applause and finished with enthusiastic ovations. The play was certainly never performed as elaborately as described in the stage directions. At the first performance, there were four actresses including the author. Very often Roussel performed a dramatic reading of the play herself.

In *Par la Révolte*, Roussel is advocating a radical neo-Malthusian doctrine. The neo-Malthusian movement in France started at the beginning of the Third Republic in reaction against the conservative pro-natalist movement. Inspired by France's defeat in the Franco-Prussian war, the pro-natalists believed that the country's military strength depended on an increase in the population. The neo-Malthusians maintained, on the contrary, that it was necessary to limit the number of births in order to improve the living conditions of the working class. The movement was named for Malthus (1766–1834), an Anglican pastor, economist, and demographer, who explained the need to reduce the birth rate for economic reasons. The Malthus law stated that population growth will always tend to outrun the food supply and that the betterment of the lot of mankind is impossible without stern limits on reproduction. He recommended that people should get married later in life and abstain from sex both in and out of marriage. The goal of the neo-Malthusian movement was somewhat different. Rather than recommending abstinence, they fought for the widespread use of contraceptives. France was particularly receptive to neo-Malthusian ideas for several reasons. First, by the end of the nineteenth century, the French population was already neo-Malthusian in practice, curiously more so than other European nations. The use of contraception, though illegal and therefore clandestine, had been widespread since the end of the eighteenth century, and the French had developed even more contraceptive methods during the Second Empire (1852–1870)—condoms, diaphragms, vaginal sponges. Moreover, with the rise of socialism, there was a decline in religious sentiment in late-nineteenth-century France, especially among the working class who were the population most targeted by the movement. Finally, in the post-Commune era, the movement found a large number of militants hungry for revolutionary social causes.

It was Paul Robin who founded the first official neo-Malthusian organization in France, La Ligue de la Régénération humaine. This revolutionary propaganda movement's goal was

Répandre les notions exactes de science physiologique et sociale permettant aux parents d'apprécier les cas où ils devront se montrer prudents quant au nombre de leurs enfants, et assurer, sous ce rapport, leur liberté et surtout celle de la femme. (Ronsin 49–50)[25]

They provided sex education, published a journal and a catalogue of materials for sexual hygiene and pregnancy prevention, and sold contraceptives. The slogan for the movement became "la grève des ventres" (the strike of the wombs). The expression came from a speech by Eugène Humbert, leader of the Ligue de la Régénération humaine after Paul Robin, in 1903:

Ne faites pas plus d'enfants que vous ne pouvez en élever convenablement (. . .) Aux jérémiades des repopulateurs répondez par la plus grande, la plus efficace, la plus puissante, la plus imposante, la première des grèves: la grève des ventres. (Qtd. in Albistur and Armogathe 387)[26]

The neo-Malthusian movement was very successful at the turn of the century, in particular among anarchists and certain socialist groups, as well as among intellectuals and the medical community.

From the start, women were the major target audience of neo-Malthusian militants who recognized that their success depended largely on convincing women. Yet, most French feminists at first were not really concerned with contraception and abortion rights. In fact, on the contrary, most feminists at the turn of the century exalted maternity. They were reformists, fighting for parental authority; for the right to file paternity suits, to work, and to vote, and to divorce; for the development of education for women and girls; and even for the recognition of maternity as salaried work. There were, however, some more radical feminists who joined the neo-Malthusian movement. Nelly Roussel was the primary link between feminism and neo-Malthusianism. She took Humbert's slogan, "la grève des ventres," and made it a feminist cause, inciting women to revolt against their state of oppression by refusing to have children. Roussel believed that women must take control of their own lives both in the political and domestic spheres. She did not agree with the socialist notion that the question of women's rights was simply part of the struggle against oppression in general and that it would resolve itself once the class system was abolished. She maintained that the first step toward political, economic, and social emancipation for women was to obtain absolute reproductive freedom. Like many turn-of-the-century feminists, Roussel also believed that motherhood was a form of labor that should receive economic compensation. Motherhood is a system of production in which women are the workers. Roussel simply advises women to cease to exercise this function until they have obtained the material and moral advantages they demand.

The form of Roussel's play, the dithyrambic style of the language and the obvious symbolism, is a bit disconcerting for us today, but they corresponded well to the declamatory, emphatic style of orators of the pre-television era. Roussel's allegory is less didactic than impassioned, its purpose not being to instruct but to rally and to agitate. Moreover, she seems to have effectively fulfilled her mission. Roussel's play was well appreciated by the socially conscious audiences for whom it was performed. It received glowing reviews from critics in newspapers such as *La Fronde* (an all woman run paper that Roussel wrote for), *L'Ouvrière*, *L'Action*, and *La Régénération* (put out by La Ligue de la Régénération Humaine). For example, Sébastien Faure, an important anarchist militant, wrote the following review of *Par la Révolte* in *L'Action* in 1905:

> Il serait utile que les Syndicats, les Coopératives, les Universités Populaires, les Cercles d'études sociales et tous les groupements qui travaillent au grand œuvre de libération intégrale connussent et fissent

connaître ce petit bijou d'une pensée robuste . . . Je le recommande
à tous.[27]

In fact, I only found one critic who had anything negative to say about it.
In another review published in *L'Action*, a journalist writing under the
pseudonym Flammèche criticized the conclusion of the play. He or she
grants that the play was moving, but maintains that the advice was futile.
The critic claims that women themselves are not willing to engage in
such a strike. Furthermore, for Flammèche, a violent revolt is not the
solution to the problem. She or he advocates a long, sustained struggle
leading to an "entente cordiale." Nelly Roussel responded to
Flammèche's criticisms in an article published in the same paper. First,
citing the *Dictionnaire Larousse*, she defined the word "révolte" as "la
rébellion contre l'autorité," the legitimate refusal to suffer, the struggle
against injustice, and the resistance to oppression. Revolt is not, she adds,
synonymous with violence; in fact, the best revolts are peaceful. As to
Flammèche's objection that women would not accept the strike, she
explains that she is not asking women to give up lovemaking. It is not a
lovers' strike, but a mothers' strike. She wishes love to remain sterile as
long as the society remains ungrateful:

> . . . si nous enfantons encore, ce sera *pour nous*, non pour [la société];
> ce sera *librement*, consciemment, à *notre* heure, parce que cela nous
> *plaît*, et non parce qu'un dogme, religieux ou social, nous l'ordonne
> comme un devoir. ("Eclaircissements")[28]

Flammèche's criticism of the play is typical of the reaction of most feminists in turn-of-the-century France who believed more in reform than in
revolution. While anticlerical feelings were common among feminists and
leftist Republicans, Roussel's anti-Republican sentiment was more radical. For many, the Third Republic, founded in 1870 after nearly a century
of often violent political struggles, was the only safeguard against the
return of the monarchy. The Republic was the symbol of hope, freedom
and equality, and progress. Roussel, on the contrary, attacked the Republic
and its many symbols, such as the *Marseillaise*, symbol of the French
Revolution, forbidden throughout much of the nineteenth century, and
sung again as a song of victory at the declaration of the Republic in 1870.
Officially made the National Anthem in 1879, the *Marseillaise*, for
Roussel, had lost its Revolutionary appeal. No longer a song of revolt
against the oppressor, it had become representative of the establishment
and of a belligerent nationalism. To the *Marseillaise*, Roussel opposes

L'Internationale, the international revolutionary anthem of the socialists and communists written in 1871 by Eugène Pottier.

This overtly anti-Republican propaganda, in addition to the fact that Sébastien Faure, one of the leaders of the anarchist movement, had joined the neo-Malthusian movement in 1903, may explain an intensification of the anti-Malthusian efforts. In 1907, the newspaper *L'Autorité* refused to print a letter Nelly Roussel wrote in response to an anti-Malthusian article. The court upheld the paper's decision not to print her letter on the grounds that her neo-Malthusian arguments were an attack against the nation.

> Considérant que c'est là une théorie immorale et antisociale, dont la pratique arrêteraient le progrès de l'humanité et serait, pour la nation chez laquelle elle prévaudrait, une cause certaine d'affaiblissement et de décadence; Considérant que la réponse de Mme Nelly Roussel heurte donc ce devoir patriotique sur lequel repose la vie des peuples civilisés et qui inspire une grande partie de nos lois [. . .]; Considérant enfin qu'elle qualifie de "mensongère République" le régime constitutionnel sous lequel nous vivons [. . .]. (Qtd. in Albistur and Armogathe 386)[29]

This incident, which only led Nelly Roussel to increase her neo-Malthusian activism, was soon followed by more severe repressive measures after anarchist Eugène Humbert became the leader of the neo-Malthusian movement in France in 1908. In spite of these measures, the movement continued to develop and was at the height of its activity when the war broke out in 1914. Neo-Malthusianism had always been linked to pacifism. While the natalists claimed that a large population was crucial to the balance of power necessary to prevent and win wars, the neo-Malthusians claimed that overpopulation was one of the causes of war: "la procréation excessive provoque la surabondance de travailleurs, et donc le chomage et la misère, ainsi que la pléthore de soldats et donc la guerre."[30] Ironically then, the movement as a whole became relatively inactive after Humbert, a pacifist, left for Spain. Nelly Roussel, however, continued to speak out in favor of the principles she had defended before the war in *La Fronde*, *L'Action*, and *La Voix des femmes*, a journal founded in 1917 by socialist Colette Reynaud. In 1920, in response to the *loi scélérate* that made all neo-Malthusian propaganda illegal, Roussel wrote:

> La dépopulation cause la guerre! . . . Parmi toutes les sottises dont on farcit le cerveau du pauvre peuple, il n'en est pas plus énorme

que celle-là. La "dépopulation" n'a rien pu causer du tout, pour l'excellente raison qu'elle n'existe pas! [. . .] ou du moins qu'elle n'existaient pas avant le massacre volontaire de dix millions d'hommes en pleine force; et la mort, par le chagrin, la famine et les épidémies, d'un nombre à peu près égal de femmes et d'enfants. (Qtd. in Bard *Les Filles de Marianne* 215)[31]

Both *Pourquoi elles vont à l'église* and *La Faute d'Ève* are stagings of another of Nelly Roussel's major spheres of activism: *la libre-pensée*. In these plays, she brings to the stage themes developed in a lecture on "La Femme et la Libre Pensée," which Roussel gave at numerous occasions in the early years of the century. La Libre Pensée began as a movement in France in the mid-nineteenth century and blossomed during the Third Republic when over a thousand Sociétés de Libre Pensée were founded. Their goal was to complete the work of the French Revolution and to secularize all sectors of French society. Roussel participated in the founding of L'Association des Libres Penseurs de France in 1902. Unlike most orders of Freemasons,[32] the freethinkers movement did not ostensibly discriminate according to sex. Indeed, 14 of the 95 members of the original administrative board were women (Maignien and Safwan 94). In her lecture, Roussel explains that the feminist movement and the freethinkers movement should work together against a common enemy: the church. She claims that all religions are instruments of oppression and are responsible for the inferior status of women:

Si la femme, aujourd'hui encore, dans les pays les plus civilisés, est traitée, par les divers Codes, en inférieure et en incapable, c'est parce que toutes les religions, *inventées exclusivement par les mâles, désireux de justifier la suprématie que leur sexe avait conquise à l'aide de la force brutale,* ont insulté et méconnu le nôtre. (*Trois conférences* 60)[33]

Christianity is no exception.

Si nous rencontrons encore, nous, féministes, tant d'adversaires et tant d'indifférents . . . c'est parce que l'atavisme chrétien n'est pas tout à fait mort . . . parce que la légende biblique, qui fait de la première femme l'auteur de tous les maux humains et l'instrument de damnation de l'homme, n'a pas encore perdu toute son influence aux yeux de nos contemporains—même "libres-penseurs." (61)[34]

Roussel goes on to analyze the representation of women in Christianity and to reexamine the so-called "faute d'Eve." She claims that Eve's disobedience was evidence of "une noble curiosité scientifique, un impérieux *désir de savoir.*"[35]

> En face d'Adam respectueux de l'autorité et acceptant l'ignorance, Eve nous apparaît comme la personnification symbolique de la révolte consciente et de la Pensée libre! (66)[36]

Roussel's play, *La Faute d'Eve*,[37] is a staging of this idea. In this *scène symbolique*, first read by the author at a meeting of the Union des Femmes Française in March 1912[38] and published in 1913 in *Le Movement Féministe*, there are only three characters: Adam, Eve, and an Angel. The two short scenes take place in Eden where a bored Eve laments the monotony of her surroundings: "Je voudrais du nouveau, de l'inconnu, de l'extraordinaire."[39] She covets the forbidden flower of Science. When Adam warns her against picking it, she counters: "Dieu, en nous donnant l'intelligence qui conçoit, la raison qui discute, la parole qui exprime, Dieu a préparé lui-même et voulu notre rébellion. Et je ne puis me résoudre à admettre que je ne comprends pas!"[40] She seizes the flower and breathes in its empowering perfume. Adam watches first terrified, then fascinated. The Angel arrives and proclaims them banished from Eden: "Allez vous perdre dans ce monde que vous avez voulu connaître. Vous y trouverez la souffrance, la peur, la faim, le froid, l'inquiétude; vous y mangerez un pain amer, payé de vos efforts, arrosé de vos larmes."[41] While the poor Adam breaks down in tears, Eve is exalted. She sees her banishment from paradise not as a punishment, but as deliverance. Freed from the boredom of a comfortable, sheltered and passive existence, she is thrilled to discover Life, with all its action, struggles, and dreams.

> EVE: Je pars sans détourner la tête, ne laissant rien ici de moi, que le lourd manteau d'ennui enfin tombé de mes épaules, et le voile qui, couvrant mes yeux, leur dérobait la vraie lumière (*prenant la main d'Adam, qui peu à peu s'est redressé et qu'elle entraîne*). Viens, ami, donne-moi ta main. Entrons sans crainte et sans regret dans l'immense inconnu du monde. Viens vers les luttes qui meurtrissent, et les conquêtes qui enivrent; viens vers l'angoisse qui torture, et vers l'amour qui console. Viens vers l'action et vers le rêve; vers les ténèbres qui peu à peu s'éclaircissent; viens vers la découverte éternelle et le mystère sans cesse renaissant. Viens vers les douleurs, vers tous les espoirs, vers tous les orgueils. Viens vers la vie enfin, énorme, tumultueuse![42]

Roussel recognizes, however, that most women do not interpret the Bible as an incitement to revolt. On the contrary, they accept the traditional male interpretation condemning women to obey and suffer as punishment for the original sin. She analyses why women love their religion in spite of its misogyny. The first reason is ignorance:

Elles aiment leur religion *parce qu'elles ne la connaissent pas*, ou, du moins, qu'elles la connaissent mal; parce qu'elles n'en voient que le côté extérieur et séduisant, les cérémonies fastueuses et les poétiques légendes. (*Trois conférences* 72)[43]

Roussel concludes that the freethinkers movement must teach religion: "Faisons-la voir telle qu'elle est, sans fard et sans guirlandes. Arrachons le masque hypocrite et les oripeaux brillants" (73).[44] More importantly though, women are attached to religion because they are imprisoned in the *home* and excluded from other more fulfilling activities and pursuits.

Si elle pouvait . . . trouver dans des occupations professionnelles intéressantes et aimées, ou bien dans l'étude, dans la Science, dans les joies artistiques ou philosophiques, ou encore dans la propagande, dans les ardeurs et les fièvres de l'Idée, l'emploi de ce qui reste en elle d'énergie, de passion, de désir de vivre et d'agir, . . . elle serait sauvée. (76)[45]

For Roussel, in order to secularize the society, the freethinkers movement must work with feminists to increase women's opportunities to participate in fulfilling activities outside the home. She deplores the fact that the majority of male freethinkers perpetuate the Christian ethic with respect to women in both the public and private spheres.

It is this hypocrisy that Roussel denounces in her play *Pourquoi elles vont à l'église*. Very different in genre from the first two symbolic scenes, this one-act play is a realist drama set in a modest working-class home in a small town. The female protagonist, like Eve in *La Faute d'Eve*, is bored; she is shut up in the house all day doing household chores while her husband is at work, at political meetings, and in the café. Monsieur Bourdieu, a member of the Société de Libre-Pensée, spends all his free time with his fellow male comrades promoting a nonreligious moral code in which all men in all classes of the society would have access to truth, knowledge, and freedom. When Madame Bourdieu asks her husband what they discussed in the meeting, he replies that it would not interest her: "Politique, propagande; enfin, pas des affaires de femmes" (159).[46] She suggests that an intelligent woman would learn to appreciate such issues if her husband took the time to discuss them with her. Monsieur Bourdieu exclaims with irony: "Ça doit être agréable d'avoir des discussions philosophiques dans son ménage! . . . Quand on rentre chez soi, c'est pour manger tranquillement la soupe, sans s'inquiéter d'autre chose. Moi c'est ainsi que je comprends la vie de famille" (159).[47] Indeed, in this play, Bourdieu only comes home to eat the lunch his wife has prepared before running off to the café "comme d'habitude." After he leaves, Madame Bourdieu becomes even more aware of her husband's hypocrisy and of the injustice of her situation upon reading a report of a lecture given by an eminent orator at a banquet of her husband's Société de Libre Pensée. In his lecture, enthusiastically applauded by Monsieur Bourdieu, the orator recognized that people turned to religion as a refuge from the monotony and hardships of life. The remedy is to enlighten the people:

> Il faut que, en dehors des manifestations qui s'adressent au grand public, chacun de nous, dans sa petite sphère, *n'imposant rien*, mais discutant, raisonnant et persuadant, prépare le triomphe de la morale laïque, la morale de l'avenir, basée sur le respect de l'individualité humaine, librement épanouie. Il faut *intéresser tous ceux qui nous entourent* à nos efforts, à notre idéal, et le leur rendre sympathique *par une conduite personnelle au-dessus de tout reproche.* (160)[48]

Madame Bourdieu realizes that she, as a woman and a wife, has been excluded from the freethinkers' universal *all*, and that her husband's interest in the freethinkers movement is based as much on homosociability as on ideology. She decides in the end to accompany her neighbor to church as a modest revolt against both her boredom and the sexual double standard of the freethinkers movement.

It is surprising, and perhaps regrettable, that Roussel did not find a more positive dénouement in this play as in *Par la Révolte* and *La Faute d'Eve.* Madame Bourdieu does not become a rebel; she is not saved by an enlightened character who might have presented her with an alternative to the church; she does not leave the comfort of her home to brave the dangers of "l'immense inconnu du monde." Unlike Véra Starkoff, who provided realistic positive role models for the men and women of her audience, Roussel simply criticized the status quo in this play without explicitly staging a viable alternative. Nevertheless, the solution must have appeared obvious to all but the most obtuse members of the audience.

Roussel's plays are a form of agitprop theater: "forme radicalisée du théâtre politique, faisant passer avant toute autre considération les objectifs de la lutte" (Corvin 19).[49] According to Corvin, the aesthetic principles of agitprop theater, "Clarté d'objectif, brièveté, concision des textes, langue percutante . . . sont systématiquement recherchés pour mettre à nu les rapports sociaux, transposer le propos politique ou éducatif en un langage simple et compréhensible" (Corvin 19).[50] The language in these plays must be easily remembered by both the actors and the audience. After all, these were most often not professional actors accustomed to memorizing vast amounts of text, and the majority of the audience was not used to profound intellectual endeavors. Agitprop theater, in its pure form, targets a single issue with strategic precision, thus creating a "powerful short-term shock effect, striking at the heart of on issue with piercing accuracy" (Szanto 78).[51] Furthermore, this type of social protest theater must also be inexpensive and uncumbersome so that it can be performed anywhere, anytime, with minimal sets and costumes: "La pauvreté matérielle est sa règle . . . Le costume est celui de la vie" (Corvin 19).[52] Agitprop theater is perhaps most effective in "noninstitutionalized theatrical performance conditions" (Szanto 78). The bourgeois theatergoing audience is likely to have a stronger reaction (positive or negative) to an agitprop performance in a nontraditional theatrical setting in which they are destabilized and alienated, unprotected by the reassuring environment of the theater institution. Working-class audiences, on the other hand, may be more receptive to the message of agitprop theater in a nontraditional theater setting in which they feel a sense of community: political meetings, Maisons du Peuple, Universités Populaires. In these circumstances, rather than being subjected to a representation of bourgeois values, the audience may feel more implicated in the performance and thus be more deeply affected by the propaganda. As Barker points out in "Alternative Theatre/Political Theatre," theater performed in alternative venues is perceived as being more subversive and therefore as a greater political threat by the authorities than drama performed in traditional venues, regardless of the intention of the playwright or director.

For authors like Roussel, the quality of this type of theater was not so much in the poetry of the language, the magnificence of the sets and costumes, or in the technique of the acting, as in the Truth of the message, the ideological content, and the contact with the audience. Roussel sought to exalt her audience through her use of dithyrambic allegory, as in the propaganda plays performed in the national festivals during the French Revolution, ancestors to the educational and artistic events at which *Par la Révolte* was performed. These plays were not meant to be subtle or profound; nor were they meant to become literary masterpieces. Roussel, like Véra Starkoff, whose plays we study in chapter four, wrote for a specific audience, at a specific moment. In fact, she could only have hoped that the issues brought to the stage in their plays would not be relevant a century later.

CHAPTER FOUR

Theater of a Tolstoïenne: Véra Starkoff

Véra Starkoff[1] is the most enigmatic of the authors discussed in this book. Though her name appears frequently in archives about turn-of-the-century feminism and the Université Populaire, little was known about her life or in fact her true identity until recently. In an introductory essay to Starkoff's plays published in 2001 in *Au temps de l'anarchie, un théâtre de combat 1880–1914*, Monique Surel-Tupin wrote, "On sait peu de choses sur cette militante d'origine russe qui s'engagea dans le mouvement des universités populaires" (287).[2] After much intriguing research in such unusual places for a literary scholar as cemeteries, police archives, and genealogical databases in France, the United States, and Russia, I was able to discover a minimum of biographical information about her. Unfortunately, many aspects of her life and career remain unknown.

Véra Starkoff was born Tauba Efron[3] on April 1, 1867, into a privileged milieu in Russian-occupied Poland. Her grandmother, Taube Wilner, was a direct descendant of the famous eighteenth-century rabbi Gaon of Vilna (Yarin), though her immediate family appears to have converted to Protestantism, perhaps to avoid persecution in Czarist Russia. In the early years of the twentieth century, her father, Ilya Efron, had a publishing house in St. Petersburg. His firm published books on social, cultural, and economic history, as well as the highly respected *Brockhaus-Efron Encyclopedia*. In 1884, like many young Russian women, Starkoff went to Switzerland to study. Then going by the name Thérèse, she lived in Geneva where she reportedly attended classes in philology at the University of Geneva.[4] Starkoff moved to Paris in 1889 at which time the Efron family came under investigation by the Czarist police due to her close association with Véra Davidovna Gurari, a Russian revolutionary and labor organizer.[5]

It is still unclear why Starkoff emigrated from Russia, settled in Paris, and chose to publish under a pseudonym, though none of these facts is surprising. While growing up in Russia in the 1870s and 1880s, Starkoff would certainly have been aware of the fervent activities of the Russian revolutionary movement in which women represented about a quarter of the militants (Burnet-Vigniel 33; Hillyar and McDermid 28). The majority of these female revolutionaries were, like Starkoff, young women of the privileged classes. Gurari, with whom Starkoff was allegedly in association, organized covert circles in St. Petersburg in the 1880s. In 1884, Gurari founded a military group that met clandestinely to study social democratic texts and developed plans for a military coup against the government. She also carried out revolutionary propaganda with the Bestuzhev women's circle (Naimark 123, 128). The Bestuzhev Higher Courses for women, founded in 1878 in St. Petersburg, were fertile ground for female revolutionaries. A report of the secret police in 1886 claimed that "in the last five years there has not been a single more or less large revolutionary organization that did not have Bestuzhev students in considerable numbers among them" (Qtd. in Hillyar and McDermid 167). It is not inconceivable that Starkoff met Gurari while attending these courses and participated in their covert revolutionary activities. Nor would Starkoff have been the first in her family to participate in revolutionary activities. Her uncle Jean Effront was exiled from Russia after being arrested for revolutionary activities during this period.[6] Was Starkoff forced into exile or did she simply choose to study in Switzerland like so many young Russians in search of greater intellectual freedom? This question, like many others concerning Starkoff's youth, remains to be answered.

What is known is that by 1889 Starkoff had settled in Paris where she would live until her death in 1923.[7] Paris was a favorite refuge for expatriates from the Russian Empire in the final decades of the nineteenth century, whether they be Polish rebels, persecuted Jews, exiled nihilists, or simply intellectuals attracted to Paris as a cultural capital of Europe. In Paris, they formed colonies, often segregated by religion and political ideology. The fifth arrondissement, where Starkoff was married in 1892, was the residence of a large number of Russian émigrés; Rue Flatters was purportedly inhabited almost exclusively by Russian students in the late nineteenth century ("Historique de l'émigration" 6). In 1893, following the reinforcement of a law requiring all foreigners living in France to register at the town hall of their place of residence, approximately 35,000

Russians were legally declared living in France. According to the 1901 census, 10,925 Russians were then officially residing in Paris. This number would grow to over 25,000 by 1907 ("Historique de l'émigration" 14–16). The use of a pseudonym for women authors was common practice in the late nineteenth century when Véra Starkoff began publishing. In Starkoff's case in particular, she may have had personal reasons for wishing to keep her identity secret. Though some members of her family, like her uncle Jean, may have shared her political opinions, others were supporters of the Czar. Her uncle Akim Effront (1855–1909), with whom she is buried in the Montparnasse Cemetery, came to Paris in 1889 for the World Fair and returned two years later to found "La Correspondance russe," a publication whose goal was to maintain good relations between France and Russia. Five years later, when Akim was under investigation prior to his election as Chevalier de la Légion d'Honneur, police reports indicate that Akim was most certainly a secret agent of the Russian government; his official title was "attaché à la chancellerie de sa majesté l'Empereur de Russie."[8] With an uncle hired to report to the Russian government, it may indeed have been judicious for Thérèse to use a nom de plume. Her secret was exceptionally well kept since her true identity was never revealed in any publications about her work as a writer or as a militant.

Throughout her life in exile, Starkoff would continue to be interested in Russian culture, from her first published original work, an essay entitled *Siberia* (1899), to her last, *Le Bolchevisme* (1922). She translated works by Pushkin[9] and Chernyshevski,[10] and gave lectures on various related topics. Starkoff was particularly influenced by the philosophy of Tolstoy. In her essay *Le Vrai Tolstoï*, Starkoff cites Tolstoy's own writings in order to rectify certain misconceptions about him. She applauds his opposition to all forms of exploitation and violence, notably his anticlericalism and antimilitarism. While Tolstoy was Christian, he strongly criticized the Church for oppressing the people and for its moral corruption: "La religion de Tolstoï est une sagesse de la conscience humaine, une morale de la bonté, une sociologie du travail. . . . La religion de Tolstoï était l'humanité" (17, 34).[11] Starkoff hoped that when the people learned the truth about his philosophy, "tous les exploités de la terre et tous ceux qui souffrent glorifieront en lui le plus grand, le plus attachant, le plus noble défenseur des hommes" (37).[12]

Starkoff was also involved in the activities of the Union Fraternelle des Femmes (UFF), a feminist association founded in 1901 by Marbel, a former member of the Ligue Française pour le Droit des Femmes (LFDF) and journalist for *La Fronde*, a newspaper run entirely by women

(1897–1905). The UFF, which had socialist, anticlerical leanings, organized debates on a variety of themes from clothing reform to reproductive freedom. An article in *La Française* listed the association's goals:

1. Intéresser les femmes à toutes les questions qui les concernent et de leur faciliter l'étude de ces questions à l'aide de conférences, livres, journaux, documents et communications de toute nature;
2. De travailler, en outre, à l'amélioration du sort de la femme et de favoriser l'évolution féminine par les moyens qui lui paraîtront les plus efficaces. ("Union Fraternelle des Femmes")[13]

The UFF also encouraged collaboration with other groups like the Union Française pour le Suffrage des Femmes (UFSF), the Conseil National des Femmes Françaises (CNFF), the Alliance d'Hygiène Sociale, and the Ligue Nationale contre l'Alcoolisme (Bard 34). In 1903, an article in *La Fronde* on the activities of the UFF mentions the fact that Véra Starkoff donated two copies of her play *L'Amour libre* to the association's library and discussed in length a lecture given by Starkoff defending a legal reform that would facilitate divorce. At this lecture, she also introduced the novel *Deux Vies* by Paul and Victor Margueritte, which she feels all women should read:

C'est tout d'abord la conception nouvelle de la famille "pierre qui porte la cité" opposée à la famille patriarcale, où, entre parenthèses, manque actuellement le patriarche; le foyer domestique alimenté par l'amour du progrès et non en guerre avec l'humanité; puis c'est la critique parfaite des lois actuelles du mariage qui désorganisent et corrompent la famille; et surtout, c'est affirmation, on pourrait dire unique, des deux grands écrivains, de l'individualité féminine, c'est leur préoccupation aussi précieuse que rare de donner à la femme les moyens de mettre son cœur et son esprit en harmonie avec la conscience universelle. ("Les Réunions féministes")[14]

Inspired by Russian playwrights Tolstoy and Pushkin, as well as by Ibsen and Zola, Starkoff became interested in the theater and participated in the theatrical activities of Université Populaire. Starkoff wrote at least five plays in the first decade of the century: *L'Amour libre, L'Issue, Le Petit Verre, Tolstoïenne*, and *Le Concierge antisémite*. All were performed and the first three were published by P. V. Stock, one of the primary publishers of anarchist texts. Starkoff's published plays were written *for* and *about* the Université Populaire. *L'Amour libre* was dedicated to

"les soirées ouvrières":

Chers camarades,

Je vous dédie mon premier essai dramatique en témoignage de ma profonde gratitude. Votre admirable effort de pensée et de courage a raffermi ma foi au Progrès, ébranlée par la désespérante mentalité bourgeoise. Vous détenez la clef de l'avenir, le travail régénerera le monde, selon la parole prophétique de notre grand maître regretté, Emile Zola.[15]

In the preface to Le Petit Verre, Starkoff defined le théâtre populaire. She explained the importance of abolishing the monopoly of knowledge held by the privileged classes in order for Art and Science to progress. Here we note the direct influence of Tolstoy. In her 1911 essay about Tolstoy, she wrote: "La science et l'art actuels sont accaparés par les capitalistes qui s'en servent pour exploiter les masses humaines. Tolstoï se dresse contre cette exploitation" (6).[16] She quoted a letter that Tolstoy had written to Romain Rolland:

Le faux rôle que jouent dans notre société les sciences et les arts, provient de ce que les gens soi-disant civilisés, ayant à leur tête les savants et les artistes, sont une caste privilégiée comme les prêtres. Et cette caste a tous les défauts de toutes les castes. [. . .] Elle a le défaut de peser sur les masses, et par dessus cela, de les priver de ce qu'on prétend propager; et le plus grand défaut—celui de la contradiction du principe qu'ils professent avec leur manière d'agir. (7–8)[17]

For Starkoff, the Université Populaire, and particularly the people's theater, allows the proletariat to fight against the usurpation of Art and Science in order to supplement their economic emancipation with a richer intellectual life and a new, *social* morality:

A côté de ses revendications de l'estomac et de la raison, la classe ouvrière éprouve la nécéssité d'élever son cœur et de mettre en harmonie des idées, ses sentiments et ses actes, d'élaborer, en un mot, une morale sociale. C'est là le rôle du théâtre populaire. (*Petit Verre* 5–6)[18]

Rejecting both the Church and the *Code Napoléon's* definition of "moral," Starkoff thus redefined the word in socialist terms and claimed that the theater is an ideal school for this new moral code:

> Il ne s'agit pas, bien entendu, des préjugés et des superstitions enseignés par l'Eglise et le Code Napoléon. Il est question ici de la mise en pratique des idées de Justice et de Vérité, de l'amérioration du sort humain. Les esprits théologiques voient une incompatibilité entre le réalisme et la morale, car ils considèrent les phénomènes de la nature comme des manifestations du diable. Contrairement à eux les grands génies dramatiques . . . admirent et reproduisent la nature dans toute son intégrité avec les ténèbres et sa lumière. [. . .] Profitons de leurs leçons. [. . .] Ce ne sont pas les manuels de préceptes qui élèveront le niveau moral de la masse, mais des spectacles de la vie observée fidèlement. Ils contiennent des enseignements précieux, ils éveillent dans la conscience des spectateurs le désir de combattre les erreurs, les vices et les mauvaises lois qui rendent les hommes malheureux, ils dévoilent le cœur humain et font connaître les conditions du bonheur. (6)[19]

In her three published plays, in addition to propaganda for the Université Populaire, Véra Starkoff introduced a variety of ideological themes such as solidarity, anti-clericalism, the refusal of paternal authority, free love, and the work ethic. All three plays also bring out major feminist themes of the early twentieth century.

The action in *L'Amour libre* actually takes place in a Université Populaire just prior to a lecture. The main characters are mostly workers: an embroiderer, a mason, a carpenter and his wife, and a day laborer. As the play begins, the female protagonist Blanche, who is working as secretary for the day, explains to the speaker, Ruinet, that lectures in the Université Populaire are an exchange; both the lecturers, who are usually of bourgeois origins, and the workers in the audience can learn from the experience:

> L'*Université populaire* n'est pas une école composée d'élèves qui acceptent toutes les leçons! C'est une coopération, un échange d'idées entre le conférencier et les ouvriers . . . C'est la conscience, la parcelle de justice et de vérité qui est en chacun de nous que nous cherchons ici à dégager, à accroître par nos efforts communs. Et la conscience du conférencier, élevé dans les conditions bourgeoises, est quelque fois inférieure à celle de l'ouvrier, et dans les réunions,

il reçoit souvent plus qu'il ne donne. Il nous apprend la science, nous lui révélons la justice!" (11)[20]

Blanche criticizes lecturers who show disrespect for the workers or who simply use the Université Populaire as a venue for free publicity. In the second scene, one worker informs Ratule, a mason who arrives for the first time, about the workings of the Université Populaire. He is surprized to see a woman at the reception, and to learn that he can read books and newspapers for free, and that there is no fixed fee for attending the lecture. He thinks the topic, *l'amour libre* (free love), sounds entertaining. Misunderstanding the expression "l'amour libre," he interprets it to mean free sex: "on a du plaisir ensemble, c'est bon, puis on s'en va chacun de son côté, bonsoir" (12).[21] Cropest, who is more enlightened, replies sarcastically: "Comme des chiens, quoi? Le plaisir et pas de conscience, comme la bête" (12).[22] He asks Ratule what happens if the woman gets pregnant. Not unexpectedly, Ratule answers that it's not his problem: "qu'elle se débrouille!" (12).[23] He doesn't care if he has a bunch of children running around as long as he doesn't know them. He doesn't think it particularly fair, "mais que voulez vous que j'y fasse?" (12).[24] Cropest explains that *free* does not mean *dishonest*. *L'amour libre* means love that is free from the institution of marriage and from the biological constraints of maternity. Since the mid-nineteenth century, marriage had come under harsh criticism by socialists, anarchists, and utopianists. For them, marriage was a capitalist socioeconomic contract which they equated with slavery. The preferred alternative was *l'union libre*, a mutual agreement between consenting adults to be living partners.

In a later scene, Cropest and Ratule continue their discussion, this time on the topic of parenting. Cropest explains that he and his wife take turns coming to the meetings and taking care of their daughter. Ratule predictably thinks this is hilarious: "Ha! Ha! Ha! C'est donc les hommes qui gardent les mioches à présent . . . ce n'est pas l'affaire des hommes de garder les mioches" (17).[25] Cropest disagrees:

Et pourquoi pas? J'aime bien les enfants, moi. La mienne est si drôle! Elle me fait tant rire! Et quand bien même elle serait mauvaise, elle est à nous deux, à sa mère et à moi. Pourquoi donc que ma femme aurait tout le mal? Chacun sa part. (18)[26]

To Ratule's claim that men work harder than women, Madame Gaillard joins the discussion: "et avec ça qu'elle ne se fatigue pas! Et qui fait la lessive? Qui racommode les nippes? Qui fait la soupe? Et qui lave et

récure partout, du matin au soir? Je voudrais bien vous voir à sa place, avec les mioches qui crient et qui trottent dans nos jambes" (18).[27] Her husband adds that women need to be educated as much as men since they are primarily responsible for bringing up the children:

> Et puis, camarade, vous oubliez le principal; la femme non seulement nourrit l'enfant, elle l'élève, et si elle est ignorante, elle l'élèvera dans l'erreur, dans les idées fausses, des les préjugées et la dévotion. La femme a besoin d'instruction comme nous, et peut-être encore plus que nous, car elle tient dans ses mains l'avenir. Nos enfants, camarade, c'est l'avenir. (18)[28]

In the following scene, we learn about Blanche's past. She is a single mother; seduced and abandoned by a wealthy law student, she had suffered from both a precarious financial situation and a tainted social status until she started to frequent the Université Populaire where "on ne s'occupe pas de savoir si on est marié ou non" (11).[29] Blanche is skeptical about free love; she has suffered from her experience of it. Ruinet defends the practice in principle, claiming that the abuses are to be blamed on unfair laws. For example, Ruinet deplores the law preventing paternity suits;[30] women should be able to take legal action to force a man to take responsibility for his illegitimate children. But Blanche points out that a father who does recognize an illegitimate child as his may declare that the mother is unknown, thus taking away all her rights. Blanche claims that she would prefer to bring up her child alone rather than have him taken away from her. Ruinet then makes a thinly veiled plea for reproductive freedom. In his view, the main tragedy in Blanche's case is the unwanted pregnancy. His solution to women's suffering is reproductive freedom: "Je voudrais que la maternité fût volontaire!" (24).[31] Again, Blanche disagrees. It is not having the child that is the problem for her, but rather the legal status of the illigitimate child: "Abolissez donc la loi qui proclame la bâtardise, donnez à tous les enfants le même droit au bonheur, et vous détruirez la misère! Et la maternité ne sera plus une chaîne, mais un titre de gloire, l'amour—un épanouissement de vie!" (24).[32] Blanche's main combat is against the injustice of the laws that harm the innocent children.

Though the issues discussed in *L'Amour libre* are very serious and Blanche's situation less than optimal, the play is none the less a social comedy. The final lines of the play leave us with the feeling that Ruinet will convert the neophytes in his audience (like Ratule). We are also led to believe that Blanche and Ruinet will be able to work through their differences of opinion in order to build a happy partnership, thanks to open communication and mutual respect.

Starkoff's second play, *L'Issue*, contrasts the bourgeois mentality of Monsieur and Madame Rouet with the enlightened ideas of Roche, a schoolteacher who tutors their nine-year-old son, Henri. As the play opens, Roche, the authorial voice in the play, is giving a lesson to Henri on the meaning of the word liberty. Like Cropest in *L'Amour libre*, he explains that freedom doesn't mean doing whatever one wants to the detriment of others. In order to be truly free, one must not only think of oneself, but also of one's neighbor. Freedom involves respecting the ideas, feelings, and beliefs of others. Henri asks how he is supposed to know what to believe when his mother spends all her Sundays at church and his father does not believe in God. Roche answers that he will have to decide for himself when he's older and has studied and thought a lot about it. He adds that Henri may end up not agreeing with either of his parents, but developing his own beliefs. This lesson has the double role in the play of instructing the audience and of catalyzing a crisis in the Rouet family. When Henri tells his father what he has been studying, Monsieur Rouet accuses Roche of teaching his son subversive thoughts:

> C'est honteux que nos enfants soient confiés à des hommes privés de sens moral, car c'est immoral, entendez-vous, immoral de saper l'autorité paternelle. Le devoir d'un instituteur laïque est d'inculquer à ses élèves le respect du père et les lois. (156)[33]

Roche admits that he is against the principle of paternal authority given that not all fathers are respectable. The discussion then turns to the theme brought to the stage in *L'Amour libre* of illegitimate children and paternity suits. Roche explains that he was illegitimate, that his father was a coward and abandoned his mother. While Rouet defends the law that forbids paternity suits on the basis that it protects the family, Roche questions his definition of "family." For Rouet, the family is centered on the father, "le chef, le cerveau" (159). Roche disagrees; for him, the family should center on what's best for the children not the father:

> Le père, le chef comme vous dites, investi de sa puissance au lieu de favoriser le développement normal des enfants, le paralyse; la puissance paternelle, loin de la fortifier, désorganise la famille! Elle fait entrer au foyer l'idée mortelle de l'oppression et en bannit l'amour et la conscience. (159)[34]

Rouet maintains that his children and his wife should not only obey him but also unconditionally espouse his opinions. Here, his apparently

submissive wife joins the discussion: "Ça c'est trop fort! Alors pour toi, la femme ou les enfants c'est la même chose . . . Pour les enfants, je n'ai rien à faire, la loi te les donne . . . Mais quant à sauver mon âme . . . C'est autre chose . . ." (160).[35] Seeing that Roche's presence is causing even his wife to revolt, Rouet fires him for his subversive ideas.

Rouet's 22-year-old daughter, who had attended all of Henri's lessons and was witness to this argument, rebels in turn. In a tête-à-tête with Roche just after Henri's lesson, she asks his advice. She has been seeking a way to escape from her oppressive family environment, but the only *issue* she saw was marriage, a common solution for young women that often led to a rude awakening and a disastrous marriage. She does not love her suitor, but believes that he will give her the freedom to pursue her charitable works. Roche, who is in love with Lucie, says that it is a crime to marry a man she does not love. She must not sacrifice herself at any cost: "Se sacrifier, c'est abandonner le meilleur de soi, sa conscience. Le premier devoir de tout être humain est au contraire, d'affirmer sa conscience et non de la sacrifier!" (150).[36] Lucie is an attentive pupil; she asks for nothing better than to be convinced not to marry her suitor: "C'est très beau ce que vous dites, parlez, je vous écoute. Instruisez-moi" (151).[37] Though their conversation is cut short by the appearance of her mother, it will bear fruit by the end of the act when Lucie announces that she has decided not to marry Toudoux. She stands up to her father in spite of his threats and claims of authority:

ROUET: J'ai exprimé ma volonté, et j'entends qu'on
   m'obéisse; j'ai tout droit sur mes enfants, que diable!
LUCIE (*avec fermeté*): Pardon! Jusqu'à l'âge de vingt-et-un ans; j'en
   ai vingt-deux, et je te prouverai que je suis majeure! (171)[38]

The first scene of the second act takes place at a meeting of the committee of a Université Populaire at the modest home of its founder: Roche. His fifth floor garret, sparsely furnished with a table, some chairs, and lots of books, contrasts with the pretentious bourgeois salon of the first act. The main theme in this scene is solidarity. One of the members of the committee, Madame Favre, explains that she cannot take on the role of a secretary at the moment because she has to take care of a neighbor's children on top of her own ill-paid work as a laundress. The neighbor, whose husband died, is in the hospital after a difficult childbirth, and the family has no money. Madame Favre appeals to her comrades to help the

family out:

> C'est une misère . . . tout manque dans la maison . . . . les enfants n'ont rien à se mettre sur le dos et ils se promènent nu-pieds sur le carreau. On a froid à les regarder. Camarades, nous parlons tant de solidarité, si nous achetions des chaussures aux enfants? (175–176)[39]

When someone protests that they too are poor, Madame Favre replies: "Nous pouvons toujours faire quelque chose, puisqu'il y en a de plus malheureux que nous" (176).[40] The proposition is adopted, and Roche offers to pass around a collection at the lecture the following day.

A short scene follows in which Roche admits to Monsieur and Madame Favre that he loves Lucie but cannot dream of marrying her because of "une barrière de préjugés." He does not believe she is strong enough to break away from her milieu, and he doesn't want to impose a life of poverty and work on a woman who could live in luxury and idleness. In the final scene of the play, Lucie arrives at Roche's apartment. She has realized that marriage was not her only option and has run away from her comfortable bourgeois life in order to seek salvation in work:

> LUCIE: Je suis lasse de tâtonner dans les ténèbres, et j'ai enfin trouvé l'issue qui me mènera vers la lumière!
>
> ROCHE: Et cette issue?
>
> LUCIE: Elle est toute simple. Vous me l'avez indiquée un jour sans que je m'en aperçoive; je me rappelle vos paroles: "Le salut est dans le travail." Eh bien, je suis décidée à travailler, à gagner ma vie. (189)[41]

Roche confesses that he loves her but that he is afraid she will be unhappy. He explains to her at length what it means to be of the proletariat:

> Ma chère Lucie, je ne doute pas de votre sincérité. Je vous crois capable des plus hauts élans de solidarité. La solidarité est une part importante et belle de la vie prolétarienne. Par là vous êtes des nôtres. Mais il y en a une autre, pénible celle-là, et qui fait reculer les âmes les plus fortement constituées. C'est la tâche quotidienne et prosaïque de la vie matérielle et si secondaire qu'elle soit, on ne peut s'en décharger sur les autres sans retomber dans l'erreur séculaire, l'erreur qui divisait autrefois l'humanité en maîtres et en esclaves, qui les divise maintenant en patrons et domestiques. Les ouvriers actuels

sont des esclaves déguisés! Dégager le travail de toute servitude, c'est
le but de ma vie . . . (194)[42]

He asks her to accept a trial period before living with him (there is no
mention of marriage). He suggests that she first live and work with
Madame Favre: "vous vivrez pendant quelque temps de sa vie, une vie
belle et noble, et si ce cadre de misère et de travail ne change en rien
votre résolution, je n'ai pas besoin de vous dire que je serais heureux . . ."
(195).[43] Finally, in the closing lines of the play, Roche warns Lucie not to
be his echo. She must discover Truth for herself; not following behind
him, but rather accompanying him in a mutually supportive partnership:

> *L'homme, bêtement s'est arrogé le monopole de la vérité. Il a enlevé à la*
> *femme ce qui compose l'essence même de la vie, la pensée et la liberté! Il en*
> *a fait un cadaver, et sa cohabitation avec une morte les précipite tous deux*
> *dans la tombe! Il faut que l'homme relève sa compagne jetée à terre, pour*
> *qu'il reste debout.* (196)[44]

In this play, Véra Starkoff paints a romanticized portrait of the working
class. Though Roche admits the work is difficult and that there remains
progress to be made, he primarily depicts the working-class life as beautiful
and noble. This is very different from the representation of the working
class by Madeleine Pelletier as we see in chapter five. While Pelletier
wishes to raise the working class out of their current state of depredation,
Starkoff sees the working-class lifestyle as superior to that of the bourgeois.

In *Le Petit Verre*, Starkoff brings to the stage a theme popular among
social reformers at the turn of the century: alcoholism in the working
class. Alcohol consumption had risen dramatically in the late nineteenth
and early twentieth century. In 1904, when Starkoff published and performed her play, the consumption of pure alcohol in France had risen to
about 35 liters per adult from 20.7 in 1860 (Prestwich 24). The dangers
of excessive alcohol consumption had been recognized by the medical
field for decades, and the first major temperance organization, the Société
française contre l'abus des boissons alcooliques, was created in 1871
(Prestwich 61). This association, which changed its name to the Société
française de tempérance (SFT) in 1873, fought alcoholism from a scientific
point of view, as opposed to the moralizing approach of religious anti-
alcohol campaigns. Their efforts included publishing posters warning of
the effects of alcohol abuse and awarding prizes for temperate behavior.
Although they believed in principle that education was key to curbing
alcohol consumption, they failed to reach the working class; in reality, the

association concentrated more on scientific prizes and research than on popular propaganda (Prestwich 64). The 1890s brought a new wave in anti-alcohol efforts thanks to increased emphasis on social reform and solidarity, as well as to the development of the hygiene movement. Women also became involved in the anti-alcohol movement during this period. The Union Française Antialcoolique (UFA), founded by Paul-Maurice Legrain in 1895, which was primarily committed to popular propaganda, was probably the first nonreligious anti-alcohol organization to admit women as equals. Both the UFA and the SFT, which changed its name to the Ligue Nationale contre l'Alcoolisme in 1895,[45] were very active during the next decade. The Ligue in particular reached out to all groups sympathetic to the cause and developed close alliances with associations like the Alliance of Social Hygiene, the League against Tuberculosis, the Musée Social, the Association of Industrialists against Work Accidents, and several women's rights associations: the Conseil National des Femmes Françaises and the Union Française pour le Suffrage des Femmes. In exchange, the Ligue advocated women's suffrage (Prestwich 73).

As we mentioned previously, the Université Populaire was also involved in the efforts to reduce alcoholism among the working class. The workers' excessive consumption of alcohol was seen as a result of a number of socioeconomic factors, notably insalubrious housing, poor education, and a want of more beneficial activities. It was also blamed on the increased production of industrial distilled alcohol, notably absinth,[46] and on proliferation of *débits*, cabarets, and cafés-concerts. The effects of alcoholism were equally complex. In addition to the obvious deleterious effects on the drinkers' health and to the high risk of alcohol-related accidents, the militants of the Université Populaire recognized equally catastrophic socioeconomic results. Alcoholic workers earned less money and were more likely to lose their jobs. Too stupefied with alcohol, they are unable to pursue intellectual or cultural endeavors that might better their lot. Alcoholism was further held responsible for the disintegration of the family and the degeneration of the French people. The more militant activists emphasized in addition that alcohol prevented workers from developing a political conscience, becoming aware of their exploitation, and fighting for their interests. Alcohol reduced their capacity to revolt.

The Université Populaire thus fought alcoholism on several fronts; they ideally wished to provide temperance restaurants,[47] to educate the workers about the dangers of excessive alcohol consumption, and to provide alternative recreational activities to draw the workers away from drinking establishments. The fight against alcoholism was generally

written into the statutes of each Université Populaire as one of the primary goals of the institution. In the "Préambule des statuts provisoires de la Société [des Universités Populaires]," Deherme wrote:

> Les heures de loisir sont pour l'ouvrier, l'employé et le paysan, s'ils n'ont pris le goût des saines et fortes lectures, les plus tristes et les plus dangereuses, alors qu'ils pourraient non seulement les employer agréablement et dignement, mais encore les utiliser pour leur développement physique, intellectuel et moral, ce qui veut dire pour leur émancipation sociale.
>
> En face du cabaret, du café-concert, nous nous proposons d'édifier nos Universités Populaires. (*Bulletin* 24)[48]

In keeping with this philosophy, the first lecture at the Coopération des Idées was "L'alcool, des alcoolisés, des alcooliques" by Dr. Lucien Jacquet, one of the doctors who had been influential in drawing attention to the problem of alcoholism among workers. In his 1899 report on the incidence of alcoholism in Paris hospitals, he revealed that 45.9 percent of his patients suffered from the disease. He warned of the "destruction of the 'noble and intelligent' working class" (Prestwich 79) and called for major reforms: "Now we need action, not just personal and timid, but collective and bold" (Qtd. in Prestwich 67).

The fight was not an easy one. Throughout France, the number of cafés increased fivefold between 1789 and 1914 (Haine 4). The café or *débit* at the time was much more than a place to have a drink. While working-class homes were often cramped, dark, and cold, the café provided workers, mostly men, with a warm, well-lit, friendly place to socialize in the evening after work or on weekends. When factories didn't have a canteen or allow workers to eat on the premises, cafés often provided a practical lunchtime venue. Bachelors could even rent a room from the café owner. Cafés were also a popular meeting place for work-related discussions and political meetings as we see in our discussion of Madeleine Pelletier's play, *Supérieur!* Furthermore, drinking alcohol had become part of the working-class identity. Even those workers who understood the dangers of excessive alcohol consumption, often defended the practice on the grounds that the anti-alcohol campaign was just another way the bourgeois were trying to control the lives of the working class.

In the preface to *Le Petit Verre*, Starkoff explains her goal. There is no doubt that her play is intended to enlighten her audience by making them aware of the dangers of excessive alcohol consumption and by

instructing them how to improve the situation:

La comédie *Le Petit Verre* s'attaque à l'erreur commune qui consiste
à croire que l'ivresse procure des jouissances tandis qu'en réalité elle
conduit à la brutalité et à la mélancolie. Dans les deux cas, elle ruine
la famille. L'alcoolisme est un obstacle à toute organisation sociale, il
est le grand ennemi des syndicats et des coopératives. (6)[49]

In *Le Petit Verre* Starkoff stages a village on the banks of the Seine.
The action takes place in front of the *marchand de vin* (wine merchant)
"A la Gaîté." In the first scene, Cantin, schoolteacher in the winter,
farmer in the summer, is sitting on a bench reading a socialist journal.
He is joined by another farmer, Laferlu, who complains about not having
enough money. Cantin accuses him of spending all his money at the bar.
Laferlu responds with the "erreur commune" mentioned in Starkoff's
preface: he needs to enjoy himself and a little drink doesn't do any harm.
Cantin disagrees: "l'absinthe mène à l'abrutissement ou à la folie" (10).[50]
He suggests an alternative distraction; instead of drinking, he should help
Cantin form a union.

Un Syndicat sert à vous empêcher de vivre comme des loups, de
vous regarder comme des ennemis, et lorsqu'un voisin est dans la
gêne, à l'aider d'en sortir et non de l'abandonner à sa misère, au
point qu'il laisse à pourrir son champ et s'en va mourir de faim à la
ville. Lorsqu'on est uni, on a plus de facilité pour le travail. Un
Syndicat permet d'acheter des outils en gros, ils reviennent moins
chers . . . Si nous étions syndiqués, tu aurais ta faux toute neuve
aujourd'hui, on aurait une batteuse en commun, des chevaux, des
voitures . . . On terminerait les travaux plus tôt . . . on aurait un
peu de bon temps pour le repos, d'autres distractions que "le petit
verre." Les gens qui boivent ne s'amusent guère, ils sont maussades
ou brutaux. L'alcool, c'est du poison. (10)[51]

Like in *L'Issue*, Starkoff is advocating working-class solidarity, but here
she goes further by recommending a system of communal property, an ideal
that she would discuss in more depth in her 1919 article, "Les Origines profondes du communisme russe," which is discussed later in the chapter.
    Madame Millot, the wife of the shoemaker, arrives and joins the con-
versation. She laments the fact that so many men in the village drink; in her
native village, the *marchands de vin* don't serve hard alcohol, only coffee and

wine in the winter, and cider and beer in the summer. Moreover, in her village they had other places to gather: unions, cooperatives, and a Université Populaire. When Cantin hears this, he cries out:

> Pays de cocagne! Si on pouvait en faire autant ici, on enlèverait un peu de cette torpeur qui engourdit les cerveaux et les cœurs de nos paysans. Et dire qu'ils ont dans leurs mains le métier le plus sain, le plus utile, le plus élevé; qu'ils sont les maîtres des champs, des blés, du pain, de la vie en somme, et ils courbent leurs existences comme des esclaves abrutis [. . .] ils ne se reposent jamais, ils vivent comme des sauvages, ils ne se fréquentent pas, ils ne connaissent ni la causerie, ni la lecture, ni la promenade. Le seul plaisir qu'ils s'offrent c'est cette goutte qui détruit en eux jusqu'aux derniers vestiges de conscience! (13)[52]

Madame Millot says that she and her husband hope to open a Université Populaire in the village and that they would like Cantin's help. As a schoolteacher he has a lot of influence.

In the following scene, Monsieur and Madame Miret arrive and introduce another theme: anticlericalism. Monsieur Miret, who has been mayor of the village for 30 years in addition to his work on the farm, explains that the greatest obstacle to progress in the area is the Church and its accomplices, the aristocracy, and the bourgeoisie. He says that the Baroness de Conchy denounces workers who don't go to mass, and they are fired from the factory owned by the regional representative in government: "La misère des travailleurs fait la fortune de l'église" (16).[53] Madame Millot concurs: "Du moment qu'un curé règne dans le pays, on est certain que l'ivrognerie y prospère; c'est le péché mignon qui empêche de voir clair" (16).[54]

Starkoff's religious beliefs were inspired by her *maître de pensée*, Tolstoy. She was a Christian but believed that the institution of the Church was detrimental to the working class. Her religious beliefs were based on the notions of generosity and solidarity rather than ritual and dogma. In her essay *Le Vrai Tolstoï*, she explains that he believed in a sort of primitive Christianity, but that he was opposed to the Christianity of the Church, which he criticized for its moral corruption:

> D'après la religion de l'Eglise, tout est permis. Posséder des esclaves . . . Amasser une fortune prise sur le travail des frères opprimés . . . Etre riche au milieu des Lazares rampant sous les tables du festin . . . Défendre sa fortune par la violence contre

les besogneux . . . Passer toute sa jeunesse en débauches, et ensuite appeler une de ces débauches mariage et avoir la bénédiction de l'Eglise . . . tuer pour punir . . . tuer pendant la guerre . . . (15–16)[55]

According to Starkoff, Tolstoy held the Church responsible for all the iniquity of the society. Tolstoy's religion, on the contrary, was based on "une sagesse de la conscience humaine, une morale de la bonté, une sociologie du travail":

Il s'agit de développer en nous cette parcelle divine, cet amour de tous les hommes, par l'exercice de la solidarité. Se sentir étroitement uni à ce tout immense, à cette conscience universelle, c'est là le vrai bonheur de l'homme, l'objet de toutes les religions. La religion est la recherche du lien qui nous uni à l'univers. (17)[56]

Starkoff does not, however, develop this notion of a different form of Christianity in her published plays perhaps because most of the leftist militants and free-thinkers like Nelly Roussel with whom she worked at the Université Populaire were not only anticlerical, but also antireligious.

The next three scenes of *Le Petit Verre* center on the relationship between alcoholism and domestic violence. Cantin explains to Madame Millot that he is waiting outside the bar hoping to catch his fiancée's father as he comes out drunk. When he has had one drink too many he becomes furious and tries to beat his wife and Mariette, and Cantin has to defend them. When Mariette arrives on stage, the conversation turns to another variation on the theme of paternal authority. Cantin commiserates with her about the fact that paternal authority gives a father the right to beat his children: "il est grand temps qu'on l'abolisse" (19).[57] Finally, the father Biquet comes out of the bar drunk, but wanting to drink more. He plans to return home to ask his wife for more money:

Faudra bien qu'elle m'en donne, ma bourgeoise . . . et si elle ne veut pas, je saurais la forcer . . . j'avons les bras solides . . . je veux mon argent . . . je suis maître chez moi . . . si elle s'obstine . . . cré nom de Dieu . . . elles y passeront toutes les deux . . . la mère et la fille . . . (23)[58]

When Cantin tries to intervene, the farmer continues his tirade:

Les femmes, c'est fait pour garder la maison . . . c'est fait pour obéir . . . ça n'a pas de raison . . . ça n'a pas de force . . . c'est bon à rien . . . Je veux mon argent . . . *Cantin essaye de nouveau de le calmer mais il continue:* La femme . . . c'est fait pour servir l'homme . . . c'est son devoir . . . elle me cache ses sous . . . je saurais les retrouver . . . sans quoi je lui casserai les reins . . . elle n'a pas le droits de toucher à mon bien . . . elle n'a rien à elle dans la maison . . . tout est à l'homme . . . C'est moi le maître . . . (23)[59]

Fortunately Cantin manages to accompany him home and protect the women this time. Obviously, the representation of the working class, particularly the men, is less romanticized in this play than in *L'Issue.* The only really positive male role in the play is Cantin, the schoolteacher. Though Cantin works as a farmer in the summer, it is more as a gesture of solidarity with the peasants in his village than a real identification with the working class.

As Biquet and Cantin leave the stage, Laferlu, the farmer who claimed in the first scene that he had the right to enjoy himself and that a little drink doesn't do any harm, comes out of the bar depressed and in tears. As Starkoff claimed in the preface, drunkenness causes melancholia rather than pleasure. Even Millot, the shoemaker who wants to open a Université Populaire in the village, is not without reproach. In the final scene, he comes out of the bar having spent his dinner money on drink. His wife accuses him of hypocrisy:

Tu n'as pas honte, le militant, qui est venu t'installer ici pour faire de la propagande. Elle est jolie, ta propagande [. . .]. Est-ce qu'un homme qui a de la conscience se laisse entraîner au mal! . . . C'est bon pour ceux qui ne savent pas lire, ni raisonner, ni vivre . . . Est-ce qu'un homme qui aime sa femme et ses enfants se laisse entraîner à la débauche! . . . (26)[60]

Monsieur Millot apologizes and promises it will never happen again. His wife accepts his apology. The play thus ends on a note of reconciliation and hope.

Domestic violence was a major problem in Third Republic France. Thanks to the unrelenting efforts of Naquet, divorce was finally made legal in 1884 for "excès, sévices et injures graves,"[61] as well as for adultery and a degrading prison sentence. The first was by far the most common cause for divorce; in 1909, 77 percent of divorces were motivated by domestic violence (Adler 197). It is not surprising then that Véra Starkoff was not the only woman playwright to bring this issue to the stage. In 1911, for example, Berthe Reynolds' female protagonist in

Les moutons noirs decides not to marry her fiancé, a peasant from her village, when a student from the city describes the life that awaits her: "Tu n'as pas peur du sort qui t'attend quand tu seras mariée? Une brute d'homme qui te battra. Une nichée d'enfants qui te feront passer les nuits sans dormir; et du matin au soir, un travail de servante" (Reynolds 145).[62] The protagonist in *La Lame sourde* by Jeanne Neis is married to a brutal, jealous, and alcoholic husband who beats her regularly and forces her to do her conjugal duty. The whole village knows about it, but no one except her son is willing to defend her. Anna's suffering finally ends with her suicide.

It is interesting to note that while Starkoff tried to correct one myth, showing that alcohol leads to melancholia and brutality rather than enjoyment, her play, like those of Reynolds and Neis, perpetuates another myth: that the problem of alcoholism, like that of domestic violence, is primarily a male working-class phenomenon. While it is certain that alcoholism was a serious problem in the working class in turn of the century France, it is less clear that there was a higher rate of alcoholism in the working class than in the other sectors of the society. In fact, according to Theodore Zeldin, the family atmosphere may have been more harmonious in working-class families where there was often more of a sense of equality and companionship (Zeldin 352). The problem was however more visible within the working class due to several factors. For example, members of the working class were more likely to end up in hospitals, which were primarily the domain of the less privileged classes until well after World War II (Prestwich 79). The wealthy received their health care at home. The workers were also more likely to have serious accidents at work, and their alcohol-related digestive problems were compounded by malnutrition. Moreover, the interest in social reform and the "worker problem" in general brought this class of society under intense observation and investigation to which no other group of the society was subjected to the same degree (Prestwich 82).

On the other hand, Starkoff does not perpetuate the myth that alcoholism was primarily an urban problem since her play is set in a village and her characters are peasants. In the early twentieth century, the anti-alcohol movement was centered in urban areas. Many believed that modern urban life was in large part responsible for the problem; since rural life was less stressful, peasants had less need to drink. In *Le Petit Verre*, Starkoff shows that peasants too have their worries, notably financial, and that they lack the variety of recreational and educational opportunities available in urban areas. Her play could therefore be understood as a subtle reproach to the anti-alcohol movement, which with the exception of schoolteachers like Cantin, had little contact with the rural population (Prestwich 83).

Another myth about alcohol consumption that Starkoff reinforces in her play is the widespread belief that wine (and in some regions cider and beer) is not harmful; indeed, "wine is not alcohol." Wine is natural and good for the health of both mind and body. Drinking wine is a symbol of sociability, of community, and of festivity; it may even be an aesthetic experience. Wine drinking leads to a state of *ivresse*, a typically French concept related to ecstasy, rapture, and exhilaration. Finally, wine is simply French and thus a symbol of a national identity. *Alcool*, on the other hand, is toxic and leads to unpleasant or dangerous drunkenness and chemical dependency (Nahoum-Grappe 75–87; Prestwich 19–24). Like wine, beer, and cider, also fermented as opposed to distilled, were often considered hygienic drinks and were important to the regional identity of certain areas in eastern and western France (Prestwich 21). The highly toxic and very popular alcohol, absinth, was the main villain for anti-alcohol movement until it was made illegal in 1915.

Five years after *Le Petit Verre*, Starkoff founded her own theater company, appropriately called le Théâtre d'Idées. The inaugural performance, in January 1909 at the Comédie Royale, featured Starkoff's play *Tolstoïenne* along with *Le Jobard*, a one-act play by Jacques Nayral and a lecture by Armand Charpentier. An article in *L'Action* informs readers that reduced price tickets are available to members of the Federation of the Universités Populaires upon presentation of their membership card. The second performance of the Théâtre d'Idées in March of the same year included *Les Vaincues*, a drama in three acts by Poinsot and Normandy, and a short "fantaisie extra-légale" by José Monnet and Henri Clerc entitled *La Loi fait peur*. Starkoff, who performed in *Les Vaincues*, first introduced the play. She explained that her intent was to draw the audience's attention to the exploitation of women—primarily seamstresses and laundresses—who work from the home in the *sweating-system*. She advised the women in the audience to form unions to fight against this oppression. *Les Vaincues* also brought to the stage the theme of alcoholism and domestic violence among the working class, which Starkoff had explored earlier in *Le Petit Verre*. In the third performance of the Théâtre d'Idées in May 1909 at the Théâtre Mondain, Starkoff staged her one-act comedy, *Le Concierge antisémite*, as well as *Empereur!*, a comedy by Jacques Nayral, and *Jusqu'à l'âme*, a drama by the anarchist novelist, playwright, and philosopher Han Ryner, introduced in a lecture by the author.[63]

The following year, an actress, Hélène Slatoff, who had performed in Starkoff's *Tolstoïenne* in 1909, appears to have usurped the name Théâtre d'Idées. In a letter dated May 3, 1910, Slatoff wrote to feminist Céline Renooz: "Faites moi le plaisir de faire partie du comité d'honneur du théâtre d'idées. [. . .] je tiens à avoir dans le comité d'honneur des féministes de valeur, votre place y est toute tracée."[64] In 1912, an article in *La Française* announces a performance of the Théâtre d'Idées, supposedly in its fourth year of existence, founded and directed by Madame Hélène Slatoff. Véra Starkoff responded in a letter to the director of *La Française*: "Je lis avec stupéfaction le prospectus du Théâtre d'Idées avec le nom de Mme *Slatoff* comme fondatrice. Sous prétexte que je n'ai pas déclaré le titre du théâtre que *j'ai fondé*, elle se l'est approprié."[65] This conflict may explain Starkoff's decision in December 1910 to apply to become a member of the Société des Gens de Lettres, the organization responsible for protecting the intellectual property rights of authors. Championed by authors Camille Le Senne, Paul Margueritte, and C. M. Poinsot, Starkoff was admitted as a member in January 1911.[66]

As of 1910, Starkoff published primarily nonfiction. In her portrait of Chernyshevski, for example, she introduces the French public to a Russian socialist philosopher who was a leader and inspirer of the nineteenth-century revolutionary movement. He was imprisoned in 1862 and later exiled to Siberia for writing proclamations to the peasants (Zenkovsky 324). In addition to his socialist populism, Starkoff certainly appreciated both his belief in a scientific foundation for ethics and morality, and his aesthetic theory as developed in his Master's dissertation, *The Aesthetic Relation of Art to Reality*, published in 1855. Chernyshevski rejected idealist aesthetics. For him, the purpose of art is not only "to reproduce phenomena of real life that are of interest to man," but also "to explain life" (Qtd. in *Russian Philosophy* 24). Chernyshevski's aesthetics thus favored both philosophical and literary realism in which the artist passes judgment on the reality portrayed in his/her works. This type of art would therefore have a moral and social dimension.

> His paintings or his novels, poems, and plays will present or solve problems that arise out of life for the thinking man; his works will be, as it were, essays on subjects presented by life. . . . In such a case the artist becomes a thinker, and works of art, while remaining in the sphere of art, acquire scientific significance. (Qtd. in *Russian Philosophy* 27)

Like Ibsen and Zola several decades later, Chernyshevski outlined the role of "the playwright as thinker,"[67] a role that Starkoff adopted in her own writing and appreciated in the playwrights whose works she staged.

In 1912, Starkoff turned her attention to the Russian author Pushkin. She gave a series of lectures on his drama and performed her translation of his play *Mozart et Salieri*. In a letter to the president of the Union Fraternelle des Femmes inviting her to a lecture and performance, Starkoff describes Pushkin as "un poète féministe."[68] Her adaptation of *Mozart et Salieri* was performed once more at the Athénée St. Germain in December 1912, along with Pushkin's one-act drama *La Roussalka*.

As of 1913, when the advent of war began to appear more and more likely, Starkoff concentrated her efforts on pacifist propaganda. In March 1913, for example, she suggested in a meeting of the UFF that French mothers should appeal to German mothers in order to prevent the war (*La Française* March 15, 1913). This type of maternal pacifism, which was quite popular on the eve of the war, became less so once the hostilities began. As usual, Starkoff was primarily influenced by Tolstoy's pacifist ideals. In early 1918, Starkoff applauded the Soviet's attempt to get out of the war and mistakenly attributes it to a pacifist agenda:

> Trotzky se révèle un pur disciple du "grand écrivain de la Terre russe." Il met en pratique le moyen d'éclairer le peuple d'un pays agresseur préconisé par le chantre de la conscience humaine. Le moyen est de dévoiler le mensonge d'un gouvernement belliqueux en refusant d'adapter sa doctrine. Le peuple russe ne relève pas le gant meurtrier. Il rejette avec dédain les armes que le Kaiser veut imposer au monde et ses féroces méthodes de guerre empruntés aux âges primitifs. Le peuple russe ne veut pas combattre les Allemands militaristes par leurs propres armes. Car Tolstoï lui avait appris que toute la fausseté de la doctrine militariste est précisément dans les armes; les adopter c'est en adopter la doctrine . . . Le refus de se battre était pour lui le vrai moyen de combattre les vio- lences . . . . ("C'est Tolstoï qui triomphe")[69]

Starkoff's financial situation suffered greatly during this period. At the onset of the war, she founded an organization that collected funds to come to the aid of Russians like herself living in France without financial resources. The following year, she resorted to giving Russian lessons in an effort to make ends meet.[70] In letters written to the Société des Gens de Lettres justifying her inability to pay her dues, she claimed that her income had been reduced by half because of the war, and that the Russian Revolution in 1917 had ruined her completely.[71] In 1921, she was obliged to resign from the Société due to lack of funds.

Like most democrats and socialists in France, Véra Starkoff welcomed the February Revolution in Russia in spite of the disastrous consequences on her personal finances. In May 1917, she spoke at a celebration "à l'honneur de la libération du peuple russe"[72] organized by Le Libre Examen, the first women's Freemason Lodge, which would become Lodge number one of the Grande Loge Féminine de France.[73] As of 1918, Véra Starkoff came under investigation by the police for her pro-Bolshevik activities. In a report about the innumerable other Russian émigrés living in France suspected of subversive political activities, Starkoff was categorized as having an "Attitude politique douteuse" (Questionable political attitude).[74] In 1920, she was suspected of using her Russian language classes to recruit communist militants and was included in a list of Russian Freemasons established by an anti-Bolshevik organization in 1922.[75]

By 1919, Starkoff had, however, become disillusioned with the Russian Revolution. In April of that year, she published an article entitled "Les origines profondes du communisme russe" in the communist newspaper, Le Populaire. As an introduction to this article or perhaps as a justification for printing an article by a dissident, the editors of the journal wrote:

> Il est intéressant de montrer comment un écrivain de la valeur de Véra Starkoff, dont les idées sont extrêmement éloignées de celles des bolchevicks, s'efforce de comprendre la grande transformation communiste et la rattache à l'histoire politique et sociale de la Russie. (Le Populaire April 6, 1919).[76]

In this article, Starkoff traces the origins of communism in Russia to two institutions of the former Republics of Novgorod, Kief and Pskof, for whom the love of the land and freedom was a veritable religion: Obstchine, "la propriété en commun de la terre," and Mir, "l'univers de la campagne, c'est-à-dire tous les paysans qui travaillent en commun . . . une sorte de parlement rustique qui régit et juge toutes les affaires du village."[77] She relates Obstchine and Mir to the contemporary institution of the Soviet:

> Dans le mot du soviet (conseil), comme dans celui de Mir et de l'Obstchine (la chose commune), il y a à la gravité d'une pensée en commun, le recueillement de la conscience collective de la terre. La préoccupation religieuse de la conscience humaine, gardienne de la terre libre, dans les affaires publiques est particulièrement russe. Et s'il est vrai que chaque peuple est porteur d'une idée universelle, celle du peuple russe semble être la libération de la terre.[78]

After quoting Tolstoy in length on the disadvantages of private property, Starkoff concludes that while it would be paradoxical to call the

Bolsheviks *Tolstoïens*, the fundamental ideas behind the Revolution are in fact *Tolstoïennes*: "on peut supposer que leur succès est dû à la mise en pratique de certaines maximes chères à Tolstoï, issues de la sagesse populaire. Les Bolcheviks ont cherché à coopérer véritablement avec le peuple."[79] In her last original publication, *Le Bolchevisme*, published in 1922, a year before her death, Starkoff develops the ideas outlined in this article adding a critique of the violent methods employed by the Bolsheviks. Repression is a bourgeois method: "la Terreur rouge et le militarisme révolutionnaire retardent l'ère du communisme" (45).[80] Starkoff recommends ending the Terror and the reign of intolerance. Always faithful to the ideas of Tolstoy, she calls for unilateral disarmament.

In her drama, Starkoff seeks to share Tolstoy's philosophy as she understood it, by adapting it to a realist, contemporary context to which the audience could relate. Her choice of genre corresponded to her goal not only to criticize existing institutions but also to provide a positive outlook for the future based on "une sagesse de la conscience humaine, une morale de la bonté, une sociologie du travail," in short on "l'humanité" (*Le Vrai Tolstoï* 17, 34).[81] Unlike male authors such as Brieux and Hervieu, who remained "bound to the [naturalist] theory that forceful drama must expose a bad situation" (Millestone 385), Starkoff chose to adapt the naturalist approach to comedy. By portraying women who succeeded in becoming autonomous beings and men who encouraged them, Starkoff provided positive role models for both the men and women in her audience, thus leaving them with a feeling of hope.

It is difficult today to evaluate the actual impact of this type of social protest theater. It probably didn't directly influence political decisions and laws. Yet, theater was regularly cited as witness to social questions in the legal discourse of the period. As to the more individual level, Starkoff and Roussel's plays certainly made the workers more aware of the issues. While some of the members of their audience may have known about and agreed with the views put forth in her plays, they were not simply preaching to the converted. Many of the activists of the Université Populaire were in fact quite conservative in their views about women. In a debate at the Congrès des Universités Populaires in 1910, about the role of the working-class woman, the conclusion was unequivocally that "La femme hors du foyer, c'est la ruine morale de la famille" (Mercier 1986: 158).[82] The Université Populaire's position on feminism was indeed ambiguous: such conservative positions were held by the same group who advocated coeducation, reproductive freedom, and sex education for girls. As one part of a broader educational program, which is after all the purpose of the theater in the Université Populaire, the plays of both the authors certainly served to educate the audience, to reinforce social ideas, and to rally feminist and socialist activists. Their plays, like those of Madeleine Pelletier discussed in chapter five, must not be thought of as an end in themselves, but rather as one of many tools used in conjunction to form new individuals (both men and women) for a new society.

Braving the Law: Madeleine Pelletier

Like the other authors we have discussed, Dr. Madeleine Pelletier (1874–1939) is best known for her activities as a militant feminist and political activist.[1] However, Pelletier was the only one of them born into a working-class family. She grew up in an insalubrious one-room apartment behind her mother's fruit and vegetable shop in the neighborhood of Les Halles. Though her mother earned the money for the family—her father was paralyzed and confined to a chair—she was not a positive role model for Madeleine. An ardent Catholic and royalist, uneducated, dirty, and a slave to her work and her family, Pelletier's mother symbolized the working-class woman's plight. This may explain why Pelletier would never romanticize the working-class lifestyle like Starkoff and other leftist militants. On the contrary, she fought to raise the proletariat out of the degradation in which they lived.

Pelletier left school at the age of 12 and began to frequent feminist and anarchist circles. At the age of 20, she decided to go back to school. She prepared her baccalaureate on her own and attended medical school from 1898 to 1903. While studying medicine, she developed an interest in the new science of anthropology, which was at the time closely related to the field of medicine. In 1900, Pelletier began to attend meetings of the Anthropological Society of Paris, founded by Paul Broca, professor of clinical surgery, in 1859. "Both her medical and anthropological studies confirmed her bias toward the scientific/positivist current in French thought" (Gordon 31). During the early years of the century, Pelletier carried out research on craniometry (skull measurement) under the supervision of Léonce Manouvrier of the Anthropological Society. Craniometry was being used at the time to prove racist and sexist theories about the intellectual superiority of the white male. At first,

Pelletier did not question the validity of the initial presupposition—the relationship between brain size and intelligence—but attempted to use the same premise to prove the opposite conclusion: in a study of Japanese skeletons, women's skulls were in fact proportionally larger than men's given their body size; hence the women were more intelligent. Pelletier then continued her research in the field of craniometry in collaboration with Nicholas Vaschide, a member of the Anthropological Society and director at the experimental psychology laboratory at the Villejuif insane asylum where Pelletier had also worked briefly as a substitute intern in 1901–1902. Together they produced a study entitled "Les Signes physique de l'intelligence." By then, Pelletier had also become interested in psychology. In 1903, she applied for the competitive exam for an internship in psychiatric hospital service, but was prevented from participating because of a stipulation that candidates for the *concours* must hold political rights, a requirement that effectively banned all women. Pelletier appealed the decision and led such an effective campaign in the press that the requirement was repealed the following year. In 1903, Pelletier was admitted as a psychiatric intern. For the next four years, Pelletier worked as a psychiatric intern in three different hospitals, collaborating with some of the most important psychiatrists of the time: Paul-Maurice Legrain, Edouard Toulouse, Auguste-Armand Marie, Alix Joffroy, and Paul Dubuisson. In spite of this experience and the number of articles she published during her studies, Pelletier was unsuccessful when she participated in another *concours* to become a resident in a psychiatric hospital. She was accepted as a doctor for the postal services, a sector that was eager to hire women doctors to treat its numerous female employees.

In Pelletier's first play, *In anima vili, ou un crime scientifique*, published by the anarchist group L'Idée Libre in 1920, Pelletier returns to these early interests of psychology, medical experimentation, and the structure of the brain. Here she combines a commentary on war with a staging of a debate about the ethics of scientific research. Paul Bernard, a brilliant scientist, has invited two of his colleagues, Delage and Wagner, to a laboratory in an isolated house that he had built in order to carry out his vivisection experiments "en paix." After a general discussion on the ethics of vivisection, he announces that he has brought them together to carry out a dangerous and revolutionary experiment and that they must abduct a passerby in order to conduct an experiment on the brain of a live person. After much hesitation, Delage and Wagner abandon their scruples and accept the challenge. They abduct a drunkard, administer chloroform, open up his skull, and apply electrodes to his brain. Projected onto a screen, they see an animated image of the man's thought. All three agree that the breakthrough discovery was worth the death of an individual. Even as they are exalting over the success of the experiment and deciding how to hide the evidence of their crime, a bomb falls on the house destroying the corpse and killing Wagner. The two surviving scientists, totally indifferent to the destruction of the house and the death of their colleague, start planning for the future: "sans plus tarder, nous irons au laboratoire creuser ton idée d'excitation du cerveau au travers le crâne" (24).[2]

While the main conflict in the play centers on whether or not human experimentation is valid if it leads to a groundbreaking scientific discovery, the overriding philosophical question concerns the meaning of life. The action in the play takes place during World War I and reflects Pelletier's despair and disillusionment during the hostilities. Like Starkoff, Pelletier had been frustrated by the reaction of the majority of socialists and feminists, who had abandoned their pacifist ideals in favor of patriotic nationalism. She criticized the socialists for not encouraging the workers to band together to prevent the hostilities, and she refused to revert to traditional gender roles in which women maintain the home front knitting socks and making babies to replace the fallen soldiers. Instead, motivated more by her feminist agenda and personal ambition than by her pacifist ideals, she sought to use her professional skills to serve the war effort and applied first to work in an army medical unit at the front, then to join the ambulance corps. Both attempts being unsuccessful, she settled for the Red Cross. In September 1914, Pelletier decided to visit the battleground of the battle of the Marne to observe the effects of the war first-hand. After this decisive experience, Pelletier became discouraged by the absurdity of war, the horror of the senseless killings, the chauvinistic attitude of the majority, and the hypocrisy of fellow militants. In moments of despair, she lost her faith in the possibility of human progress. Her pessimism led her to abandon her activities as a militant for the remainder of the war, opting instead to return to the study of science, this time chemistry.

In *In anima vili*, Pelletier's characters talk about the war as an arbitrary and senseless activity.[3] Before accepting to kill a random passer-by, Delage, who understands the importance of the experiment, offers himself as the guinea pig:

> Prenez ma vie, allez, elle ne vaut pas cher: j'ai 40 ans et je suis tuber-
> culeux, vous le savez. Qu'importe quelques années de plus ou
> de moins. Si j'avais été pris dans cette horrible guerre, peut-être

serais-je déjà mort. Je n'ai qu'à m'imaginer que nous ne sommes pas dans ce laboratoire, mais dans une bataille. Vous n'êtes plus le professeur Bernard, vous êtes mon chef militaire, vous êtes Napoléon, que vous égalez, je vous le dis, par le génie . . . et vous me confiez une mission dont on ne revient pas. J'y serais allé et je serais mort comme tant d'autres . . . pourquoi faire? . . . la guerre est une stupidité . . . Je suis certain ici de mourir pour quelque chose qui vaille la peine. (13)[4]

Later, as Delage is trying to convince Wagner to participate in Bernard's experiment, he refers explicitly to Wagner's experience in battle:

Tu as passé deux ans au front, tu as participé à des charges à la baïonnette: tu n'es pas un sentimental. Un meurtre de plus ou moins qu'est-ce que cela peut te faire; car c'est la même chose, tuer à la guerre ou tuer ici, c'est toujours tuer. (17)[5]

In these passages, Delage underscores the arbitrary nature of war. If by chance, Delage had not had tuberculosis, he would very likely have been killed in battle. He draws a parallel between scientific experimentation and war. If a military leader can order his soldiers to battle and to certain death with impunity, why shouldn't a leading scientist be allowed to sacrifice human life for the good of science? Moreover, Wagner, as a soldier, has already committed murder. Pelletier thus questions the notion that killing a man in battle is not murder. Furthermore, for Delage, Bernard's cause is much more worthwhile than any battle; war is futile while a scientific breakthrough brings progress.

We may ask ourselves whether Pelletier sanctions the actions of the characters in her play. She describes Paul Bernard as a "savant de premier ordre, homme de génie" (2).[6] He has made tremendous discoveries and is virtually revered by his disciple Delage. Wagner, on the other hand, also recognizes Bernard as a genius, but is convinced from the opening of the play that he is a bit mad: "*Nihil est ingenium sine aliqua stultitia*, autrement dit, il n'y a pas de génie sans quelque grain de folie. Le patron est certainement un génie, un grand génie; il est forcément un peu loufoque" (3).[7] Wagner's opinion might not hold much value coming from the least sympathetic of the three main characters, but it does serve as foreshadowing for the apparently crazy idea Bernard would propose at the end of Act I. Whether or not Bernard is in fact crazy is left to the interpretation of the reader or audience. The performance would, of course, influence this interpretation. A melodramatic staging might give Bernard the appearance of a mad scientist driven by an irrational monomania, while a more realist staging might represent him as a lucid researcher who, unswayed by moral or legal considerations, has made a conscious decision to push the scientific method to its limits. The text itself seems to support the second interpretation. Bernard recognizes that his ideas may be perceived as crazy. He explains to Delage and Wagner that he had originally planned to request permission to conduct his experiment on a prisoner awaiting the death penalty but subsequently decided to carry out his experiment in secret because the authorities, the press, and even some of his colleagues might think him mad. Furthermore, it is doubtful that Pelletier intended him to be seen as delusional. In the stage directions, she describes Bernard as a genius. Moreover, in an earlier pamphlet entitled "La Prétendue Dégénérescence des hommes de génie" (Paris, n.d.) in which she challenges the conclusions of Lombroso of the School of Anthropology, Pelletier had rejected the idea that geniuses were either physically or psychologically degenerate. Contrary to Lombroso, Pelletier defended the genius' right to difference:

> The man of genius does not resemble other men. Gifted with a more active brain, he carries his intelligence into everything; where other men blindly follow routine, he thinks: this is a source of those eccentricities which psychologists reproach him with. These eccentricities make him into a man who, in addition to his superiority, is different from others, and this is what his fellows will not forgive. (Qtd. in Gordon 46–47)

Pelletier was not only willing to accept these eccentricities, she apparently admired them. In the light of this, we might conclude that Pelletier did not intend Bernard to be mad, but rather an exceptional individual willing to brave the law and transgress accepted ethical practices in the name of science.

This interpretation is also reinforced by the characterization of Delage. Pelletier describes him as "intelligence supérieure aussi, quoique moins brillante. Grand caractère" (2).[8] Delage appears to be the authorial voice in the play. In the opening scene, he and Wagner discuss vivisection. When Wagner derides antivivisectionists, Delage counters that general public's reaction against vivisection is understandable:

> Il est regrettable d'avoir à faire souffrir des bêtes pour faire des recherches. Tu vas peut-être te moquer de moi; mais ce n'est pas sans

répugnance que je pratique la vivisection. [. . .] Je fais taire mon cœur, je dompte mes nerfs; mais je n'ouvre les bêtes qu'en cas de nécessité absolue. Toutes les fois que cela est possible je leur donne du chloroforme et si je puis éviter de les tuer, je le fais. (5–6)[9]

Though Pelletier certainly believed in the scientist's right to perform experiments on animals, she was in no way insensitive to the animals' suffering. In an essay entitled "La Morale et la loi," she wrote:

A future society would forbid the murder of animals; one would no longer have the right to poison the unhappy cat who has ceased to please, the dog who one wishes to get rid of. Animal aid would be part of the national budget; well-furnished refuges would shelter abandoned dogs and cats. (Qtd. in Gordon 190)

Delage plays the role of mediator; he is open-minded and able to see all sides of an issue. For example, he and Wagner discuss their lifestyles. Wagner distinguishes between his work and his life: "Certes, moi aussi je travaille: docteur ès sciences, docteur en médecine et je prépare maintenant le grand concours: mais enfin, j'ai aussi ma vie; ma femme, mes enfants . . ." (6).[10] He is somewhat disdainful about Bernard and Delage's exclusive dedication to their research, accusing Delage of having no time for love. Delage counters that he and Bernard do not limit themselves to their specialization, that they are interested in a wide range of intellectual pursuits. He also distinguishes between love and marriage:

WAGNER: Je parierais qu'il ne te reste plus le temps pour l'amour.
DELAGE: Il ne m'en reste pas pour le mariage. Le mariage, cela rétrécit la vie en l'encombrant de soucis matériels. Avec le célibat, nous réduisons à leur simple expression les préoccupations terre à terre: au restaurant, je lis les journaux; la nuit, quand je ne dors pas, je lis les mémoires historiques. (6)[11]

Just as Pelletier chose a life of militant celibacy for herself, Delage appears to prefer the freedom of bachelorhood. When Wagner takes a pro-natalist stance, typical of World War I period—"s'il n'y avait que le patron et toi pour assurer la repopulation . . ." (6–7)[12]—Delage replies that he does not recommend this life for everybody. In a surprising comparison for a anticlerical author, he compares himself and Bernard to monks in the Middle Ages:

> Le moyen âge avait ses moines qui, déchargés du fardeau de la vie
> matérielle, se consacraient tout entiers dans leurs couvents à la
> prière et à l'étude. Nous sommes des moines à notre façon, avec les
> avantages de la vie libre, sans l'assujettissement d'une règle faite pour
> les inférieurs. (7)[13]

Wagner categorically refuses Bernard's plan, not for moral reasons, but
for fear of being caught: "Et si nous sommes découverts songez-y donc,
patron: c'est un scandale épouvantable. La cour d'assises, la prison, la
guillotine . . ." (11).[14] Delage is also shocked by Bernard's suggestion at
first, but for very different reasons. First, he wonders how three honest
men could commit cold-blooded murder. He thinks about the stranger
they would have to kill: "peut-être un brave homme: un père de famille
que ses enfants et sa femme attendent à la maison" (11).[15] He too recognizes the legal consequences of Bernard's plan, but he is more critical of
both the public and the "misérables lois" (12). The world is simply not
ready for such a revolutionary idea. Even scientists are too blinded
by prejudice to understand. It would take a great man to defend
this "meurtre sublime": "l'homme réunissant au génie scientifique, la
grandeur du caractère, l'audace magnifique qui le ferait se placer au-
dessus des lois et de l'humanité" (12).[16] Delage is, in fact, such a man. He
believes that exceptional men are above the law: "La loi, la morale sont
pour les hommes et les circonstances ordinaires" (15).[17] It is he who
finally convinces Wagner to accept the proposition by coming down
to his level and addressing his mundane concerns. Wagner is ambitious;
he is afraid of the scandal the experiment might provoke, but he is also
attracted by the career advancement possibilities of a breakthrough
discovery.

> Je suis dur mais enfin, il ne faut pas te faire illusion. Cette réalité
> matérielle qui seule t'impressionne, elle t'échappera. Pour s'imposer
> il faut faire des travaux seul, tu en es incapable: tu resteras petit
> agrégé. [. . .] Ici, c'est une carrière brillante qui t'attend. (17)[18]

Careerism is a characteristic that Pelletier attributes to inferior men
whether it be in science as in the case of Wagner, or in politics as we see
later in the chapter in our discussion of *Supérieur!*

Nevertheless, in spite of all these considerations, we are still left with
an innocent victim in this play. Or are we? Pelletier may have been trying

to solve this problem by making the victim seem less innocent. Bernard prevented his colleagues from abducting the first two passersby: a young girl and an old man. The person he finally chose was a drunkard who, they would later discover, had been a pimp. If Bernard and Delage thought themselves above the law and moral considerations, the man of the street apparently was not. For Pelletier, both alcoholism and prostitution were symptoms of a diseased capitalist society. The fact that the victim was a drunken pimp was perhaps intended to make the murderers seem less guilty. As Delage says: "résultat à part, ce n'est une grande perte" (21).[19] Bernard's crime is in fact portrayed as a form of scientific direct action. If, as we see in our analysis of *Supérieur!*, Pelletier was not opposed to the anarchist practice of using violence to make a political statement, could she, a doctor committed to saving lives, have believed that the death of a man for the benefit of science could be justified? In any case, whether or not the author sanctions her characters' behavior, her judgment was made on neither religious nor legal grounds. Pelletier had long rejected the Church, and she certainly was not afraid of braving the law herself; she wore men's clothing at a time when cross-dressing was illegal, performed abortions when such interventions were a crime, and published her second play, *Supérieur!*, in which she alludes to contraception and abortion, after the 1920 *loi scélérate* (villainous law) had formally banned all neo-Malthusian propaganda.

Supérieur! is similar in genre to Véra Sarkoff's plays written for the Université Populaire. Pelletier often spoke at the Universités Populaires, and though she might not have actively participated in theatrical activities, she may well have seen the types of drama that were performed there. Pelletier was also well aware of anarchist cultural politics. As an adolescent during the final years of the nineteenth century, she had rebelled against her reactionary, Catholic mother and began attending anarchist meetings. Though she claimed that she was not really an anarchist[20] and would spend the majority of her career as a militant for socialist factions and the Communist Party, she would always retain ties with the anarchists who were often more open to her undoctrinary ideas. When her play *Supérieur!* was published by L'Idée libre in 1923, in the wake of her eye-opening trip to Russia, Pelletier had already become disenchanted with the Communist Party and had begun publishing articles in anarchist journals. Three years later, after her official rupture with the Party, she again found refuge in the anarchist circles of her youth.

In *Supérieur!*, Pelletier stages the making of an anarchist revolutionary. As the play progresses, the young self-taught protagonist revolts against his boss and his parents, joins the anarchist milieu, receives the death penalty for an assassination, escapes, and, as the play closes, leaves for Russia under a false identity. Though Pelletier would not have had to look far to find any number of models for her protagonist,[21] the autobiographical elements of the play are strikingly evident. Like her protagonist, the young Madeleine rebelled against her parents, became involved in anarchist circles and went back to school as a young adult. Also, in 1921, like her protagonist, she took a clandestine trip to Russia under a series of false identities.

Pelletier weaves into the melodramatic and meteoric transformation of her protagonist, a serious critique of both the bourgeois society and the political arena in which she participated actively. The play begins with the mise-en-scène of Pelletier's criticism of the family. In the opening monologue of the first act, entitled "famille," we learn that Pierre feels alienated in his own milieu and wants nothing more than to leave home:

> Oh! M'en aller, m'en aller, fuir pour toujours ce milieu qui n'est pas le mien; où on ne me comprend pas, où on me méprise, où on me hait, je n'exagère pas. Comment ai-je pu naître ici? Car, enfin, je n'ai rien . . . , rien de commun avec eux. (3)[22]

Pelletier maintained that the nuclear family is, as an institution, detrimental to both women and children since it enslaves the wife and mother, and restricts the free development of the individual. The family should thus be suppressed and replaced by the collectivity. Sociability would no longer depend on the arbitrary, imposed relationships between family members, but on relationships which were chosen and voluntary, based on common interests and sensibilities:

> Le couple devenant deux camarades unis par l'amour, le mariage sera supprimé, les couples s'uniront et se désuniront à volonté; l'état prendra en charge les enfants. A la famille égoïste se substituera une sociabilité plus large. Des femmes et des hommes d'idées et de goûts communs se réuniront . . . (Qtd. in Sowerine and Maignien 108)[23]

Pierre also complains in his opening monologue that his parents forced him to leave school when he was 13 in spite of his superior grades. Here Pelletier introduces two interdependent themes: equal opportunity education and meritocracy. For Pelletier, both access to education and the possibility of advancement should be based neither on sex nor on socioeconomic factors, but rather on ability and achievement.

Education should be an instrument of social advancement for the hardworking and intellectually superior. Pierre has been able to elevate himself in spite of his parents. Pelletier symbolizes his progress in her description of the set: in his "pauvre chambre d'ouvrier," Pierre has constructed "un coin de l'intellectuel"[24] with a desk, bookshelves, a gas lamp, and a portrait of a nineteenth-century mathematician. Pierre's advancement is again evident in the difference between his language and that of his parents; while Pierre speaks standard French, his parents speak a more uneducated jargon. This is an interesting reversal from the valorization of slang in the late nineteenth century when anarchist propagandists—journalists, orators, café owners—exalted argot as both an expression of popular culture and a political tool: "Anarchists emphasized the gulf that separated the formal language of the political elites from the subcultural idiom of the Parisian faubourgs in order to reinforce class conflict and promote working-class solidarity" (Sonn, *Anarchism and Cultural Politics* 95). In *Supérieur!*, on the contrary, popular language is not a means of solidarity among the working class, but rather a sign of division between the complacent working class—accomplices to their own oppression—and the enlightened few, who, by their own merit, have been able to lift themselves up from their working-class origins. While Pelletier herself never denied her working-class origins—she was proud of them and felt insulted during her trip to Russia when she was taken for a bourgeoise (*Mon Voyage aventureux* 34)—she was only proud of those origins in so far as she had risen above them.

Not only do Pierre and his parents speak a different language, they also have a different value system. Pierre's parents despise his superior attitude and disdain his intellectual activities: "*Monsieur* est bien supérieur au patron, il est supérieur à nous; à tout le monde. Il lit dans les livres et personne ne lui va à la cheville du pied" (4).[25] His parents are shocked when they learn that he has stood up to his boss, has revolted against oppression, and has, as a result, been fired. In their value system, all that matters is earning a living and being able to feed oneself. Without a job, Pierre is a useless burden on the family. Since he has voluntarily broken the unwritten socioeconomic contract of the milieu, he must leave.

In the second act, entitled "Seul dans la vie" (Alone in life), we find Pierre in another symbolic setting, the archetypal room of a struggling intellectual in a garret in the Latin Quarter. Pierre has become a teacher of math, philosophy, and German thanks to superior intelligence, hard work, and material deprivation, but no thanks to the official educational system. He complains in the opening monologue of the act that because of his poverty, he has been obliged to learn everything on his own.

Though he knows as much as a professor in his areas of specialization, he lacks diplomas, general culture, advice, and friendship. At the end of this monologue, his neighbor Jacques, an aging anarchist, comes to visit and thus begins a filial relationship built on common interests and respect, so different from his relationship with his biological father. Jacques complains bitterly about "la sale société bourgeoise"[26] in which intelligent, enthusiastic young men like Pierre must suffer cold and hunger while rich cretins live a life of comfort and luxury. In the course of the act, he convinces Pierre that he too is an anarchist and invites him to a meeting the following day.

During Pierre and Jacques' conversation about politics in this act, Madeleine Pelletier introduces a new theme based on her disenchantment with the various political parties in which she has been involved. She brings to light the hypocrisy and ambition of leftist politicians in general and the rigidity of the Communist Party in particular. Pierre has a very negative view of politics: "La politique, cela ne me dit rien . . . Quelques hommes médiocres avec du bagout et de l'aplomb qui bernent les masses pour s'en faire un marchepied" (11).[27] Jacques explains that he must not put all the parties "dans la même boîte à ordure. Tu as raison cent fois pour les partis parlementaires. Les politiciens ne cherchent qu'à s'assurer un fromage, il se foutent de l'idée, c'est entendu" (12).[28] Later in the play, Pelletier provides an illustration of a dishonest and ambitious politician who admits that he is just using the anarchist movement as a stepping stone in order to become a leader in the Communist Party without having to work his way up in the ranks.[29] True anarchists, according to Jacques, are different: no politicians, no elected representatives, no *arrivisme*. What's more, anarchism is not a secret society; there are no statutes, no official membership; anarchism is open to everyone "comme dans un café" (like in a café). Though her characters never name any specific parties in this act, Pelletier is obviously taking a stab here at the excessive dogmatism and exclusionist attitude of the Communist Party, thus braving the law of the Party from which she would soon be barred for disagreeing with the official doctrine.

Jacques' comparison of the anarchist movement to a café serves as a transition into the following act, entitled "anarchiste," in which the action takes place in a meeting hall adjacent to a café, again a highly symbolic setting; according to Kropotkin, the French anarchist movement originated in Parisian cafés (406). As we saw in the discussion on Starkoff's *Le Petit Verre*, the café had traditionally been a place of sociability among the French working class, but by the end of the nineteenth century, working-class cafés would take on an overtly political character.

This was particularly true in anarchist circles. All forms of propaganda by the word took place in cafés: political meetings, *goguettes*, even plays. Moreover, the anarchist press was often written, published, read, and discussed in cafés.[30]

The café in Pelletier's play is being used for an anarchist meeting. The crowd of some 50 men and women represent the spectrum of various anarchist types from the naturalist to the terrorist to the ex-Russian princess. The act is divided into a series of tableaux each presenting a different anarchist perspective. In the opening tableau, Pelletier brings to the stage a crucial debate within the French anarchist circles in the years following the Russian Revolution. At first, nearly all the anarchists applauded the Russians for having accomplished a social revolution, however flawed the resulting system; but they would become more and more disenchanted with the Bolshevik state. Though some still maintained that a faulty revolution was better than no revolution, most anarchists as of 1921 strongly criticized the Bolsheviks and the Communist Party as promoting dictatorship, a form of government opposed by both communist anarchists and anarchist individualists (Maitron II: 41–55). In Pelletier's play, the crowd is listening to a speech by an anarchist leader, Roidel, who harshly criticizes the Communist regime in Russia. He maintains that anarchists must not associate themselves with Bolsheviks. Duval, another anarchist in the hall, disagrees: "pour la première fois, dans un pays, le socialisme sort de l'idéologie pour passer à la réalité, je trouve que ce serait un crime de ne pas l'aider" (14).[31] Duval is dissatisfied with propaganda by the word: he calls for deeds.

In the next tableau, Pelletier again braves the law by staging an apology of propaganda by the deed. Since the *lois scélérates* of 1893, all anarchist propaganda not only inciting individuals to commit terrorist acts, but even simply advocating propaganda by the deed, was considered a crime (Maitron I: 252). In Pelletier's play, two members of the assembly, Jacques and Duval, explicitly support propaganda by the deed and agree to put their ideas into action by assassinating an unnamed "homme néfaste":[32]

DUVAL: C'est à tort que l'on pense que les actes individuels ne servent à rien. Le meurtre d'un gouvernement, que la classe ouvrière déteste, peut, aujourd'hui, surtout que la Russie donne l'exemple, déclencher la révolution. (15)[33]

Duval's lines here echo Pelletier's position on propaganda by the deed years earlier, during her association with the insurrectionist faction led by

Gustave Hervé from 1907 to 1911. Though Hervé was only moderately favorable to feminist issues, his ideology corresponded well to Pelletier's on other fronts, notably neo-Malthusianism and revolutionary militancy. Pelletier was not à priori pro-violence, but she was tempted by the use of propaganda by the deed and direct action in both feminist and socialist activism. She was impressed by the results of violent tactics in the suffragette movement in England and tried to convince French suffragists to use similar methods. She found little enthusiasm, and her violent militancy limited itself to leading a group of about ten women to a polling station and throwing stones at the window in 1908 (Gordon 101). In her articles in Hervé's journal *La Guerre Sociale*, Pelletier defends individual acts of terrorism. An article published on July 14, 1909, entitled "La Tactique de l'attentat" is most explicit:

> Aux époques d'agitation, les actes de propagande par le fait peuvent avoir une utilité de premier ordre en dénonçant par exemple une situation qui ne se serait pas dénouée sans eux. [. . .] Pour être utile, l'attentat doit, dans une époque donnée, viser un but précis; modifier une situation en supprimant l'homme qui l'incarne; corser une grève, un mouvement insurrectionnel en créant de l'irréparable entre les révoltés et le gouvernement.[34]

In 1923, Pelletier would reiterate her theoretical revolutionary stance while denying any personal role in terrorist activities: "Révolutionnaire, je le suis en théorie; en pratique je ne tue que les puces [. . .] et je laisse vivre les araignées" (Qtd. in Sowerine and Maignien 81).[35] Can we not then understand Duval's comments as the author's self-criticism when he says to Jacques: "Préconiser [la propagande de fait] ne suffit pas. Et je trouve même une lâcheté à conseiller aux autres de risquer leur peau, alors qu'on se tient tranquille au coin de son feu" (15)?[36]

In a later tableau, Pelletier again openly brings to the stage a discussion of subjects strictly outlawed: abortion and contraception. Though this scene seems tangential to the plot of the play, its theme is central to Pelletier's thought and activism. Pelletier, as both a doctor and a feminist, had always been active in the neo-Malthusian movement. She demanded reproductive freedom for women. Pregnancy kept women in a position of inferiority and dependency, if not slavery. Though Pelletier recognized that depopulation may have been a real concern for the nation, she believed that the rights of the individual were more important, more sacred. The woman has an absolute right over her own body, and this right includes both contraception and abortion.[37]

Neo-Malthusian propaganda was tolerated through most of the Third Republic but as of about 1910,[38] repressive measures would begin to have a more serious effect. After the war, in order to repopulate the country, the government passed a series of even more draconian repressive measures. Like the anti-anarchist legislation of 1893, the *loi scélérate* of 1920 made all neo-Malthusian propaganda illegal, and in 1923, the year in which Pelletier published *Supérieur!*, a particularly devious law made abortion a misdemeanor rather than a crime so that it would be judged more severely by a magistrate alone rather than by an overindulgent jury. Abortion had become such a common practice that the government feared jury members were likely to condone it. As Pelletier wrote hyperbolically in 1933, at the time when she was under accusation for allegedly performing abortions: "aujourd'hui on peut avancer que pas une femme, les stériles et les vierges mise à part, ne s'est pas faite avorter, au moins une fois dans sa vie."[39]

It is in this political and historical climate that Pelletier published a play in which a militant anarchist informs another young woman that there are ways to deal with an unwanted pregnancy and to avoid such situations in the future. Though she never pronounces the words "abortion" or "contraception," the feminist and neo-Malthusian message is perfectly clear. At the end of the tableau, Marianne, the anarchist, invites Léonie to her home that night: "Venez chez moi, ce soir, on causera, et vous verrez qu'il n'y a pas de quoi se jeter à l'eau" (20).[40] Marianne quite obviously is the voice of Madeleine herself in this scene and the invitation, if the play had been performed, would have been extended to each member of the audience. Though the play did not provide much practical information about abortion or contraception, it would have taught the uninformed spectator that such possibilities existed.

Now, according to the law of 1920, even simply giving advice about contraception or abortion was illegal and cause for imprisonment. Why then, when Pelletier was recognized as being a leading neo-Malthusian propagandist, was she not arrested for publishing *Supérieur!*? One reason is that the play may never have been performed. Agitprop theater is only dangerous in performance. If it was staged, it was certainly in a well-controlled, private venue far from the eyes of the censors and police. Another reason might be the veiled nature of the play's language concerning sexuality and the body. *Supérieur!* was perhaps not explicit enough to cause Pelletier any trouble with the police. Throughout the tableau, we must read through the silences, through what is not said, to understand the women's stories. Therefore, Pelletier's play was certainly much less worrying to the natalists than her work as both orator and abortionist since in the domain of neo-Malthusianism, Pelletier practiced what she preached. Indeed, she would eventually be arrested and committed to an insane asylum for having performed abortions. Pelletier also reinforces in this tableau her critique of the nuclear family. Léonie explains through a series of ellipses why she chose to become her boss's lover; the only alternative was marriage: "que voulez-vous? . . . , se marier . . . comme ma mère . . . Un homme qui vous colle un gosse par an et vous flanque des raclées quand il est saoûl! Enfin, bref, j'ai fini par céder" (19).[41] But being a kept woman, for Pelletier, was obviously not much better than marriage. Rather than being beaten by a husband, Léonie is beaten by her lover: "C'est un homme brutal . . ." and very quickly, like a husband, her lover "lui a collé un gosse": "Au bout d'un mois, vous savez, rien . . ." (19).[42] The difference is that predictably her lover left her when he found out she was pregnant. Obviously for Pelletier, the best solution for a woman is to stay single, child-free, and independent like Marianne. Moreover, as a militant, a woman *must* take the necessary steps to remain child-free in order to devote herself to the ideological cause. When asked whether she has any children after she admits to having practiced free love for years, Marianne replies:

Des enfants! Que vous êtes godiche, ma pauvre petite! Je suis militante sérieuse, moi; or, une anarchiste n'a pas d'enfants, sachez cela. D'ailleurs, qu'en ferais-je de mes enfants? Je gagne tout juste pour moi et je tiens à honneur de ne rien demander aux hommes. (167)[43]

Pelletier herself opted for a life of militant virginity. In a letter to her friend Arria Ly, she wrote: "Comme vous, je ne me marierai pas et il est probable que je ne prendrai jamais d'amant parce que dans les conditions actuelles les relations sexuelles sont une source de diminution pour la femme qui est mariée et de mépris pour celle qui ne l'est pas."[44] She goes on to say, however, that virginity should not be a definitive solution: "elle n'est que la conséquence de la situation injuste qui est faite à la femme";[45] virginity is "une attitude de combat."[46] Ideally, women, like men, should have the right to sexual pleasure:

Au sujet de la virginité je l'ai pratiquée toute ma vie, mais je pense qu'elle n'est à préconiser que dans la société présente où il n'y a pas de choix qu'entre la virginité et l'esclavage. Dans une société à base d'égalité sexuelle, la femme pourra se livrer aux . . . plaisirs de l'amour.[47]

Pelletier's character Marianne represents this ideal of "free love": child-free, free from the ties of marriage—"une femme mariée n'est jamais une bonne militante"[48]—free to enjoy sexual pleasure without prejudice, and thus free to dedicate her time and energy to anarchist militancy. In the fourth act, entitled "Par le crime," Pelletier brings to the stage not the crime as the title might imply, but the motive for the crime. Here, she paints an extremely negative portrait of the university system. In the final tableau of the previous act, a philosopher had suggested that Pierre contact an eminent and influential mathematician with a reputation of being very enlightened and without bourgeois prejudices. Contrary to his reputation though, the professor is in fact a hypocritical, conservative bigot. When Pierre arrives to show Bigorneau his work and to ask for a job as calculator based on his merit, the illustrious master shows his real colors: merit counts for nothing; in order to get a good job, you must be well connected, rich, and, most of all, born into the right class.

> Vous êtes fils d'ouvriers; travaillez comme ont travaillé vos parents. C'est dans le travail que vous trouverez le bonheur, la stabilité de la vie. Mariez-vous et faites beaucoup d'enfants; la Patrie en a besoin . . . (26)[49]

Pierre's meeting with Bigorneau was all that was needed to push him over the edge: "Ah! La société, la sale société! Rien à faire, il faut la détruire" (27).[50] And before the opening of the following act, Pierre will have received the death sentence for murder.

Pierre's metamorphosis from frustrated working-class intellectual to anarchist terrorist again echoes Pelletier's writings in *La Guerre sociale*. In June 1909, a month before her article on "La Tactique de l'attentat," Pelletier had published an article in which she analyzed how a young man becomes an "Apache," a term used to describe young Parisian hoodlums or delinquents. Far from critical, she sympathizes with the plight of these young men, born into a working-class family but fed up with the monotony and poverty of the working-class life. Being an Apache is an exciting, relatively lucrative alternative: "La profession d'apache, au contraire, est pleine d'imprévus agréables. D'abord, il y a la préparation des coups; puis l'émotion au moment d'agir, la joie intense lorsqu'on réussit sans se faire prendre; enfin, après un 'coup chic,' on se donne un peu de bon temps" ("Être apache").[51] Pelletier believes that such young men could be useful to the revolution. While most honest workers are afraid of the risks of illegality, Apaches have already tasted danger: "Il ne serait pas mal . . . qu'il y ait dans notre armée révolutionnaire quelques apaches conscients. [. . .] Pour préparer la révolution, pour favoriser ces escarmouches qui feront l'éducation révolutionnaire des masses, nous avons besoin de gens à qui l'illégalité ne fait pas peur" ("Être apache").[52]

The final act of *Supérieur!*, entitled "Vers la Vie" (Toward Life), takes place near the prison where Pierre has been incarcerated. This act contains very little ideological material and serves primarily to resolve the plot. Pierre does not die a martyr like his accomplice Duval but escapes from prison thanks to his adopted father Jacques and leaves for Russia, where Jacques believes he will serve the Idea: "Je l'envoie en Russie, où son grand esprit contribuera à édifier le monde nouveau" (28).[53] The conclusion to Pelletier's play is thus optimistic, if not idealistic. As Felicia Gordon points out in the *Integral Feminist*, Pelletier may have turned to fiction writing in the decades following her trip to Russia in order to compensate for her disappointment in the real world of socialist and feminist militancy (Gordon 193). Like in her utopian and autobiographical novels, the conclusion to *Supérieur!* offers a glint of hope. After harshly criticizing a variety of existing forms of socialism throughout the play, Pelletier reveals in the conclusion a desire to believe in the possibility of the new world, the ideal socialist state which would appreciate and make the most of men and women of superior intelligence.

Like the plays of Nelly Roussel and Véra Starkoff, Pelletier's play must be considered in terms of social protest theater whose goal was to educate the workers and to inspire them to transform society, whether it be on an individual level or an international scale, through reform or revolution. In order to understand the success of this type of theater, we must therefore ask ourselves if the plays made the workers more aware of the issues or incited them into action. Had Pelletier's play been performed, would the audience have come to her for birth control advice? Would members of the audience have been as inspired as after a performance of Ibsen's *An Enemy of the People*, exclaiming: "What dynamism and what dynamite! What bombs did we not intend to explode . . . "? (Weir 205). Certainly not in any significant numbers. But, as just one of many "armes de combat" (Lumet 120) in the struggle to enlighten the people, plays like *Supérieur!* undoubtedly served to reinforce revolutionary ideals and to rally the people in order to form new individuals like Pelletier's Pierre "[qui contribueraient] à édifier le monde nouveau." Unfortunately, Pelletier's play came too late. In 1923, the French government had become much less tolerant toward neo-Malthusian propaganda, the Universités Populaires had all but disappeared, culture was no longer high on the anarchist agenda, and propaganda by the deed had long been a thing of the past—in fact, the movement itself was no longer very active except in Spain. Had she written for the stage 20 years earlier, her art might have better served the revolution by, in the words of Kropotkin, "enflaming young hearts with the beautiful revolutionary breath" (Qtd. in Sonn, *Anarchism and Cultural Politics* 190).

CHAPTER SIX

Theater of Ideas: Marie Lenéru

Marie Lenéru (1874–1918) was the only author among those studied here who can be identified above all as a playwright rather than an activist. In fact, though her plays are all but forgotten today,[1] Marie Lenéru was one of the most admired women playwrights of the first decades of the twentieth century and she received the most consistently glowing reviews. Of her eight known plays, five were performed in mainstream theaters, and all but one were published. Unlike the other authors discussed, Marie Lenéru did not originally intend to write political plays to be used for propaganda. Her preferred genre was the play of ideas, a form of socially conscious drama that developed in the final years of the nineteenth century. Her mentor was François de Curel (1854–1928), a major playwright in the first decades of the twentieth century elected to the Académie française in 1918. The play of ideas is similar to the better-known genre of the social thesis play by dramatists like Eugène Brieux and Paul Hervieu. Thesis plays had become quite mainstream by the turn of the century and both of these authors were elected to the prestigious Académie française: Hervieu in 1900 and Brieux in 1909. In a thesis play, the author exposes a problem and gives the solution. These well-made plays are often pessimistic and generally didactic in the sense that the author imposes his or her views on the audience. A play of ideas is generally more intellectual or philosophical than a thesis play. It exposes a problem or an issue, but rather than give a solution, the author shows all sides of the debate, allowing the members of the audience to form their own conclusions.

Frank Chandler, in his 1920 study of contemporary French drama, distinguishes between the drama of moralists and reformers:

> The dramatic moralist is one interested to present impartially upon the stage the reactions of men and women concerning certain problems of conduct. The dramatic reformer is one who takes the still further step of urging upon the stage specific modifications in our ethical, social, or political life. The moralist simply enunciated or proves a thesis. The reformer strives to move men's hearts to adopt and carry into practice such a thesis. [. . .] The reformers tend to become too concrete for good art, the moralists too abstract. But both must be regarded as significant in any attempt to interpret the main tendencies of the contemporary drama. (190)

While all the other playwrights we have studied in this book were reformers according to Chandler's definition, Lenéru was primarily a moralist.[2]

Serious, taciturn, reclusive, provincial—Marie Lenéru was neither a political activist nor the sort of woman who usually frequented the theater milieu. More surprising was the fact that she was a playwright who was deaf and nearly blind. Furthermore, when she began writing, she had no connections at all with the theater world. She did have talent and superior intelligence, a room of her own, sufficient time to work,[3] self-discipline, and ambition. Lenéru believed strongly in her talent and was willing to fight to promote and defend it. As early as 1898, she wrote in her journal: "Je ne me vois que deux avenirs: une stalle dans le chœur d'une abbaye bénédictine, ou bien un des ces grands talents qui donnent toutes les pairies" (156).[4]

Lenéru was also very daring. In 1907, she sent the manuscript of her first play, *Les Affranchis*, to Catulle Mendès, an important novelist, playwright, and critic of the time. In the letter she sent with her manuscript, she presented herself candidly and apologetically as a young, bourgeois woman and challenged him not to let a negative prejudice prevent him from reading her play:

> Je suis donc une femme, et même une jeune fille, et même une jeune fille "du monde" et enfin j'ai écrit une pièce! Dans ces condi-tions déplorables, Monsieur, consentirez-vous à la lire? Je sais que des jeunes gens vous envoient leurs manuscrits; je vous prie, ne vous

laissez pas arrêter par un préjugé de mésestime que je redoute d'autant qu'à votre place, je n'en démordrais pas. (Qtd. in Lavaud 91)[5]

Mendès accepted the challenge and was immediately struck by the quality of Lenéru's writing. He replied, "Mademoiselle, votre œuvre est extrêmement remarquable et, par endroits, infiniment belle, haute, poignante. J'en suis plein d'admiration et de joie" (Lavaud 91).[6] Lenéru thus became Mendès's protégée and was introduced into the milieu of the Parisian literary elite.

Having an influential protector was even more important to Lenéru than for most authors in that, because of both her sex and her handicap, it was nearly impossible for her to negotiate directly with theater administrators and to follow the rehearsals of her plays as closely as was necessary. Successfully navigating the theater milieu was one of the greatest challenges to women playwrights who wished to have their plays staged in professional theaters during the first decades of the century. As Pierre Mille pointed out in an article about the difficulties facing women play-wrights in 1924: "Il ne suffit pas d'écrire une pièce, il faut encore la faire accepter, puis la faire représenter."[7] Many women wrote plays, but few had the courage to submit their plays to professional theaters given the deprecatory attitude of most directors and actors toward women writers. In the same year, *Le Cri de Paris* conducted a survey asking "Pourquoi, quand il y a tant de romancières, voit-on si peu de femmes auteurs dramatiques?"[8] Gabrielle Bruno, one of two women respondents, wrote:

> Vous demandez, mon cher confrère, pourquoi si peu de femmes sont auteurs dramatiques? Que me demandez-vous plutôt pourquoi il y a si peu de femmes *dont on joue les pièces*. Nombreuses, en effet sont les femmes qui ont en tiroir des manuscrits de pièces refusées—ou non offertes parce qu'assurées de n'être pas lues—et plus nombreuses seraient-elles si l'espoir de leur faire un sort soutenait les auteurs ou autrices. ("Notre enquête," September 14, 1924)[9]

Régis-Leroi, journalist for *Minerva*, came to a similar conclusion in 1932. Women playwrights were less numerous than women novelists not because writing for the theater demanded more objectivity as some claimed, but because of the difficulties involved with getting plays staged: "Peut-être faut-il voir dans l'abstention féminine un simple recul devant les difficultés de se faire jouer" ("Souvenirs des heures laborieuses").[10] According to Régis-Leroi, women's plays were not being refused by theaters so much as women were refusing to submit their works to the theaters.[11]

Furthermore, having a play produced depended on much more than the talent of the author and the quality of the play. A theater production was very costly. Few women had the financial backing to produce their own plays, and few theaters were willing or able to take the risk of producing a play that was not sure to be a financial success. Women who succeeded as professional playwrights often had some form of guarantee to offer the theater; either they were already well-known as writers in another genre or they had influential connections. Unfortunately, having a play accepted by a theater was not the final difficulty. The obligation to attend rehearsals was an equally formidable obstacle. As Judith Barlow points out in her introduction to a collection of early twentieth-century plays by American women, "All women writers face . . . 'negative expectations', but the playwright—who must deal with producers, directors, and actors, and whose efforts can be destroyed in one night by hostile critics—is particularly vulnerable" (Barlow xxxii). Even confirmed playwrights complained about their obligation to attend rehearsals: "Il n'y a pas d'amour-propre qui résiste à cette épreuve,"[12] wrote Madame Ancelot, author of 25 plays performed on the Parisian stage in the nineteenth century, four at the Comédie-Française. George Sand, who had eight plays performed at the Comédie-Française with over 400 performances, bemoaned her duty to sit through rehearsals at the national theater: "c'est à faire abandonner la partie cent fois pour une."[13] Sand fortunately became famous enough to be able to refuse this ordeal: "Je suis trop vieille pour supporter cette fatigue" (Chevalley 44).[14]

Pierre Mille recognized that the theater milieu might be in part responsible for the lack of successful women playwrights. He pointed out that the theater world could be very hostile for women writers. Actors and actresses were unwilling to take orders from a woman, and directors like Antoine, who staged Lenéru's first play, could be brutally authoritative:

Il n'en est pas moins vrai que "la manière" pour mettre une pièce en scène ressemble quelquefois à la manière de caporaux et de sergents pour instruire les recrues. Une femme se trouve alors, pour imposer ses vues, si elle a composé une pièce et veut la faire jouer, désorientée, intimidée. De surplus, les artistes lui obéissent plus difficilement qu'à un homme par défaut d'habitude peut-être. On obéissait à Sarah: Mais c'était Sarah. D'autres y ont plus de peine, mêmes directrices et le disent . . . . C'est ainsi qu'une femme, auteur dramatique, se heurte à des obstacles matériels, pour la mise en place de son œuvre, que ne connaissent pas ses concurrents masculins.[15]

In the 1924 survey mentioned above, the two women respondents also blamed the milieu. Actress Suzanne Devoyod witnessed:

> Jamais une femme ne se hasarderait—si elle n'a pas été habituée dès l'enfance au milieu théâtral. Elle en sortirait aussitôt, horrifiée. Le roman peut s'écrire chez soi . . . Mais voyez-vous une bourgeoise paisible, une jeune fille du monde venant dans les coulisses? Vous imaginez-vous Mme de Noailles dont les poésies sont splendides donnant des ordres aux machinistes ou discutant avec le souffleur? Voyons . . . ("Notre enquête," September 7, 1924)[16]

According to Gabrielle Bruno, a woman playwright was considered out of place in the theater milieu.

> Dans le monde des théâtres, c'est très ennuyeux d'avoir affaire à une femme. Les pourparlers qui se font au café entre un bock et une pipe, les collaborations, où on se dispute jusqu'à l'engueulade, les répétitions où l'on se tutoie, ça n'est pas, croit-on, la place d'une honnête femme. Si bon garçon soit-elle, sa présence vous gêne et vous déroute. ("Notre enquête," September 14, 1924)[17]

The woman playwright, as opposed to the actress it would seem, was *une honnête femme* who should not be subjected to the crass, impolite, and informal intimacy of the theater. Not only would she expose herself to an unpleasant environment, but her presence would also make the men uncomfortable. In 1924, the theater had evidently not yet lost its reputation as immoral and promiscuous, a reputation that had kept so many "honest" women from pursuing a career as actress or playwright in earlier periods.

Even without her handicap, Marie Lenéru, as a "jeune fille du monde," would have had difficulty overcoming all these obstacles. Fortunately, she had the support throughout her career of well-known authors and theater professionals who believed in her talent as a playwright and who promoted her work in various ways. While Catulle Mendès was negotiating having *Les Affranchis* performed, his wife, Jane Catulle Mendès, also a writer, submitted the play to the jury of the literary prize *La Vie Heureuse*. This prize, the future *Prix Fémina*, had a jury comprised solely of women writers. Many of these, including Séverine, Judith Gautier, Marcelle Tinayre, Jeanne Marni, Gabrielle Réval, Lucie Delarue-Mardrus, and Jane Catulle Mendès, also wrote plays during some time in their career. The jury decided to award the prize to Marie Lenéru, and, as a result, *Les Affranchis* was published by Hachette before it had been produced.

When Catulle Mendès died in 1909, before Lenéru's first play had been performed, Rachilde assumed his role as her promoter. Rachilde (1860–1953) was herself an excellent example of a well-known woman author whose important work in the theater had been neglected by literary history until recently.[18] When Paul Fort founded the Théâtre d'Art in 1890 in an effort to bring symbolism to the stage, Rachilde's play, *La Voix du sang* was the highlight of the opening night. She became one of the main supporters of the nascent symbolist drama as playwright, critic and member of the play selection committee of the Théâtre d'Art.[19] A good friend of Alfred Jarry, she played a key role in convincing Lugné-Poe, founder of another symbolist theater, le Théâtre de l'Œuvre, to put on *Ubu Roi*, a play that had an unprecedented impact on avant-garde theater in France (Deak 229; Lively "Introduction" 4).

Rachilde's experience and reputation as a promoter of young, talented playwrights became very valuable to Lenéru. It was she who showed *Les Affranchis* to André Antoine, founder of the avant-garde Théâtre-Libre. Though the symbolists had often criticized Antoine's naturalist stagings at the Théâtre-Libre, they also recognized his enormous contribution to revolutionizing the theater at the turn of the century.[20] Always interested in discovering and promoting young, innovative playwrights, Antoine organized a series of matinees dedicated to the new plays by unknown authors. He chose Lenéru's play to inaugurate the series on December 10, 1910, at the Théâtre de l'Odéon that he then directed. The performance received glowing reviews.

Les Affranchis brings to the stage the issue of divorce, an important debate in both legal discourse and literature in the early twentieth century. After divorce was finally legalized again in 1884, thanks to the unrelenting efforts of the radical Naquet, the number of divorces skyrocketed: from 1,879 divorces in 1884, to 4,227 in 1885, 7,363 in 1900, and 15,450 in 1913. The number finally levelled off at about 20,000 in the 1920s.[21] At the turn of the century, when many playwrights and novelists used contemporary social debates as the focus of their literary works, divorce became a popular theme. In a legal treatise on divorce published in 1903, J. Dépinay recognized the importance of this issue in literature:

La question du divorce est de toute actualité; elle forme le sujet des chroniques, des principales revues de droit et de sociologie; elle sert de thème aux auteurs dramatiques, et elle constitue le fond de la plupart des œuvres littéraires de notre époque. (5)[22]

In 1908, René Doumic dedicated an entire chapter of his *Théâtre Nouveau* to "le théâtre contre le divorce" (the theater against divorce). He observed a *volte-face* in the treatment of divorce at the beginning of the twentieth century:

> Pendant vingt ans, ils nous attendrirent sur le sort des malheureux époux rivés à leur triste chaîne, soupirant vainement vers la délivrance . . . Devant l'empressement que mettaient tant de conjoints libérés à profiter de leur liberté reconquise, il devenait de plus en plus difficile de se plaindre du trop petit nombre de divorces. Les moralistes de la scène durent chercher un thème qui fût moins en flagrant désaccord avec la réalité. Peu à peu ils firent leur conversion. A mesure que le divorce entrait dans les mœurs, le théâtre se retournait contre lui. Il ne voulait plus en voir que les inconvénients, les injustices, les cruautés. (172–173)[23]

Lenéru's position on the debate in *Les Affranchis* is less clear. She brings to the stage a philosophy professor tempted to leave his marriage of convenience with an unintellectual wife for an intelligent young soul mate, Hélène, a young novice who had been living at Fontevrault, a Cistercian abbey, for six months. The Abbess felt that Hélène was not ready to take her vows—"Vous n'êtes pas une Cistercienne, vous êtes libre . . . La carrière que vous m'avez demandée, je ne puis vous l'offrir"[24] (7)—and brought her to stay with the Abbess' sister, Marthe Alquier, and her husband Philippe. While staying with the Alquiers, Hélène has spent most of her time studying in Philippe's library and reading books that he has recommended to her, such as Nietzsche's *Par delà le bien et le mal* and *Le Lys rouge* by Anatole France, readings more suitable for a nihilist philosopher than for a Cistercian novice.[25] Eventually, Marthe becomes jealous and confronts Philippe and Hélène. She does not suspect any sexual relations between them; it is their *intellectual* proximity for which she reproaches them: "Ah! j'aurais tout, tout pardonné. Que tu l'aimes, que tu aies succombé . . . Mais cela, cela, ce rapprochement, cette communauté . . . Je n'ai plus qu'à m'en aller, à m'en aller" (18).[26] In the final scenes of the play, the characters debate and discuss all sides of the situation. As in nearly all of Lenéru's plays, there is no clearly recognizable voice of reason, no thesis, and no resolution: all points of view are given equal weight. Though Hélène has lost her faith in God, she is still torn between her newly discovered freedom and a deeply ingrained, though undefined, sense of moral and social order. She is advised on the one side by the Abbess, the voice of the Church, and on the other by Philippe, the philosopher, who has spent his life trying to "démontrer l'insuffisance de l'ancienne morale, la nullité de son système de persuasion" (19).[27] He is described by his secretary as "un homme qui n'a pas l'ombre de sens moral" (12).[28] Finally, though the action is given a conclusion—Hélène decides to leave—the ending of the play brings that conclusion into question: "Sommes-nous des lâches ou des héros?"[29] This impartiality was applauded by most critics, but the audience in general seemed to feel cheated: "Le public réclame . . . des thèses" (Mondadon 207).[30]

I would argue though, that the real thesis of *Les Affranchis* has as much to do with the role of the intellectual woman in French society as with divorce. This theme is introduced early in the play, when the Abbess is introduced to Philippe and Marthe's 13-year-old daughter, Marie:

L'ABBESSE: Qu'apprenez-vous?
MARIE: Tout . . . et le catéchisme.
L'ABBESSE: Ah! Et qu'aimez-vous mieux, tout, ou le catéchisme?
MARIE, *qui s'intéresse*: Le Théodicée.
MARTHE, *intervenant*: Mais elle n'en fait pas! elle ne sait pas ce qu'elle dit, ni ce que c'est!
MARIE: Je n'en fais pas à ma leçon, mais j'en lis.
MARTHE, *coupant court*: Elle bafouille, et tu l'intimides!
L'ABBESSE *un sourire brillant à Marie qui la dévore des yeux*: Mais non, tu vois bien qu'elle me disait un secret. (*Suivant du regard la petite qui s'éloigne sur un signe de sa mère*). A son âge aussi, je lisais les *Élévations sur les Mystères*.
MARTHE, *vivement*: Ah! Mais j'espère bien qu'elle n'entrera pas au couvent.
L'ABBESSE: Elle sera une femme érudite et spirituelle comme Marie de Rabutin.
MARTHE: Elle sera une femme comme toutes les autres. On ne lui en demande pas davantage!
PHILIPPE: Mais pardon! Je ne verrais pas d'obstacles à ce qu'elle fût distinguée.
MARTHE: Est-ce qu'elle a besoin de ça pour être heureuse? Est-ce que je suis une femme distinguée? Est-ce que tu ne m'aimes pas comme je suis? (6)[31]

For Marthe, an intellectual woman only has one option: the convent. A woman of superior intelligence can be neither normal—"comme toutes les autres"—nor happy in the secular world. Philippe disagrees. By simply ignoring Marthe's final question, he confesses his dissatisfaction with his marriage, thus foreshadowing the ensuing events. The social bond that his marriage of convenience represents is no longer enough for him—"un homme ne vit pas de cela" (14)[32]—especially now that he has met a woman with whom he could share more than just habit and history. Philippe has found in Hélène a veritable partner and is ready to leave everything to be with her. Hélène, on the other hand, does not particularly want Philippe to leave his wife; she does, however, claim the right to have an intellectual relationship with him: "Que ceux qui sont aussi intelligents, aussi actifs, aussi sérieux que nous vivent comme nous le faisons. Que vous soyez un homme, une femme, un célibataire, un mari, cela ne me regarde pas" (15).[33] While Lenéru demonstrates in *Les Affranchis* that society was not yet ready for such intellectual partnerships between men and women in 1910, she does seem to defend the idea that marriage should ideally be a partnership between intellectual equals, and that men and women should be able to work together on intellectual endeavors without society condemning their relationship.

Lenéru may have been speaking from experience. Several years later, she complained in her *Journal* about the rumors that began each time she worked closely with a man: "Dès qu'on a su que je voyais Curel, on a fait courir le bruit d'un mariage. Pour Blum, cela venait d'ennemis il est vrai, on a dit des choses plus graves" (342).[34] Her defense was to assert that she was not a woman. Since it was impossible to be a woman colleague without being a wife or lover, Lenéru claimed the right to be genderless. Hélène, on the other hand, claimed the right to perceive her colleagues as genderless. Lenéru's demand is more radical given that the masculine is traditionally perceived as generic or universal.

Antoine's staging of Lenéru's *Les Affranchis* in 1910 at the Théâtre de l'Odéon was a critical success, particularly within the circle of Parisian intellectuals. Léon Blum, theater critic and future leader of the French socialist movement, who had enthusiastically acclaimed the play after reading it, was even more fervent after the first performance:

> Je n'ai jamais cessé de penser à ce pauvre Mendès qui, le premier, avec Mme Rachilde, avait lu cette pièce, avait cru à cette pièce. Avait-il assez raison de crier au chef-d'œuvre ! Voilà de longues années qu'au théâtre, nous n'avions rien entendu de semblable. En l'affirmant, je ne me laisse pas égarer par une prévention, une prédilection personnelle. Ce fut l'impression unanime du public, de tout le public, quelle que fût la qualité de l'attention que l'œuvre

exigeât. Le rideau s'est baissé sur une des ovations les plus enthou-siastes que j'aie entendues. Après la représentation achevée, le même sentiment d'admiration était exprimé par les écrivains les plus distants dans leurs genres ou dans leurs goûts. (Blum 1910)[35]

Blum continued to champion Lenéru's work throughout her career. When her play *La Triomphatrice* was being considered as part of the reper-tory at the Comédie-Française, it was Blum who read the play to the company. He also regularly attended the rehearsals of *Les Affranchis* when it was performed at the Comédie-Française in 1927. Marie Lenéru's handicap may in fact have turned out to be an advantage for her in that she was obliged to find someone else to replace her in the "unfeminine" tasks associated with writing plays; she could thus concentrate on writing.

Divorce is again one of the central themes in Marie Lenéru's second play, *La Maison sur le roc*.[36] Here, a famous novelist watches his family fall apart as he struggles to uphold the conservative Catholic morals he thinks are beneficial to the society, but in which he does not personally believe. Dangennes forbids one of his daughters, Julie, to divorce her husband although they are already living separately and she loves another man: "Le divorce," he claims, "est déplorable, même à ceux qui en bénéficient . . . Je ne peux pas admettre entre vous ce mariage inférieur et bâtard, cette forme sournoise de l'union libre" (41–42).[37] His feigned conversion to Catholicism has influenced his other daughter, Alexandra, so much that she has decided not to marry the man she loves, but rather to enter a convent. Her fiancé, Marcel, tries desperately to make Dangennes admit to his daughter that he believes in the moral order of the Church, but not in God:

MARCEL: Dîtes-lui que tous les respects, vous les avez, que toutes les tendances, toutes vos inclinations vont à la règle, à la discipline chrétienne, mais qu'il n'est pas question de croire . . . (123)

Si vous avez le courage de dire à votre fille: 'Crois donc, si tu veux, mais au péril de ta tête, et surtout crois seule car, ne t'y trompe pas, moi je ne crois pas en Dieu. Je possède dans mon esprit exercé l'invincible témoignage du néant de ces promesses . . . Je le sais, je parle et je convertis; je prêche et j'im-pose des jougs; j'appelle des soumissions et des sacrifices; car, pour exploiter la terre, pour la dompter vers l'ordre et la stabilité, je n'ai rien aperçu de plus fort, de plus efficace, que cette disci-pline et cette tradition . . . (134–135)[38]

Dangennes admits to Marcel that he does not really believe in God and that his conversion is only for appearances, but he refuses to acknowledge it to his daughter. It is not a good time to secularize the family, claims Dangennes; his wife is dying and she needs the succor of her faith. Lenéru would appear to criticize Dangennes for his hypocrisy, especially given the quote which precedes the text, "On ne badine pas avec la foi,"[39] a reference to Musset's play *On ne badine pas avec l'amour.* Yet, it is also possible to see Dangennes as the hero of the play, altruistically defending what he considers to be good for society in spite of the negative consequences for himself and his family. Again, like *Les Affranchis, La Maison sur le roc* finishes with an unanswered question: "Me blâmez-vous mon enfant? Je ne sais plus. Je ne sais plus rien."[40]

As in *Les Affranchis,* Lenéru may have had a more hidden agenda in *La Maison sur le roc:* the issue of domination and authority. All three women in this play are acting under the influence of Dangennes' stated beliefs. Julie does not need her father's permission to divorce her husband, yet she respects his opinion more than anything: "Si mon divorce est un tel crime contre la société, contre mes enfants, s'il doit peiner si mortellement un homme comme mon père, j'aime mieux y renoncer . . ."(56).[41] Alexandra's decision is also based on her father's faith:

> MARCEL: C'est bien, n'est-ce pas? l'attitude de votre père, son retour au catholicisme, qui ont amené chez vous toute cette crise de conscience?
> ALEXANDRA: Comment rester indifférente à ce qu'un homme comme mon père respecte le plus au monde? (112)[42]

Finally, while Dangennes intimates that his wife's illness is the reason for imposing a strict moral order on his family, we learn that she is, in fact, killing herself with self-inflicted deprivation and austerity caused by religious fanaticism, most likely also inspired by her husband's conversion. Both the young men in the play—Julie's lover and Alexandra's fiancé—are able to see through Dangennes' façade, but the women are all victims of the moral authority he exerts over them as husband and father. Lenéru shows how paternal authority and male domination, rather than being a solid foundation for the family, the *roc* of the title, can in fact cause the family to fall apart.

In *La Triomphatrice,* Lenéru brings to the fore the role of the intelligent woman. *La Triomphatrice* was accepted by the Comédie-Française in 1914 thanks to the efforts of Léon Blum, but was not performed until 1918 because of the war. Here, Lenéru stages the difficulties a successful woman author, Claude, encounters in her personal life. Her estranged husband resents her success, mostly because she makes much more money than he does. He would have been happy to have married a rich woman if the money had been inherited: "Ce ne serait pas la même chose! C'est l'argent de son père qu'elle m'aurait apporté, ou de son grand-père . . . c'est l'argent d'un homme" (35).[43] For Henri, a woman's money is degrading; he would prefer to be poor than to live off the money his wife has earned. He also resents her intelligence and her strength. The more intelligent, active, and well-balanced Claude becomes, the less Henri finds her attractive. These qualities, along with her money and her androgynous name, make her seem less feminine. Yet, even though he no longer loves her or desires her, Henri refuses to grant Claude a divorce, simply because it is she who wants it: "on ne répudie pas encore son mari" (40).[44] While this was not statistically true—in reality many more divorces were instigated by women than by men (Adler 201)—it was evidence of a perceived double standard. Granting Claude a divorce would be just as humiliating for Henri as living off her money. With the use of the negative "pas encore" (not yet), Lenéru introduced the possibility of a future in which such double standards might not exist.

The situation is not much easier with Claude's lover, another successful writer. As long as they were equals, Sorrèze tolerated her success. Becoming Claude's lover was Sorrèze's way of dealing with her as an intellectual rival, of trying to exert his power over her:

> SORRÈZE: Je vous avoue, Claude, le rival m'a d'abord ému. J'ai tout de suite compris que je n'aurais de repos qu'en vous aimant: Celui-là me vaut, et c'est une femme. Elle est tout ce que je suis et on le verra bien. Elle m'équivaut, donc elle m'annule . . . Que faire? Elle est une femme, une femme qu'un homme aimera . . . Elle brise la gloire entre mes mains, elle m'est dangereuse, et un homme l'aimera, la tiendra dans le proche et tendre mépris de l'amour. Elle me doit son humilité, elle s'agenouillera devant moi, parce qu'elle est femme, et que, si grande qu'elle soit, moi seul peux lui donner toute sa destinée. [. . .] Dans un amour normal, l'homme doit primer la femme. (50–51)[45]

Sorrèze does not see love in terms of respect and mutual admiration or as a partnership of equals, but rather as a means of dominating, and of inflicting scorn and humiliation. He believes that the man in a relationship should be superior and the woman deferential. Sorrèze's strategy fails however when, in the final act of *La Triomphatrice*, Claude becomes more successful than him; she wins the Nobel prize and is invited to do a well-remunerated series of lectures in the United States. At that moment, Sorrèze breaks off their relationship. A superior woman, for Sorrèze, is no longer a woman:

> SORRÈZE: Claude n'est pas seulement un grand écrivain, elle est tout près d'être un grand homme.
> CLAUDE (*étonnée*): Comment cela?
> SORRÈZE: Je veux dire que la femme en vous, la femme avec ses faiblesses et ses étroitesses, n'existe pas. (*Mouvement de Claude.*) Ferme et droite, intelligente et forte, vous êtes un homme, Claude, un homme fait pour l'estime et l'admiration. (101)[46]

Again, in the eyes of the men in her life, Claude's strength and talent negate her femininity.

Finally, Claude's success compromises her daughter's happiness. Ironically, Claude is a dedicated mother; she loves Denise and would gladly sacrifice her glory for her daughter's happiness. Nevertheless, she outshines her daughter to such an extent that it negates Denise's very existence as a woman:

> DENISE: Mais il n'y a d'air que pour une femme dans cette maison. Est-ce que j'existe ici? Qui me regarde, qui m'aime? J'arrive dans le monde, qui me doit mon bonheur, j'ai tous les droits de ma jeunesse, et voilà que je viens trop tard, la place est prise . . . une femme m'a ruinée d'avance, sous sa dangereuse tutelle j'ai tout perdu . . . Ma mère est ma rivale . . . . (69)[47]

Though Sorrèze and Henri deny Claude's femininity when she becomes successful, this very success gives her a power of seduction over other younger men. One young writer, Jacques Fréville, whom Denise loved, killed himself for Claude. Another young writer, Flahaut, who has been coming to the house every day, confesses in Act 2 that he loves the mother not the daughter as Claude had thought. Suffocated and annihilated in her mother's house, Denise chooses to leave home and to live with her grandmother. Like Denise, Henri blames Claude for their daughter's unhappiness. He claims that there comes a time when it is the mother's duty to be less of a woman:

> BERSIER: Il arrive un moment, ma chère amie, où le devoir est de charmer un peu moins et de s'effacer un peu plus.

CLAUDE: Je ne comprends pas bien la leçon que vous me donnez là.
BERSIER: Je veux dire que la meilleure mère est celle qu'on ne
remarque pas . . . Voilà ce qui manque à votre fille . . .
cette enfant a compris mieux que vous, avec votre esprit, la loi qui
régit les générations, la mère est une femme abdiquée. $(75)^{48}$

Ironically, the successful professional woman is not being accused here of
neglecting her family, as has often been the case, but rather of being too
seductive. As her daughter becomes nubile, it is a mother's duty to repress
her sexuality. In this play, Lenéru explores a theme that became prevalent
in women's theater in the post-1968 period: the mother–daughter
relationship. Like many daughters in late-twentieth-century plays by
women, Denise feels suffocated and seeks to escape the mother–daughter
bind. Claude, like many contemporary mothers, is struggling to be a
good mother without relinquishing her sexuality.

Today's readers would certainly interpret the message of this play as
feminist. Lenéru must have believed that a woman should be able to be a
mother and a sexual being without sacrificing her daughter's happiness.
She must have wished to denounce the attitude of Henri and Sorrèze
who claim that the man must be more successful than his wife or lover.
A woman's success should not negate her femininity. In fact, an intelligent,
active, and well-balanced woman should be more attractive rather than
less. However, in 1918, most of the audience understood the opposite:
that in a successful, happy relationship, the woman must be dominated by
a superior man. For them, the obstacle for Lenéru's protagonist, Claude,
is not male chauvinism or society's attitude toward women, it is her own
ambition. She is her own antagonist. In his 1920 analysis of
La Triomphatrice, for example, Frank Chandler clearly blames Claude herself for her misfortunes: "In her struggle to maintain her position as a
bluestocking, she snubs her husband, alienates the affections of her
daughter, and obscures the renown of her lover, thus forfeiting his
esteem" (217).

Lenéru's opinion about her character was more nuanced. She
remarked in her *Journal* that no one understood her play:

Passé deux heures hier entre Curel et Mme Duclaux; ni l'un ni
l'autre n'aime *La Triomphatrice* et, si je l'ose dire, n'y comprennent
rien. Mme D . . . l'appelle "cette tigresse." A quoi je remarque:
"mais, madame, c'est elle qui est dévorée." (344)
    Ma pauvre *Triomphatrice* est jugée par mes plus bienveillants amis:
"une hypertrophie du moi." Alors que le reproche qu'on devrait

m'adresser est de l'avoir faite trop grande et trop magnanime, cette femme qui méprise si passionnément la gloire et qui, dans toutes les répliques de toute la pièce, ne veut que sa fille et son amant. (361–362)[49]

For Lenéru, Claude is a victim of her own talent. Her success is not due to an excess of ambition. She has not tried to surpass Sorrèze; she never intended there to be any rivalry between them. Her relationships are more important to her than her career. In her preface to the play, Lenéru explained her intentions when writing *La Triomphatrice:*

> La vraie donnée de *La Triomphatrice,* celle qui en faisait pour moi l'intérêt, donnée que je retrouve dans l'esprit de chaque scène et sous chaque réplique est simplement et uniformément celle-ci: La femme a besoin d'aimer au-dessus d'elle, d'aimer en adorant; en s'élevant, elle donne à l'homme la tâche amoureuse de la dominer de plus haut . . . Je reste persuadée que la femme qui vaut mentalement, mais bien plus sûrement encore si elle vaut professionnellement, souffrira, sera gênée, déçue dans son amour jusqu'au détachement peut-être, si elle ne se sent dominée, à tout le moins égalée par l'homme aimé. (8)[50]

Here, Lenéru put the emphasis on the woman's need to be dominated by the man she loves. Yet, in her play, it is the men in Claude's life who reject her because of her success. There is no indication that she desires to be dominated. She simply desires to be loved. Claude suffers from her intellectual superiority and professional success, not because she does not feel dominated, but because Henri and Sorrèze cannot accept her talent and her success.

In his introduction to *La Triomphatrice* in 1922, Léon Blum similarly insisted on the necessity of the woman's subordination in a love relationship. He claimed that Lenéru's play was not feminist since it did not criticize this premise or defend the superior woman. Lenéru did, however, offer a glimmer of hope to feminist readers in the conclusion to her preface. She claimed that *La Triomphatrice* was a transitional play. She wrote that, today, even the most successful woman wished to love a superior man, but in the future, when it would be easier and more common for women to succeed professionally, they would probably learn to love without being dominated. Lenéru did not, however, comment on whether men would eventually be able to love a successful woman, whether it would be possible in the future for a woman to succeed and still be perceived as feminine. Nor did she express an opinion on mother–daughter relationships discussed earlier.

Lenéru's goal in writing *La Triomphatrice* was to expose a problem, not to solve it or denounce it. Had Lenéru written a more feminist play, it would certainly have fallen into the category of a thesis play rather than a play of ideas. Lenéru was most disturbed by the reductive interpretations of her critics. In her opinion, a well-written play of ideas should allow for multiple interpretations: "Évidemment une œuvre organisée a bien des points de vue" (355).[51]

Elle me demande de lui expliquer ma pièce qu'elle ne comprend guère et devant mes interprétations: "Eh bien, il faut dire cela." Eh! non, il ne faut pas le dire! Il n'est pas nécessaire à ma pièce que vous tombiez exactement sur cette interprétation-là. Moi-même, en l'écrivant, je n'y pensais pas du tout. Et il importe extrêmement à ma pièce qu'elle ne contienne pas de définitions et d'explications d'elle-même . . . Une œuvre profonde n'est pas un problème à résoudre . . . (361)[52]

Here, Lenéru is defending the play of ideas against the thesis play. A play of ideas is more profound than a thesis play since the audience members themselves must analyze all the ideas presented and search for their own solutions.

In her final play, *La Paix*, written during World War I, Lenéru attempted to be faithful to her preferred genre, the play of ideas. She still presented all sides of the debate about pacifism, though we know from her *Journal* and her published articles from the period that she herself was passionately pacifist. In this case though, her thesis was evident. She primarily gave a voice to anti-pacifist arguments only to refute them. By showing that she was aware of the complexities of the debate, she was able to develop with precision the subtleties of her own opinion and thus protect herself from accusations of defeatism. Expressing pacifist ideas in public was dangerous during World War I when pacifism was nearly always equated with unpatriotic defeatism, the idea that France should simply lay down its arms and capitulate.[53] Lenéru was not antimilitaristic, nor did she lack a sense of patriotism. She grew up in a military family: her grandfather had been an Admiral and her father, a decorated naval lieutenant killed while on active duty. There is no evidence before the onset of the war in 1914 that she had any pacifist leanings. In fact, in 1913, she wrote in her *Journal* of her deep admiration for military men (353).

By December 1914, though, her position as a pacifist was already well defined. She described the war as *la boucherie* and criticized those intellectuals who accepted the war. She refused the argument that war is inevitable, that men are inherently belligerent: "La vérité est qu'il n'y a pas eu une guerre en Europe depuis 500 ans, que très peu de chose dans la cervelle d'un seul ou de quelques-uns aurait suffi à éviter" (*Journal* 365).[54] Moreover, she regretted the tendency to confuse pacifism with antimilitarism. Lenéru's position was that as long as the current war continued, it was her duty to support the soldiers, but as soon as it was over, it was imperative to insure a permanent peace. The soldiers were not to blame, but rather the governments who were not able to find another way of resolving their conflicts. She praised Wilson and Churchill for not equating pacifism with utopianism. Lenéru, who had until this point almost entirely limited her journal entries to a discussion of literature and philosophy, now turned her thoughts and her pen exclusively to the war: "Je ne veux plus écrire que contre la guerre, car on ne peut tout de même agir que dans l'opinion" (*Journal* 366).[55]

In her next entry in 1915, she had formed the plan to write a pacifist play dedicated to those who died for France:

Ô morts pour ma patrie, à qui je veux dédier mon plus grand effort, mon plus grand travail, une pièce dont je ne sais rien encore, si ce n'est qu'elle s'appellera *La Paix* et que je vais à elle, que je m'y prépare religieusement, comme à une vocation, car il faut qu'elle agisse, ce n'est pas en artiste que je veux exploiter la catastrophe,— je veux faire représenter sur la scène du premier théâtre français, la plus forte machine littéraire qui ait jamais fonctionné pour la paix. Puisque j'ai eu ce crève-cœur de ne pouvoir faire mon métier de femme auprès de vos agonies, je ferai qu'à l'avenir on ne vous massacre plus, "mon fils et mon soldat." (367–368)[56]

Unable to help in the war effort as a nurse due to her disabilities, Lenéru had a more ambitious goal: to write a play that would prevent future wars. This is a very strong statement about what Lenéru felt to be the power of the word to influence opinions and have an important effect on society. As she wrote in "Le Témoin," ("Witness") published in 1915: "Les actes d'aujourd'hui sont les paroles d'hier. Si nous faisons actuellement cette guerre atroce, c'est que, jusqu'ici, nous avons mal, insuffisamment parlé de la paix" (244–245).[57] For Lenéru, the written word, including theater, had a special role to play in this campaign:

> Je crois avec Wells que c'est par une formidable "campagne d'opin-
> ion, menée par tous les moyens dont elle dispose: presse, livre,
> théâtre," et non par les à-côtés des congrès et des comités, que l'on
> amènera des résultats. C'est toujours la même loi du succès et la
> même erreur commise par la littérature: Vous voulez arriver?
> *Ne fondez rien à côté*, ni petite revue, ni petit théâtre, emparez-vous
> de ce qui est, des vraies forteresses de l'opinion publique. (372)[58]

La Paix would therefore not only be a thesis play, but a propaganda play. Her play, like the articles she began to publish in 1917 mostly in *L'Intransigeant*, was a vehicle for promoting her pacifist ideals. Lenéru urgently wanted *La Paix* to be performed at la Comédie-Française, the greatest *forteresse* of all. She believed it was on that stage that her play would best influence public opinion. She proposed that the theater substitute *La Paix* for *La Triomphatrice*, which was scheduled to open in 1918, but the Comédie-Française refused, fearing it would be too controversial. Unfortunately, Lenéru did not live to see either the end of the war or her play performed. She died in the flu epidemic less than a month before the armistice, and *La Paix* was not performed until 1921 at Théâtre de l'Odéon.

Lenéru sets the action of *La Paix* in a chateau in Brittany after the war during a peace conference that is taking place in Paris. Each of her characters represents a different opinion about war and pacifism. As in most war plays by women, Lenéru focuses on the female experience,[59] here of post-war France. The protagonist and authorial voice, Lady Mabel Stanley, is a young aristocratic Englishwoman. She and her hostess Marguerite Gestel, met as nurses during the war. Mabel has since become a militant pacifist. Her great hope is that the Paris Conference will result in a league that would bring together men of all parties and of all nations to work toward a permanent peace. Lenéru herself had followed with great interest the writings of pacifist leaders like Wilson and Briand, and particularly appreciated the idea of creating a League of Nations (Lavaud 143–157).

Marguerite, on the other hand, is resigned to the inevitability of war. Rather than fight for world peace, she is trying to come to a private peace with her own losses—two of her sons died during the war, and her forearm was amputated due to an infection from a soldier's wound. She believes Lady Mabel's plans are utopic and predicts another war within

50 years. For Marguerite, nothing can be done about it. Mabel, like Lenéru, thinks this type of silence and resignation is intolerable, especially for women. It is the role of women to perpetuate the memory of the horrors of past wars in order to prevent future wars. In "Le Témoin" she wrote:

> Les femmes sont d'abord, en ce moment, des mères, des sœurs, des femmes de soldats. Elles sont aussi des infirmières et des tricoteuses et tout ce que ces temps d'extraordinaire misère exigent qu'elles soient. Mais elles sont encore autre chose: frappées dans les tranchées et sur le front, dans tous leurs espoirs et leurs raisons de vivre, les femmes ne rendent pas les coups et, si unies qu'elles soient à ceux-là qui combattent, si passionnément attachées à la lutte vitale que soutient leur pays, elles ne sont tout de même pas l'acteur, ni seulement la victime, mais le témoin du drame. (241)[60]

For Lenéru, it is women's role to bear witness to the atrocities of today's war in the future: "Car le jour viendra bien enfin, où le devoir ne sera plus d'accepter et de se taire, mais de juger et de se révolter" ("Le Témoin" 242).[61] In *La Paix*, this time has come. According to Mabel, Marguerite must not mourn in silence; it is her duty to speak up against war.

Lenéru similarly juxtaposes the attitudes of two younger women. Simone, the daughter of a patriotic, war-loving poet, takes her father's position to an exuberant extreme. For her, war is beautiful because it makes heroes of men. This attitude is reminiscent of Lenéru's own admiration for military men before the war and of the general enthusiasm when World War I broke out in 1914. As another character remembers "Ils étaient si contents de partir! . . . Je me rappelle, en allant à la gare . . . C'était si beau" (324).[62] Simone proclaims that she will marry only a soldier. When confronted with Mabel's pacifism, having no solid arguments, she simply repeats her refrain, her "phrase de perroquet" ("Le Témoin" 243): "la paix, c'est une utopie! . . . Il y a toujours eu des guerres et il y en aura toujours . . . Tant qu'il y aura des hommes, on ne pourra pas les empêcher de se jeter les uns sur les autres" (390).[63] After the carnages of the war, Simone's exuberance seems inappropriate, even to her father. Jean, her fiancée and Marguerite's only surviving son, a soldier himself who fought in the war and had planned to continue his career in the army, becomes exasperated, calling her behavior revolting and scandalous. It is her attitude, rather than Mabel's discourse, that convinces him to resign from the army and to dedicate himself to the pacifist cause.

Perrine, a young villager, has a very different reaction to the war. Three of her brothers died, and she has had to abandon her wish to enter a convent in order to care for her surviving brother who lost both his legs. Instead, she has taken the vow never to have children:

PERRINE: Des enfants? . . . Je n'en veux pas ! (*Devant l'étonnement de Marguerite*) Les enfants, je sais ce qu'on en fait, plus tard. Ah ! non ! assez d'une fois . . .
MARGUERITE: Ce n'est pas d'une bonne Française, ma fille.
PERRINE: Alors, je vous dirai tout. J'ai fait le sacrifice de mon bonheur en ce monde. Et pour que Dieu ne permette pas, tant que je serai en vie, qu'on tue encore une fois les enfants des autres . . . j'ai fait un vœu de n'en avoir jamais à moi. (*Devant le silence de Marguerite.*) Vous ne trouvez pas ça bien, Madame?
MARGUERITE: Ma pauvre enfant, s'il suffisait de se sacrifier . . . Quelle est celle de nous qui ne donnerait pas sa vie?
PERRINE: Alors, qu'est-ce qu'il faut faire?
MARGUERITE, *dure*: Rien. (324)[64]

Here, Lenéru stages a variation on the theme of maternal pacifism, one of the major arguments among feminist pacifists. While it is true that only men fight in war, women too are affected and have an important role to play, not only as nurses, but as mothers of soldiers. Maternal pacifists encouraged women to refuse to give birth to children, to nourish, and nurture them, only to have them serve as cannon fodder in the next war.[65] Like the women in Aristophanes's *Lysistrata*, they believed that if all the mothers in belligerent nations worked together, they could prevent war.[66] In Lenéru's play, Perrine's reasoning is somewhat different. She claims at first that she does not want to have children because she knows what will be done to them. Marguerite's reply is predictable; "une bonne Française" would do her duty and produce future soldiers for the nation. Perrine then explains her true reason which is more mystic than feminist. She believes that thanks to her sacrifice, God will not allow other children to die. While Marguerite's reaction is discouraging— her sacrifice is in vain; nothing can be done to prevent war—Lady Mabel is more positive when she learns of Perrine's decision: "c'est déjà bien assez d'avoir eu l'idée de faire quelque chose" (324).[67] For Mabel, any pacifist action is better than no action.

Though there are equal numbers of male and female characters in *La Paix*, the male characters appear less developed and less central to the thesis of the play. Their role is primarily to underscore Mabel's personality or arguments. For example, le Général Peltier is neither particularly war loving nor pacifist. His primary interest is in marrying Mabel who had been his nurse during the war. Though Mabel loves him, she refuses to marry him as she feels being a general's wife would be incompatible with her work as a militant pacifist. His presence in the play shows us just how dedicated Mabel is to her cause.

Delisle, the patriotic poet, is the antithesis of Mabel. He too is a militant propagandist, but for the opposite cause. Peltier calls him "le grand entraîneur, la plus forte voix de France . . ." (338);[68] Perrine sang his songs in school. He speaks of war with the poetic romanticism:

Il est certain que dans le matérialisme abject des sociétés modernes, la guerre seule transfigure les peuples, réveille les vertus endormies, fait vivre encore sur la terre des heures d'idéal et de beauté. (338)[69]

He predicts, without regret, that France will again be at war within ten years. Delisle's faith in war is not unlike Dangenne's faith in the Church in *La Maison sur le roc.* The individual suffering caused by war or the Church are of little consequence; what is important is that both institutions create a strict moral code and a certain ideal. In the case of war, that ideal involves brotherhood and heroism in men, devotion and sacrifice in women.

The final character, Graham Moore, only appears in three scenes. He is a fellow pacifist militant who comes to see Mabel to bring her news of the Peace Conference in Paris. He too loves Mabel; he expresses his admiration for her intelligence and stresses her importance to the pacifist movement. He is jealous of Peltier and tries to convince Mabel that, in spite of her pacifism, she is only attracted to the military hero in him: "c'est votre cœur de femme qu'il faut arracher à la guerre, qu'il faut livrer passionnément à la vie et à la paix" (341).[70] Moore returns in the final act to tell Mabel the bad news: the measures they had proposed at the conference were voted down. There will be no league of nations, no permanent peace. In the pessimistic and visionary conclusion of Lenéru's play, Moore predicts that it will take an atomic bomb to make the nations understand the necessity of peace.

The majority of reviews of *La Paix* were enthusiastically favorable. They underscored the beauty, the boldness of the ideas, and the rare quality of the style of the play. For Antoine, it had the grandeur of a tragedy. Marie Lenéru even received the supreme compliment of not writing liking a woman:"Quel puissant cerveau d'homme se cachait sous le front sévère de Marie Lenéru. Sa dernière pièce . . . ne fait à aucun moment penser à une œuvre féminine" (Dorgeles).[71] Like Claude in *La Triomphatrice*, Lenéru's intelligence and success negate her femininity. She is often characterized as virile when critics wish to stress the exceptional quality of her theater. A few reviews, however, criticized the play for being too wordy. While they often lauded the ideas and the emotions, they questioned whether there was enough action for the theater. These reviews were an indication of major changes that were taking place in the theater world.

Marie Lenéru's drama continued to attract attention for about a decade after her death thanks to the efforts of her friend Mary Duclaux, who succeeded in publishing her plays, and to several influential protectors, like Léon Blum, who had them performed. Nevertheless, in 1927, when *Les Affranchis* was performed at the Comédie-Française, it was not sufficient to have influential protectors; the theater of ideas had gone out of favor. The play, which had been lauded in 1910 for its "vérité d'observation, portée philosophique, [et] passion," was criticized in 1927 as a "confuse élucubration": "Rien de plus déclamatoire, plus faux, plus vide" ("Les Théâtres").[72] The difference between Antoine's mise en scène and that of the Comédie-Française explained in part the radical difference in reception. Indeed, critics who had liked the original production, tended to blame the failure of the revival on the staging and the acting. Other critics pointed out that the expectations of the public had changed. Antoine, for example, wrote: "Beaucoup plus qu'en 1910, le public actuel se porte vers le théâtre facile, n'exigeant aucun effort; . . . il a perdu le goût des grands sujets et des hauts débats à la scène."[73] Robert de Beauplan concurs:

> L'évolution du théâtre ne s'est pas faite, surtout depuis l'après-guerre, dans un sens favorable à des œuvres aussi pleines de pensée et, on doit le dire, aussi hautainement sévères que *Les Affranchis*. Les spectateurs demandent de moins en moins à méditer et de plus en plus à être agréablement divertis.[74]

During the interwar years, the fashion shifted from wordy, intellectual, social drama to a more spectacular genre that could attract audiences in the age of cinema.

However, though her plays were not performed again after this failure, Marie Lenéru was not so quickly forgotten. Ten years later, in 1937, in an article entitled "Des femmes dans le sillage de Molière et de Shakespeare," Monique Forestier discusses Lenéru more than any other single author, with the exception of Marcelle Maurette whose first play was performed in 1928, the year after the revival of *Les Affranchis*, and who recognized Marie Lenéru as her most important forerunner.[75] Thanks to the recent interest in the history of women's theater, two plays by Marie Lenéru have been resuscitated and republished in English: *La Triomphatrice* (*Woman Triumphant*) in 1996 in an anthology of plays by women from 1880 to 1930, and *La Paix* (*Peace*) in 1999 in an anthology of war plays by women.[76] Moreover, Mary-Helen Becker contributed a substantial entry on Marie Lenéru to Makward and Cottenet-Hage's *Dictionnaire littéraire des femmes de langue française*.[77] In an essay on French women playwrights of the twentieth century in *A History of Women's Writing in France*, Mary Noonan cites Marie Lenéru as the first major woman playwright of the century and writes that "Lenéru's confident use of the stage space to explore gender relations constituted a significant advance in the use of the theater to stage the woman writer's exploration of her sense of self" (221). I would suggest that the success of Lenéru's plays and their importance to theater history stem from the fact that they go beyond an exploration of gender relations and the writer's sense of self. Her plays have a broader and more profound philosophical and social import. What appealed to her contemporaries—Mendès, Rachilde, Antoine, and Blum—was this depth of thought and the insightful analysis of social issues and human psychology that Marie Lenéru brought to the stage in her plays of ideas.

CHAPTER SEVEN

Conclusion and Epilogue

During the late nineteenth and early twentieth centuries, the theater developed from an art form whose primary goal was to entertain and move the audience, to a forum with educational, philosophical, social, and political objectives. All factions of socialists and feminists believed in the power of the theater to influence the audience. As feminist Harlor wrote in 1901, "[Le théâtre] est, en quelque sorte, la suprême tribune de propagande, celle d'où s'oriente définitivement l'opinion vers de nouvelles conceptions sociales ou morales" (682).[1] Indeed, for all the authors discussed in this study, theater was a form of educational or political activism. Louise Michel's plays *Nadine* (1882), *Le Coq rouge* (1883), and *La Grève* (1890) were performed as part of anarchist political and artistic events with the goal of instilling in the audience the spirit of revolt. Nelly Roussel wrote short plays to be performed for the workers in the Université Populaire and at a variety of political meetings. In *Par la Révolte* (1903), she incited the women in her audience to demand reproductive freedom. In *Pourquoi elles vont à l'église* (1910), she presented a critique of the hypocrisy of the freethinkers movement that claimed to promote equal access to truth, knowledge, and freedom, while excluding women from their meetings and discussions. She blamed the religious affiliation of women on the men who prevented them from participating in more intellectually rewarding activities. Her short allegorical scene *La Faute d'Ève* (1913) staged a rewriting of the story of Genesis in which Eve consciously rebels against the safe, monotonous haven of the Garden of Eden, embracing instead a more exciting and fulfilling life. Through her drama, Roussel thus encouraged women to seek freedom, justice, and knowledge. Véra Starkoff's plays *L'Amour libre* (1902), *L'Issue* (1903), and *Le Petit Verre* (1904) were educational social comedies written for the theater of the Université Populaire. In her plays, Starkoff strove to enlighten her audience about issues such as free love, domestic violence, paternal authority, and alcoholism. Though Marie Lenéru identified herself primarily as a playwright rather than as a political activist, her plays brought to the commercial stage debates similar to those developed in the plays of militant playwrights. While she may not have aimed to incite her audience to revolt or to dramatically change their political opinions, she certainly wished to encourage them to think about the complexities of contemporary political and social issues. In *Les Affranchis* (1910), Lenéru explores the question of divorce, as well as the difficulties posed by the intellectual proximity between men and women. Divorce is a central theme in *La Maison sur le roc* (1911), a play in which Lenéru explores the role of religion in a rapidly changing society. *La Triomphatrice* (1914) examines the difficult role of the intellectual woman. Only in her final play, *La Paix* (1918), was Lenéru's goal more militant than aesthetic. Here, she abandons the theater of ideas for the thesis play, explicitly staging an apology for pacifism. Madeleine Pelletier's first play, *In anima vili, ou un crime scientifique* (1920), like Lenéru's *La Paix*, was a reaction against World War I. In this play of ideas, Pelletier couches a philosophical reflection on the sanctity of human life and the absurdity of war within a crime drama about the ethics of scientific experimentation. In *Supérieur!* (1923), she paints a portrait of the anarchist milieu, tracing the development of a young rebel. Her play raises awareness about the injustice and hypocrisy of the bourgeois society and about different means of resistance and revolt including education, reproductive freedom, and direct action.

Women playwright-activists had to overcome immense obstacles for their plays to function as political theater. Writing the play was only one step in the process. They then had to confront publishers, censors, theater directors, and actors before they could hope to reach the target audience in order to have the intended political impact. This process entailed braving a male-dominated theater milieu that often deterred women playwrights. Staging plays in professional theaters also involved large sums of money, which were not easily available to women writers in the late nineteenth and early twentieth centuries. Both Nelly Roussel and Véra Starkoff circumvented these difficulties by staging their own plays with a minimal cast and decor in the Universités Populaires and at political meetings, where elaborate, professional stagings were the exception. Louise Michel and Marie Lenéru were able to capitalize on their connections and reputation in order to have their political plays performed in professional theaters. Louise Michel's name alone was enough to draw a full house to her first play and her status as heroine of the Commune provided her a large network of useful connections in the theater world. She was probably less concerned with the financial success of her plays—she gave away all the proceeds to charity—than with the impact of her theater on the audience. Marie Lenéru was the only author presented here whose plays were performed in mainstream, commercial theaters. When she wrote her only overtly political play, *La Paix*, she had already established a reputation as a talented, successful playwright with influential protectors within the mainstream literary milieu, such as Catulle Mendès, Rachilde, and Léon Blum. Having had previous plays performed by André Antoine and at the Comédie-Française certainly helped in securing the Théâtre de l'Odéon for the staging of *La Paix* at a time when such intellectual drama was no longer in vogue. Madeleine Pelletier was arguably the least successful of these authors given that her plays may never have been performed. If they were, they certainly did not reach as many people as, for example, Louise Michel's *Nadine*, performed to a packed house of politically engaged spectators, or Nelly Roussel's *Par la Révolte*, staged innumerable times in a variety of settings throughout the country. Political theater is most powerful when performed. Indeed, the mise en scène of a play and the atmosphere in the theater itself may potentially determine the subversive nature of the play's impact on the audience.

Though the plays studied here cover a period of nearly half a century and vary from full-length grand spectacles to short symbolic scenes, as a group they form a distinctive political voice, not only criticizing the society in which they live from a left-wing feminist perspective, but also providing positive female role models and visions of a better world for both men and women. Compared to political plays written by men of the same period, the plays studied here generally have a more equal balance of male and female roles, not only in number but also in importance. Among the 25 plays written by men included in the recent anthology *Au temps de l'anarchie, un théâtre de combat 1880–1914*, four have no women characters and four have only one. On an average, the plays have nearly three times as many male roles as female roles. In contrast, with the exception of Louise Michel's *Nadine*, the plays by women included in this anthology all include women in lead roles and have nearly equal numbers of men and women characters on an average.

Not only are there more female characters in plays by women, but they are also more often strong, lead roles. In politically militant theater by men of this period, the female characters are rarely positive role models for the audience. Working-class women are most often portrayed as victims, either passively accepting their suffering or choosing suicide or prostitution as a solution to their misery. Bourgeois women are frivolous, docile, and devoid of any political consciousness. Even women who take on a lead role as militants, such as Madeleine in Octave Mirbeau's *Les Mauvais Bergers* or Pauline in *La Grève rouge* by Jean Conti and Jean Gallien, are represented as simply continuing the combat of the men in their lives.[2] Though women are rarely the voice of reason in the plays by women that I have studied,[3] they are often strong protagonists, such as Esther and Marpha in Michel's *La Grève*, Hélène in Lenéru's *Les Affranchis*, Blanche in Starkoff's *L'Amour libre*, Lucie in *L'Issue*, and Roussel's *Eve*. These characters, while generally paired with a male protagonist who serves as an intellectual, political, or moral soul mate or mentor, do not simply continue the man's combat. They do not wait for their man to die before taking up his cause as in plays by men. The female protagonists in political theater by women evolve throughout the plays, developing into women with strong beliefs of their own. They are willing to fight for their ideas and to work hard to create a better life for themselves and a better world for future generations.

I would argue that many of the plays studied here provide counterevidence to Millstone's conclusion in her dissertation, *Feminist Theater in France, 1870–1914*. Millstone laments the fact that feminist theater fails "to successfully portray women as autonomous beings [. . .] Whatever the level of feminist awareness of the situation that she may attain, the many-faceted heroine of feminist drama of this period is shown incapable of successfully shaping or reshaping a life based on this new-found identity" (385). If this is true of the plays Millstone chose to study, of which a vast majority were written by men, it does not appear to apply to most feminist plays by women of the same period. As we have seen, the plays studied here not only criticize the status quo, but also incite their audience, men and women, to seize their rights and to fight for justice, equality, peace, and freedom. These plays give us a glimpse of a world in which women work alongside men, whether in intellectual pursuits or in political struggles; where the family is no longer an institution that enslaves women through paternal authority, unwanted maternity, and domestic duties; where the problems of domestic violence and alcoholism are reduced; where the workers are educated and exposed to culture; and where women no longer raise children as cannon fodder.

While French women and workers saw some improvement in their lives in the early twentieth century, much progress and propaganda remained necessary. Unfortunately, World War I temporarily slowed down the growth of both the political theater and the feminist movement in France. As a result, nearly half a century would pass before a new generation of women brought their feminist and political concerns to the stage in France. During this period, however, political theater was developing in other regions of Europe, perhaps preparing the way for the strong feminist voice that emerged on the French stage in the post-1968 era.

In Russia, for example, theater became an important form of political propaganda after the October Revolution of 1917. Indeed the term "agitprop" comes from the Russian *agitatsiya-propaganda*, a radical and innovative form of political theater developed by the Bolsheviks to indoctrinate the mostly illiterate masses. The Living Newspaper, for example, an early example of Soviet agitprop theater, performed simple dramatizations of news items in a variety of styles with a goal not only to inform the audience about current events, but above all to promote Bolshevik ideology and to elicit support for the party. In the mid-1920s, the agitprop movement grew throughout the Soviet Union among professional and amateur theater groups. This "Blue Blouse" movement made use of a variety of popular forms to capture its audience through striking performances that functioned successfully as political propaganda. The Blue Blouse movement was so successful, in fact, that Stalin banned it in 1928 because the views it was spreading conflicted with the official Soviet doctrine.[4]

Political theater was not, however, restricted to agitprop troupes in post-Revolutionary Russia. A. V. Lunacharsky, the Commissar of the People for Public Instruction until 1929, who strongly advocated agitprop theater as a way of preaching the new creed, also recognized the importance of establishing a state-sanctioned theater to promote communist doctrine. In 1917, a decree published by the Council of People's Commissars declared that all theaters were henceforth under the jurisdiction of the Art Department of the Commissariat of Education. Meyerhold, one of the most important avant-garde theater directors in Russia before the Revolution, was appointed head of the TEO, the theatrical division of the Education Commissariat. In 1920, Meyerhold launched "October in the Theater," a movement through which he aimed to "make a Revolution in the theater, and to reflect in each performance the struggle of the working class for emancipation" (Qtd. in Slonim 244). Meyerhold was emblematic of the effervescence of the Russian theater during the first decade after the Revolution before the doctrine of socialist realism became the exclusive form of art sanctioned by the Soviet regime. A well-established member of the Communist party, Meyerhold had the power, resources, and freedom to put his creative imagination and relentless energy to the service of his political ideas while continuing to experiment with avant-garde aesthetics on stage.

In the same year that Meyerhold created "October in the Theater," German director Erwin Piscator founded the Proletarian Theater in Berlin, an agitprop group that performed in alternative venues to a working-class audience. Piscator had come to the realization during the war that art, theater in particular, could be a powerful form of propaganda. In fact, he believed that art was inseparable from politics and was determined to infuse a broad range of theater with political ideals, from agitprop to mainstream commercial theater. Piscator became a central figure in German theatrical production as director of the Berlin Central-Theater in 1923 and the Volksbühne from 1923 to 1928, and founder of his own theater company, Piscator-Bühne. Rejecting the naturalist convention, Piscator developed what he called "epic theater," which involved integrating multimedia techniques not previously associated with the theater, such as film and slide-projection, cartoons, and newspaper headlines in order to highlight the relationship between the characters and the action in the play to the social, historical, and political reality of the world beyond the stage. For Piscator, all aesthetic criteria must be subordinated to the revolutionary goal. Theater must, above all, emphasize and cultivate the class struggle (Barker 26).

In the late 1920s, recently converted to Marxism and influenced by Piscator's political theater, Bertolt Brecht began writing *Lehrstrücke*, or didactic plays, as propaganda for Communist doctrine. Later, after his exile from Germany, he turned away from this earlier style of overtly educational drama and developed a new theory of the stage, also called "epic theater," which he felt would serve the Marxist cause better. Rejecting the naturalist theater convention like Piscator, as well as the importance of an emotional catharsis, Brecht focused instead on creating effects that would distance the audience from the action and characters on stage in order to provoke an intellectual, rather than emotional, experience:

> [Brecht] thought that the "epic" theater, which aimed at awakening the spectator's critical faculty, which concentrated in showing mankind from the point of view of social relationships, would serve as an instrument of social change, a laboratory of revolutionary enlightenment; in other words, that the "epic" theater was the Marxist theatre *par excellence*. (Esslin 149)

While Brecht's theory of the stage was highly influential as a dramatic convention throughout the Western world, it may not have succeeded

any better than overtly propagandistic plays as "a laboratory of
revolutionary enlightenment." Esslin claims that "there is little evidence
that Brecht's own, more subtle methods ever roused the audience to
a militantly Marxist point of view" (151).

In postwar France, there was little political theater until the late 1920s
and early 1930s when a number of politically militant theater groups
were founded. In 1932, the F.T.O.F. (Fédération du Théâtre Ouvrier
Français) was formed to support and encourage political theater in
France, particularly agitprop performances. By the mid-1930s, approximately 170 agitprop groups belonged to the Federation whose slogan
was "Le théâtre est notre arme et notre combat" (Spitzer 18).[5] The most
successful of these troupes was le Groupe Octobre. Though best known
for the role that Jacques Prévert played as author of the majority of their
texts, this group was originally founded thanks to the efforts of ten left-
wing militants, including both men and women, who were members of
an amateur drama group called Prémices. Dissatisfied with the lack of
political agitation in their performances, these members chose to create
a new organization called Groupe de choc Prémices in order to concentrate more on political activism than aesthetic concerns. They set out to
find an author capable of producing texts that would correspond to their
goals. Their search led them to Jacques Prévert, a member of the
A.E.A.R. (Association des Écrivains et Artistes Révolutionnaires) and of
the Surrealist movement. This proved a dynamic combination; the goal
of the A.E.A.R., founded in 1932, was to create a progressive literature
dedicated to helping the struggle of the proletariat, and the Surrealist
and Dada movements that had been the most important avant-garde theater groups in France in the 1920s. The new organization that was
formed, le Groupe Octobre, was by far the most successful of the French
agitprop groups during the interwar period. A number of women participated in this group from the start, and they were actively involved in
nearly every aspect of production. Of the ten original members, six were
women: Suzanne Montel, Virginia Gregory, Ida Lods (Jamet), Arlette
Loubès (Besset), Gisèle Prévert, Jeanne Chauffour (Fuchsmann). Actress
Suzanne Montel was the most active:

> Secrétaire du Groupe, elle s'occupait de la comptabilité, des décors,
> des achats . . . Responsable de la gestion de la troupe, elle était
> chargée, en outre, de collecter les textes écrits à droite ou à gauche
> par Jacques Prévert, les dialogues, les chœurs parlés et toute
> l'immense production des Prévert, Tchimoukow ou autres
> Decomble . . . (Fauré 347–348)[6]

However, in spite of the collective, democratic nature of most aspects of this group, playwriting appears to have been solely the domain of Jacques Prévert. Unfortunately, due to a lack of documentation about the majority of the groups affiliated with the F.T.O.F., it is unknown whether women participated in writing the texts for other agitprop groups.[7]

Unlike political theater, people's theater developed immediately after the war in France, becoming an officially sanctioned national institution. Firmin Gémier, who was inspired by the popular festivals of the French Revolution and influenced by his friend Maurice Pottecher's Théâtre du Peuple and the work of Romain Rolland, became director of the Théâtre National Populaire at its founding in 1920. Gémier's goal was not to create political theater for a working-class audience or proletarian theater, but rather a nationally subsidized theater of "communion" that would bring together all classes of the society, like the theater of the ancient Greeks.[8] Though the theater itself was successful and would continue to provide high-quality productions for many decades under the direction of such men as Jean Vilar and Georges Wilson, it did not fulfill the aspirations of Gémier to be a true theater of the people, in part because of its location at the Trocadéro in one of the most wealthy districts in Paris. The T.N.P. was certainly not exemplary in promoting plays by women. Only one play written by a French woman, *L'Amante Anglaise* (1968) by Marguerite Duras, was ever performed at the T.N.P.

Another form of popular theater that developed in France during the 1930s was the proletarian literature movement promoted by authors such as Henry Poulaille, Tristan Rémy, and Marc Bernard. A number of ephemeral journals—*Nouvel Age*, le *Bulletin des Ecrivains Prolétariens, les Humbles, Prolétariat*—appeared and disappeared during this decade, publishing literary manifestos, poetry, short stories, and personal essays by members of the movement. They struggled with the very definition of proletarian literature. Should the authors necessarily be born into the working class or should bourgeois authors who sympathized with the proletariat be allowed in their ranks? Some felt that proletarian literature must be Marxist and revolutionary while others argued that authenticity is more important than doctrine, that any work written by members of the proletariat bearing witness to the life of the working class has as great a transformative power as a work explicitly advocating Marxist ideals. The novel and the personal narrative were the genres of predilection within this movement; the theater does not appear to have had an important role and few women are cited as having participated actively.[9]

How can we explain the lack of a women's voice in people's theater during this period? One explanation lies in the fact that in French society, the universal is, in fact, masculine. Women represent the Other. Popular theater, whether defined as bringing together all classes of the society or representing the proletariat, was incapable of integrating the feminine into the universal. Practitioners of popular theater seem to have adhered to the same erroneous assumption as most leftist political activists at the turn of the century; it is not necessary to focus on women's issues since they are just part of a more general struggle for freedom and equality. This false notion of a genderless universal, in reality, led to the exclusion of the feminine voice in both political discourse and people's theater.

Women were, however, writing for the stage in other venues during the interwar period. Critics of the time recognized not only the existence but even the talent of a certain number of women dramatists. In 1939, one critic spoke of "une écrasante majorité féminine dans la production théâtrale" predicting that women might be "les artisans de la rénovation du théâtre";[10] another remarked, "l'on voit les femmes-auteurs croissant en nombre et en audace, sinon en génie, prendre possession des théâtres de Paris."[11] Marcelle Maurette, for example, wrote over 30 plays, most of which were performed. She became a member of the SACD (Société des Auteurs et Compositeurs Dramatiques) in 1939 after the success of her play *Madame Capet* directed by Gaston Baty at the Théâtre de Montparnasse and was made Chevalier of the Legion of Honor in 1950. Most of Marcelle Maurette's plays are about exceptional women of history or fiction who led tragic lives.[12] All were punished in some way, usually through a violent death, for having been exceptional. Marcelle Maurette's plays, though about women, are neither feminist nor political plays as defined in this study. She did not seek to raise consciousness though drama in order to improve women's lives; her goal was neither to educate the audience about social, economic, or political injustice nor to incite the spectators to action. Her plays corresponded to a move toward theatricalism in the interwar period, a tendency defended by Gaston Baty and the other members of the Cartel.[13] Baty, in particular, who would stage three other plays by Marcelle Maurette,[14] wanted to move away from both naturalism and the verbose, literary theater of Marie Lenéru, toward a *théâtre total* with complex, multidimensional stagings and picturesque sets (Bradby 18): "Theatre with a capital, 'T' " as one critic described Marcelle Maurette's play *Anastasia*.[15]

In the mid-1940s, a number of theater professionals had in turn become dissatisfied with the aesthetic conventions of the Cartel and were again interested in exploring ways of bringing the theater to the people. Many of their initiatives resembled those of the Universités

Populaires at the turn of the century: free acting classes to Parisian workers, establishing regional theaters, and making inexpensive tickets available to the working class (Miller 21). Inspired by these private initiatives, the public sector joined the movement in the early 1950s. Jean Vilar, director of the T.N.P. from 1951 to 1963, instigated a number of innovations in order to make the performances at the theater more accessible to the less privileged classes. The theater became a public service. André Malraux, Minister of Cultural Affaires, had an even broader vision. He claimed that every Frenchman had the "right to culture" and developed a network of Maisons de la culture throughout France to facilitate the people's access to their cultural right.

The playwrights, meanwhile, while united in their "flight from naturalism,"[16] were experimenting with different theatrical styles. Jean-Paul Sartre adapted his theory of existentialism and the necessity of political engagement to the stage, while authors such as Beckett and Ionesco were revolutionizing known theatrical conventions in the theater of the absurd. In 1954, when the Berlin Ensemble staged Brecht's *Mother Courage* at the First International Theater Festival, many French theater professionals again became convinced of the importance of political theater. Authors like Adamov, Armand Gatti, and Aimé Césaire henceforth sought to combine the two main trends in postwar theater: political engagement and the theater of the absurd. This volatile combination led to a situation by 1968 in which, according to Judith Graves Miller, "protest theater, plays of denunciation, and political stagings composed the major part of theatrical productions in France" (30).

Finally, for the first time in nearly half a century, women authors again strove to bring to the stage questions of gender and politics from a woman's perspective:

> Les femmes montent sur un plateau pour parler d'elles, de leurs vies, de leur travail quotidien, pour sortir de l'enfermement et du silence dans lequel elles sont été si longtemps murées. Elles veulent communiquer entr'elles, faire entendre aux hommes un discours nouveau, lever les tabous, tenter d'exprimer tout un non-dit si longtemps refoulé. (Surel-Tupin, "Prise de parole" 59)[17]

While most of the playwrights studied in this book identified primarily as political militants, their post-1968 equivalents were most often actresses or playwrights frustrated with the representation of women in the existing repertory of plays by men. The post-1968 women playwrights were not necessarily active in any formal political movement, and did not all identify themselves as feminists. Yet, their plays were often a theater of revolt: revolt against the image of women portrayed on the male-dominated stage and the condition of women in contemporary French society. Their works reflect the feminist notion that the personal is political. Women theater professionals felt an urgent need to create a woman's voice in the theater:

> Urgence de montrer, de dire ce que chaque femme pensait tout bas ou refoulait dans les profondeurs d'elle-même : la lassitude de l'enfermement, du sexisme quotidien, la dépendance des autres, l'impuissance apprise, l'attente permanente, les pièges de la mater-nité, la crainte du temps qui passe et vous laisse les mains vides, la culpabilité qui s'installe dès qu'on suit ses désirs, l'alternative douloureuse entre la normalisation et le déchaînement de l'imaginaire qui peut mener à la folie. Urgence de dénoncer l'incompréhension ou l'égoïsme du compagnon, l'angoisse de la solitude, mais aussi de dire l'amitié, la solidarité entre les femmes, le changement, parler de demain dans un langage simple, sans triomphalisme, préparer la subversion dans la vie quotidienne . . . (Surel-Tupin, "Prise de parole" 77)[18]

While post-1968 women playwrights were not the first to bring such issues to the stage, they certainly took women's theater further than ever before in terms of quantity, variety, and visibility. Though the women authors of this generation were undoubtedly unaware of the political and feminist plays by women from the late nineteenth and early twentieth centuries, it is thanks to these more recent authors that the earlier plays have been rediscovered. It is the success of the post-1968 plays that led literary critics and theater professionals to begin to explore the history of women's theater during the past decades. Like the plays of Michel, Roussel, Starkoff, Lenéru, and Pelletier, the theater of post-1968 women playwrights is "un théâtre d'intervention, au sens profond du terme, puisqu'il incite chacun de nous à ne plus subir, mais à oser imaginer autrement sa vie" (Surel-Tupin, "Prise de parole" 77).[19] It is gratifying to see that in spite of a period of relative inactivity, feminist and political women playwrights have again brought their concerns, their demands, and their visions to the stage.

Notes

Chapter One   Introduction: Theater, Politics, and Gender

1. *Au temps de l'anarchie, un théâtre de combat (1880–1914)*, Monique Surel-Tupin, Sylvie Thomas, Philippe Evernel, Jonny Ebstein, eds. (Paris: Séguier, 2001). The "Cabaret Anarchiste à la Belle Époque," directed by Monique Surel-Tupin, was performed at l'Espace Louise Michel in the 20th district of Paris in April 2001.
2. "devoted, for the revenues, to the bourgeois dung heap." (All translations in the text are my own).
3. "The hours and rhythm of work, the difficulties and expense of urban transport, the level of salaries, the shortage of collective institutions (nurseries, child-care centers), so many conditions that, together with unequal access to education, create a social deterrent to cultural development in general."
4. See Cecilia Beach, "De la maternité au matriciel: La Représentation du maternel dans les œuvres de femmes dramaturges française," Diss. New York U, 1993, 113–127.
5. For a general history of anarchism in France see Jean Maitron, *Le Mouvement anarchiste en France*, 2 vols. (Paris: Gallimard, 1975).
6. "because it strikes the mind more vividly, it embeds its lesson there through the memory of the image."
7. According to Krakovitch, only eight plays were forbidden after the reading of the manuscript between 1874 and 1891. Odile Krakovitch, *Hugo censuré: La Liberté au théâtre au XIXe siècle* (Paris: Calmann-Lévy, 1985), 248.
8. "What attracts me to anarchism is above all the intellectual aspect, the reign of individualism [. . .]. With anarchism, there is no more State, no more harmful government and thus, suddenly, what flight given to art, what liberty offered to thought, what a wide field open to free initiative, to the genius in each of us!"
9. "[*L'Art Social*] knows that it is time to substitute a healthy and vigorous poetry for a villainous and futile poetry. It knows that there is a place to be had next to the activists and apostles of the socialist cause. Finally, it knows that the moment has come to bring together and breathe new life into the diverse elements of the great art of tomorrow: socialist Art."
10. "*L'Art Social* does not reject any literary or artistic form."
11. "The intransigent proponents of *art for art's sake*, entrenched in the extreme limits of mystery, end up producing in isolation and for their personal use alone [. . .]. Literary masturbators, they shake up their brains and after having quivered for an instant in the ejaculation of a symbol (perhaps a monster without sex or flesh); after having felt a light spasm of unshared joy, they release it . . .—Into the sands of the desert."

12. "For the people, physical activity is always necessary. Books and newspapers are not enough. Indispensable to them are the rostrum and the theater, in other words direct communication, striking examples. Our soul vibrates more rapidly in direct contact with an idea that speech and action have brought to life."

13. "Thanks to our attempts, to our experiments, we will find the right formula. Social art will spread to all genres, from the *drame*, which is unpopular today, to *féeries* (plays with supernatural characters and spectacular theatrical effects), for which we will need a new type of stage, but also a new name since science will replace the little fairies and evil devils with other symbols."

14. "It seems to me that the farces and *sotties* (a genre of medieval satirical plays) performed long ago on the stage . . . have done as much for the people as have the great revolutions."

15. "Socialist art [. . .] is the soul of the people, a soul made of contrasts: strong, poignant, terrible emotions; great, powerful, noisy joys; our misery, too cruel reality; our love, the source from which we draw our only ideal."

16. "a social and anarchist play, but with no preaching or tirades. I am striving to create only life and direct action." The play to which he refers was probably *Les Mauvais Bergers*, performed in 1897 at the Théâtre de la Renaissance by Sarah Bernhardt and Lucien Guitry.

17. "The impact of your play will be much greater if the moral ensues from the action itself. Tirades are fine in a nonfiction book, but for a novel, and especially for the theater, a well-described situation and a succession of well-developed scenes are better in my opinion."

18. "I saw *Les Mauvais Bergers* (The Bad Shepherds) and I applauded all the praise it was given. It is just the conclusion that seems too pessimistic to me. [. . .] The allegory would have been truer, more vibrant, if Jean Roule's child had been born. Having him die with his mother is the negation of the whole effort and critique. There is nothing left to do but throw oneself in the Seine."

19. "Theater is the most active and most prompt means of invincibly arming the forces of human reason and of shining a great amount of light on the people all at once."

20. "We must clear off the stage so that reason may return there to speak the language of liberty, to strew flowers on the tomb of martyrs, to sing of heroism and of virtue, to make the people love the laws and the nation."

21. "There is no doubt that in the future the theater will be the most powerful means of education, of uniting men; it is perhaps the greatest hope for a national renewal. I speak of an immensely popular theater, a theater that corresponds to the thoughts of the people, that would travel to the most remote villages.

    Oh! may I see, before I die, national fraternity reborn in the theater."

22. "mediator of society," "primary agent of social renovation."

23. Firmin Gémier (1869–1933), one of the most important actors and directors of the late nineteenth and early twentieth centuries. He was already a well-known actor in 1894 for his roles at the Antoine's Théâtre-Libre. Two years later, he would perform the lead role in Jarry's *Ubu Roi* at the Théâtre de l'Œuvre. Gémier is perhaps best known for his role in developing *le théâtre populaire* and for founding the Théâtre National Populaire (1920). Gémier's definition of *populaire* included not only the working class but all classes of the society. He wrote: "L'art dramatique doit s'adresser à tout le peuple. Par ce mot [. . .] je n'entends pas seulement la classe populaire mais toutes les catégories sociales à la fois" (Qtd. in Corvin 669). ["The dramatic arts must speak to all the people. By this [. . .] I mean not just the working class but all social categories at once."]

24. "The theater? . . . a warehouse devoid of ornaments, similar to one of those barns where the *Roman comique* performed. To the faint light of a few gas lamps, perfectly resembling the old *quinquets* (a type of oil lamp) of yesteryear, the disorderly spectators crowding onto rustic benches."

25. "Entire families of workers appropriately in their Sunday best, with a flock of children of all ages [. . .], honest shopkeepers and quiet bourgeois from the neighborhood, very proper office workers, well dressed shop assistants [. . .]."

26. "Just one performance of the play would bring socialism more followers than all the speeches in the world."

27. "to proclaim loudly our hatred of the great modern corruptor, Money."

28. "No, we never intended to entertain or moralize. We search among the pages of the masters, among the works of young writers, for those most likely to elevate man, to give him joy rather than gaiety, to stimulate within him ideas of justice and independence. We said to the people: listen to the words of philosophers, poets, thinkers, listen to the words of Beauty and Liberty. These geniuses who foresaw the final harmony of human societies bemoan your present lot, they reveal to your poor, endarkened eyes the immortal light that must glow for man to be free. Become aware, people, of your force; be a free people!"

29. "ONE MUST NOT GO TO THE THEATER TO BE ENTERTAINED."

30. 1. "To provide physical and moral relaxation;
    2. To be a source of energy (to elevate and elate the soul);
    3. To enlighten the public's intelligence (awaken their minds, teach them to see and to judge things, men and themselves)."

31. "Art is a function of intelligence on the watch. Let us not leave any part of man's capital, body or mind, to atrophy. May the joy of exercise and fresh air strengthen the muscles of those whose work does not involve physical activity! But may art—and the theater is the most powerful of the arts—give strength to the intelligence that is left inactive by the manual labor that insures your existence. Meager though it may be, art will expand it."

32. "It is a lion's skin thrown over inanity. [. . .] Full of noise, eloquence, a semblance of bravery, striking images, false science, and false ideas; this type of theater is the bully of French art. It doesn't bother to think or to teach or to observe; there is neither truth nor honesty; it *bluffs* with virtuosity."

33. "isolated, scattered, with no connection between them, without cohesion, without sufficient publicity, without the force necessary to fight the routine of artists and the indifference of the public."

34. "Grand actions, well-defined characters, basic passions, a simple but forceful pace, vast frescoes rather than easel paintings, symphonies rather than chamber music. A monumental art made for the people, by the people.
    By the people!—Yes, for there is no great popular work in which the soul of the poet does not collaborate with the soul of the nation, which feeds on collective passions."

35. "A murder committed by a husband on his wife, as well as on her accomplice, at the moment when he discovers them in the act, in the marital dwelling, is excusable."

36. "Without claiming that women could straightaway create masterpieces comparable to those that men have already contributed to dramatic literature, I am certain that the feminine mind will bring to the theater a truly necessary revival. There are many situations in life, and therefore in the theater, in which women differ entirely from men in their opinions and sentiments. It would be both interesting and instructive to hear women tell about their impressions, their joys, their regrets, and even their complaints about society."

37. "Even those who have had the honor, oh so rare! of being welcomed in the Theater, have been obliged to expurgate their works of all new ideas, all boldness, all originality, all candor."

38. "so that they may freely make the most their talent, expose their ideas, reveal the secret of their reputedly undecipherable soul."

39. "a Theater of combat [. . .] and above all a Theater of ideas."

40. Daniel Lesueur (1860–1821). Pseudonym of Jeanne Loiseau, Mme Henri Lapauze.

41. "an outright revolt against the conventional lies."

42. "In fact, the play could have been performed at the Vaudeville, the Gymnase, or the Odéon; it would surely have pleased and moved the audience. The work was warmly applauded, and it deserved this success thanks to the sincerity of the emotions, and the proud outpouring of ideas, shaped within the rigorous form of the sentence [. . .]."

43. "CARMONA: And your daughter? What do you intend to do about your daughter? (Jean is silent) You don't answer? Maybe you think I can bring her up alone? You're wrong, my dear, my means are not sufficient. When one gets a woman pregnant, one doesn't leave her without resources."

44. "The theater posed two problems for me: first as a woman, second as a newcomer. In the first case I had to resign myself to taking unpleasant steps, in the second I had to accept modifications that altered the nature of my manuscript and that were more detrimental than beneficial to it. Given these obligations, I deemed it necessary to give up the prestige of having my plays performed in favor of having them simply read, soliciting less passionate but more impartial revues." We can appreciate even better how unpleasant the theater milieu must have been for a woman when we consider that Maria Deraismes did not hesitate to combat women's exclusion in the even more male-dominated milieu of Freemasonry. In 1882, Deraismes was the first woman to become a veritable member of "Les Libres Penseurs," part of the Grande Loge symbolique écossaise and later cofounded the first mixed order of Freemasons, Le Droit Humain. During her initiation in 1882, Deraismes said: "En France, la suprématie masculine est la dernière aristocratie. Elle se débat vainement; son tour de disparaître arrive"(Qtd. in Krakovitch, "Preface" in Maria Deraismes, *Ce que veulent les femmes: Articles et discours et de 1869 à 1894* [Paris: Syros, 1980], 33). ["In France, masculine supremacy is the last aristocracy. It defends itself in vain; its time to disappear has arrived."]

45. "Men are always and constantly represented in an abominable light; never have they been represented to us as decent beings of devotion and love. This is wrong. All men are not horrid rascals, dark scoundrels; and all women are not saints and martyrs either. We must not exaggerate, for fear of recalling the proverb: 'He who tries to hard to prove something, proves nothing.' "

46. "The career of the Théâtre féministe was short, too short, but good. During the 1897–1898 season, it held its own brilliantly among the marginal theaters; its only failure was financial. [. . .] It contributed to the definitive conquest of the theater by women."

47. "It is at the Mixed and Eclectic theater, accessible to all young playwrights, men and women, open to all efforts aimed at renovating the dramatic arts, and at social renovation, it is to this theater—which exists nowhere yet—that the future belongs."

48. See Amy Blythe Millstone, "Feminist Theatre in France: 1870–1914," Diss. U of Wisconsin-Madison, 1977; Michel Corvin, "Le boulevard en question," *Le Théâtre en France* Vol. 2 (Paris: Armand Colin, 1989), 347–349.

Chapter Two   Staging the Revolution: Louise Michel

1. See Anne Sizaire, *Louise Michel: L'Absolu de la générosité* (Paris: Desclée de Brouwer, 1995), 33; Xavier de La Fournière, *Louise Michel: matricule 2182* (Paris: Perrin, 1986), 42–44.

2. "What I sent [to Victor Hugo] now smelled of gun powder:

> Can you hear the roar of bronze.
> Stay back those who hesitate!
> The coward will be the traitor of tomorrow!
> To the mounts and to the cliffs,
> Let us go, sowing liberty.
> Breath swept away by the storm
> Let us pass, living Marseillaise."

3. "The Revolution was beginning! What good were dramas? The real drama was in the streets; what good were orchestras? We had the brass and the canons. [. . .] prose, verse and motifs were cast to the winds; we felt very close to us the breath of the drama in the streets, the real drama, that of humanity; the *bardits* (ancient Germanic war chants) told a new epic tale. There was no room for anything else."

4. "Far from blaming the perseverance [of the theater directors], we should give them the credit they deserve. They contribute to maintaining the morale of the Parisians; they make us forget for a minute the ideas of mourning that, though saddening us, must not completely demoralize us."

5. According to Labarthe, the governement of the Commune pressured actresses who were not sympathetic to the revolutionary cause into participating in these performances: "Agar, pas plus que Mme Bordas ni les autres artistes qui prirent part à ces fêtes, ne pouvaient, sans danger, refuser d'obéir à ces ordres" (130). ["Agar, like Mme Bordas and the other actors who participated in these events, could not, without danger, refuse to obey their orders."]

6. "But theaters must be considered above all as a great teaching establishment, and, in a republic, they must be nothing else. Our ancestors understood this, and the Convention, in a decree of the second of Germinal (seventh month in the Republican calendar), decided that a commission, that of public education, would oversee the theaters."

7. "As to that which concerns the performance of plays, we could do no better than to bring the theaters under the aegis of Education. It is the greatest and the best educational instrument for the people. The governments that preceded ours made the theater into a school for all the vices; we will make it a school for civic virtues; and from a corrupt nation we will create a nation of citizens!"

8. "We must try to create socialist establishments everywhere. The main character of the Revolution in the nineteenth century is that it is a social revolution. The product of the worker is the axiom of a general truth that must be applied to the artist, like to any other producer. [. . .] The general administration of theaters has been asked to transform the present organization based on property and privilege to a system of association run entirely by the artists themselves."

9. "As to patronage, to any influence whatsoever on art, I believe that it would encroach upon the liberty of human thought."

10. "Theaters are under the education delegation. All theater subsidies and monopolies have been eliminated. The delegation will set out to stop the system of exploitation by a director or a company and will substitute as quickly as possible an organization based on association."

11. See Edith Thomas, *Les "Pétroleuses"* (Paris: Gallimard, 1963); Gay L. Gullickson, *Unruly Women of Paris: Images of the Commune* (Ithaca: Cornell UP, 1996).

12. Adèle Esquiros was also a novelist and the editor of *Soeur de Charité*, a feminist journal in which Louise Michel published some of her poems.

13. She reports one to have said: "jour viendra où Canaques tueront oppresseurs." ["Day will come when Canaques will kill oppressors."] *Matricule 2182. "Souvenirs de ma vie" par Louise Michel (extraits)* (Paris: Dauphin, 1981), 117.

14. In fact, Michel considered herself to be a "social revolutionary." She had no interest in the theoretical debates that divided the various leftist political factions and believed that all socialists should unite in order to bring on the inevitable revolution (Mullany, *The Female Revolutionary* 52).

15. The manuscripts for all three plays are also available: *Nadine*, Archives Nationales ms. F^{18}1167^A; *Le Coq Rouge*, International Institute of Social History, Coll. Descaves, pf. 62, Comm. 7; *La Grève*, Archives Nationales ms. F^{18}1321.

16. Clovis Hugues attended Louise Michel's play, *Le Coq rouge*. In fact, it seems to have been his arrival in the theater that sparked much of the rucous: "L'entrée de Clovis Hugues est le signal de la reprise des jouissances. En haut, on crie: 'Vive Clovis Hugues!' et l'on entonne *La Carmagnole* . . . Le député boulangiste chante en choeur avec les masses." ["The arrival of Clovis Hugues was like a signal to start up the fun again. In the balconies, they cried: 'Long live Clovis Hugues!' and they sang the *Carmagnole* . . . The Boulangist deputy sang along with the masses."] *Le Voltaire*, May 21, 1888.

17. For more information about Lisbonne's career, see Marcel Cerf, *Le d'Artagnan de la Commune (Le Colonel Maxime Lisbonne)* (Bienne Suisse: Ed. du Panorama, 1967).

18. "The greatest success of the nineteenth century."

19. "Citizen Lisbonne, the new director of the Bouffes-du-Nord, is becoming one of the cleverest impresarios in Paris. He knows that exhibiting exotic animals and eccentricities is fashionable

and makes money. [. . .] Citizen Lisbonne wanted to outdo his fellow theater directors and found the way to exhibit one of the phenomena of the Commune: Citizen Louise Michel."

20. "that she didn't give a damn if they came to see her as a strange animal, because they would always get something out of what she said." Archives de la Préfectures de Police, B/A, September 1, 1888.

21. Her reputation as an altruistic saint surpassed that of the female revolutionary after her death. She was compared, by friends and enemies alike, to Joan of Arc, St. Theresa, St. Vincent de Paul, and St. Francis of Assisi for the fervor with which she defended her cause and her self-sacrifice on behalf of the poor and downtrodden (Mullany, *The Female Revolutionary* 63–65).

22. "In the name of the dying Nation, in the name of freedom and humanity, in the name of those who have died, let us take up arms and liberate our towns and our countryside! . . . Long live liberty! . . . Let us free our martyred brothers! To arms! To arms!"

23. "We are not building; we are demolishing. We are not revealing new ideas; we are doing away with the old lies. The world in which we live is dying, and our successors must bury it first in order to breathe freely . . . In going from the old world to the new, we can take nothing with us."

24. "We must eradicate absolutely all Tyranny, even if we must perish with it. Yes, brothers, let us proclaim the Republic and after the victory we will form a community in which each of us will take part in the banquet of life, producing according to his or her merit and abilities, consuming according to his or her needs. We no longer want privileges and oppression . . ."

25. "It seems that the author wanted to rehabilitate the Commune, but foreseeing that the censors would forbid it, she transposed the play to Poland. We only celebrate the Polish Commune— and not even that since instead of the Commune they said 'community'."

26. "Well! The great citizen's play was not any worse than others!"

27. "A work is always interesting when it depicts with sincerity the suffering and heroism of an oppressed people fighting its oppressors."

28. "I am in a difficult situation because I am not on my own ground here: I must restrict my comments to literature, and am forbidden to make any [political] allusions. I may make some without meaning to. Oh well, it won't be my fault. I wanted to revive the memory of that great man, Bakounine, for the younger generations: the censors tore apart my first two acts. What good does it do to work hard only to see your play massacred? (. . .)

But I must say no more, for the censors—under another name—are watching me. Tomorrow, I won't be able to refrain from breaking the law that forces me to speak only about literature; tomorrow I will be obliged to tell about death in Poland.

Tomorrow, perhaps, I will show you the long line of gallows that I had erected in the final act, near the prince's palace window, and that the censors mercilessly forbade."

29. In an interview with Charles Chincholle of *Le Figaro*, Louise Michel explained the title: "Vous avez le Coq gaulois, vous autres. Nous avons, nous, le coq rouge, l'incendie qui dresse parfois sa crête de flamme" (*Le Figaro*, May 30, 1888). ["You have the French cockerel (symbol of French nation). We have the red cockerel, fire sometimes lighting its cockscomb aflame."]

30. Eastern France, near the Swiss border, had become a center for anarchist activity at this time. Not only did anarchist leaders Kropotkin and Elisée Reclus live in Switzerland, but living near the border gave militants the security of being able to flee at a moment's notice to escape the police. Only after 1883 and the "Procès des 66" would the hub of anarchism move to Paris. Alexander Varias, *Paris and the Anarchists: Aesthetes and Subversives during the Fin de Siècle* (New York: St. Martin's P, 1996), 11–12.

31. "PAUL: There is more to be done than complain; we must destroy the evil.
ROSALIE: How you have changed, Paul! you, who used to be so timid and gentle.
PAUL: Gentleness is sterile; hatred will be more fecund."

32. " 'Le Coq Rouge': Conversation avec Mlle Louise Michel." Article dated September 17, 1888 in Archives de la Préfecture de Police, BA 1187.

33. "It is stupid, this censorship. There are meetings. They don't know what we will say. We can talk about anything, but because my words are called a 'play' instead of a 'speech,' there have to be these men who cut and slash . . ."

34. "*Le Coq rouge*—another invention for the dramatic armory. We have *Juarès* to thank for raw tomatoes. Thanks to *Le Coq rouge*, we have cooked snails. These projectiles were tried out with great success yesterday at the Théâtre des Batignolles, on the occasion of Louise Michel's play. Thrown from the upper balconies by a skillful hand, their shells are somewhat painful and their slime very dirty. Of the 20 some dinner jackets that were hit, not one of them escaped injury. The nice little snail will be of service from now on at all our theatrical solemnities."

35. "the sort of drama the valiant citizen could and had to write, in other words a passionate and vibrant plea in defense of the meek and the deprived."

36. "Better to be killed behind a pile of paving stones with a gun in one's hand than to die of hunger in a hovel."

37. "Death to the well fed! Death to the Bourgeoisie! Long live the workers! Long live anarchy! Long live the Socialist Revolution!"

38. Archives de la Préfecture de Police, B/a 76, December 20, 1890.

39. "Neither age nor sex matter in struggles like ours."

40. "INRIKE: Tonight is the true engagement party—the red wedding of death.
    ESTHER: It is the most beautiful. I had chosen it this way.
    MARIUS: And you Marpha, do you also want a red wedding—the wedding of the brave?
    MARPHA: Yes."

41. "Fuck, it's not often that *le père Peinard* goes to the theater; for once, he made an exception. God, it was sure worth it. It was a play by Louise Michel that was being performed. And the best thing was that it wasn't playing in a big theater, but in a little dive where the rabble can go easily: at the Théâtre de la Villette. There, at least, it's in a workers' neighborhood, by God. In another theater there'd've been little bourgeois cows, and upper-class bastards." *Le Père Peinard*, December 14, 1890. Emile Pouget was one of the leaders of the 1883 march on Les Invalides, after which both he and Louise Michel were arrested.

42. After 1895, Louise Michel moved back to Paris where she would continue her career as anarchist orator. She would, however, frequently return to London.

43. "The anarchists expelled from France, Belgium, and Italy could live in peace in the great city of London. They could even continue their propaganda and hold meetings every day . . . And nothing was stranger than these meetings. They started with a series of about ten speeches and ended with a ball or a concert."

44. See, for example, *The Commonwealth, Freedom*, and *The Torch* for announcements of anarchist rallies, as well as articles and speeches by Louise Michel.

45. "I was revising some comedies that I had begun writing earlier. I worked on several dramas that will probably never be staged."

46. "A young man, who was always honest, had always worked, suddenly becomes very poor. He tries to react, to pull himself up by any means possible, but he doesn't succeed. The society beats him down more and more, until one day he is arrested for stealing bread. Then, when he gets out of prison, this man has become fierce. He plants a bomb, blows up the house of the judge who put him in prison. He is caught; he is going to be executed when the society, which had been fomenting for a number of years, is suddenly victorious over the old world and frees the prisoner."

47. "Among the men who gather around him are the first metal workers, the first poets; they had a three-holed flute, a primitive lute; they draw the first signs on cave walls to transmit their thoughts. They make the first attempts at engraving on bone and sowing seed . . ."

48. "There rises from the earth / A magnificent and powerful song / The shadows have lasted a long time perhaps / But progress is growing."

49. "Everything is growing and transforming, / Radiant is the future. / Having seen it, death must follow."

50. An article in *Comœdia* (June 5, 1928) claims that a play by Louise Michel entitled "Prométhée et l'Ogre" was performed at Grafton Hall. However, "Prométhée" and "L'Ogre" were two different

plays. It is not clear whether both plays were performed or whether the journalist printed the wrong title for a single play.

51. "the spirit of revolt may become one of the most important virtues."

52. "It provides some thought, some gaiety and some ideals." International Institute of Social History, Collection Lucien Descaves, Louise Michel, pf. 46, biogr. 1–2.

53. "In fact, Lisbonne, who can be terrible at times, is at heart, a good-natured fellow, who talks about his hardships without the least bitterness toward society . . . It is a mystery to me how men can suffer the hardest trials of the penal colony and exile, and yet preserve their state of mind, good humor or carefree attitude. My hair turns grey just going past Mazas, and this Lisbonne, who spent 10 years in a penal colony, comes back from Nouméa all light-hearted and full of gaiety. During this memorable evening, the former colonel had moments of mad gaiety."

54. "Louise has always shown a sense of gaiety as robust as her sense of tragedy. But it seems to me that in London that tendency was particularly brought out. Contrary to what one might think, her close entourage, the milieu of the exiles—for the most part, like her, voluntary—does not breed melancholia. These libertarians, who live like birds on a branch, often have as much fantasy as anti-conformism in their opinions."

55. "we talked big but not one serious resolution was made there."

56. Charles Malato, like Michel, wrote a number of plays but of a lighter genre—a satire about Caesar, a "drame philosophico-fantaisiste" entitled *Le Nouveau Faust*, and a satirical drama in the style of *Ubu Roi* about a corrupt journalist and politician. He also wrote social novels, notably *La Grande Grève*, which is about the events of 1882.

57. For more on Michel's reputation as a saint, see Marie Marmo Mullany, "Louise Michel: The Female Revolutionary as Saint," *The Female Revolutionary* 21–85. See also Bradby and McCormick on the role of theater as a substitute for religion.

Chapter Three   Feminism and the Freethinkers
Movement: Nelly Roussel

1. An earlier "Théâtre du peuple," founded in 1885 by Maurice Pottecher in Bussang in the Vosges, was recognized by the Université Populaire as a precursor of the type of theater they hoped to develop. When Pottecher's *Liberté* was performed by the Théâtre du Peuple de Bussang at the Université Populaire convention in 1904, Maurice Kahn claimed that the Théâtre du Peuple and the Université Populaire pursued the same goal; both are "schools of liberty" (146). "Il en est du théâtre comme des journaux. Ce pourrait être un moyen d'éducation. . . . Ce qu'il faut c'est fonder des théâtres du peuple. Mais 'Théâtre de peuple' ne signifie pas théâtre à bon marché, théâtre de faubourg ou de banlieue, car il existe en grand nombre. Le théâtre du peuple est la formule, l'étiquette d'un art dramatique qui se réclame du peuple révolutionnaire et novateur parce qu'il est lui-même révolutionnaire et neuf. Un art n'est salutaire qu'à condition de fournir à la vie d'un peuple vigoureux et sain un surcroît de vie et d'action" (*Bulletin de l'Université populaire* 14). ["The theater is like newspapers. It could be a means of education . . . What we need is to create theaters of the people. But 'theater of the people' does not mean a cheap theater, a theater on the outskirts of town or in the suburbs, for a certain number of them already exist. The theater of the people is a formula, a label for a dramatic art that speaks for the revolutionary people interested in change because it is revolutionary and new itself. Art is not salutary unless it provides the lives of vigorous and healthy people with even more life and action."]

2. After 1901, in an attempt to decentralize *le théâtre populaire* to the left bank, Dargel organized performances of the Théâtre du Peuple at the Athénée-Saint-Germain, which would become the Vieux-Colombier in 1913 (Bracco 316).

3. For example, *Les Amoureux de l'art, La Société de musique et de déclamation, Le Cercle théâtral de l'Emancipation, L'Association populaire pour la propagation gratuite de l'art, La Lyre sociale de la rive gauche, le Groupe théâtral universitaire, La Marianne*.

4. "[*La Coopération des Idées*] followed a café-concert in a seedy part of town, where dirty songs and cheap alcohol represented art and life."

5. Both Véra Starkoff and Nelly Roussel were *Professeurs de Diction* (elocution teachers).

6. "Our mates are following the rules as long as they take measures, before the performance, to have the guests join the Université Populaire where it's being put on."

7. "We should note that since our mates do not generally have the time to memorize the plays, staged readings, common in many Universités Populaires, are both practical and adequate to give our evenings what they need."

8. "*Comœdia*, which does not wish to remain a stranger to any theatrical movement, will begin as of today a column specially dedicated to the 'Universités Populaires'. We know how widely they have developed throughout France in the past few years; we are thus happy to be able to dedicate to them a place in our columns where we will inform our readers about their musical and theatrical events, as long as the current events allow it, and without a partisan spirit of course."

9. "The number of women attending the events is about equal to that of men. It is a great point scored for the future of the Université and the goal it is trying to achieve."

10. "At an age when girls usually play with dolls, she loved literature, poetry, theater. She wrote stories and acted out plays she had written with her little friends, portending a veritable vocation as a tragic actress."

11. "Encouraged by all those who had appreciated her gifts as a tragic actress, she thought about following her theatrical vocation after her marriage." An article in *Le Rappel* claims that she is "professeur au Conservatoire" ("Dans le 19e arrondissement," October 13, 1903) while several articles from 1904 have her "ancienne pensionnaire de la Comédie-Française" ("Conférences de Mme Nelly Roussel de la Fédération nationale de la Libre Pensée," *Le Petit Méridional* April 3, 1904 and "Deux conférences," *La Dépêche de Toulouse*, April 13, 1904); neither information is true.

12. Notebook at Bibliothèque Marguerite Durand, Fond Nelly Roussel, entry dated December 28, 1913. In this notebook, Roussel filled out a questionnaire at different times of her life from 1889 to 1913. Her answers to questions like "Ma vertu favorite" and "mes héros favoris dans la vie réelle" are especially interesting.

13. Notebook July 2, 1889; September 11, 1892; March 31, 1895.

14. "narrow-mindedness and prejudice." Notebook February 7, 1898.

15 "Together, we soon participated in the creation of the Université Populaire. This magnificent élan for education of the critical and artistic capacities of the masses impassioned us. Nelly gave her all without holding back, organizing lectures, civic festivals, performances of classic drama."

16. "I thought I was safe from those formidable trials that so profoundly ruin my health, and I hoped to be a living example of the 'strike' I was promoting. Alas! In spite of scientific and intellectual progress, poor humanity is not yet master of its own fate; we have not definitively conquered fatality! . . . Here I am therefore condemned to bed rest for several months."

17. "The spirit of independence" . . . "all those who dare to free themselves from prejudice and conventions" . . . "rebellious" . . . "Neither god, nor master!" Notebook December 28, 1913.

18. "Her new role as a militant appeared to her the most noble and the most interesting, and she decided to dedicate her talents to defending her convictions."

19. "an excellent speaker . . . such a beautiful voice, so captivating and steady, her gestures always appropriate and sober."

20. "Madame Nelly Roussel . . . the most eloquent of French feminists, possesses all the gifts of an orator: a beautiful face, a beautiful posture, beautiful gestures, a beautiful voice, perfect diction, passionate and communicable convictions and emotions." Excerpt of a letter sent to *Annales de l'Ariège* (May 14, 1905) about Nelly Roussel and reprinted in *La Mère Educatrice* 6e année, no. 11 (November 1923), 150.

21. Also announced in *La Voix des Femmes* between 1920 and 1922.

22. "Woman, impure and cursed creature! You were born for suffering and humiliation. Giving birth with tears and without glory; submitting in silence, and always bowing down, that is your punishment!"

23. "Eternity is all!" . . . "Hope of a far-off paradise is incapable of calming my pain!"
24. "Oh! expect no more from me! . . . No work without a salary! . . . For too long, Humanity, my creation, has ridiculed and rejected its author! My womb is tired of carrying ungrateful children! The tree of life now refuses to bear fruit for its torturers! . . . Close yourself off, painful and too fertile flank! . . . close yourself off . . . until the hour of triumph: the glorious hour when the antique fortresses crumble under my infuriated protests."
25. "To spread exact notions about the physiological and social sciences in order to help parents understand situations in which they should be careful about the number of children they have, and to insure, in this respect, their freedom and above all that of women."
26. "Do not have any more children that you can bring up well . . . Respond to the whining of natalists with the greatest, most effective, most powerful, most imposing, the first of all strikes: the strike of the wombs."
27. "It would be useful for the Unions, Cooperatives, Universités Populaires, Circles of social studies, and all the groups who work in the great struggle for integral liberation to know and make known this little gem of robust thought . . . I recommend it to all."
28. ". . . if we have children again, it will be *for us*, and not for society; it will be *freely*, consciously, when *we* want to, because we *want to*, and not because religious or social dogma tells us its our duty."
29. "Considering that it is an immoral and antisocial theory, which, if put into practice, would stop the progress of humanity and would be, for the nation in which it developed, a sure cause of weakening and decadence; Considering that Mme Nelly Roussel's response goes against the patriotic duty on which the life of civilized people depends and which inspires a great number of our laws [. . .]; Considering finally that she calls the constitutional regime under which we live a 'false Republic' [. . .]."
30. "Excessive procreation causes an overabundance of workers, and thus unemployment and poverty, as well as a plethora of soldiers, and hence war." Henri Fèvre, "Et multipliez-vous," *La Revue d'aujourd'hui* (1890) (Qtd. in Ronsin 42).
31. "Depopulation causes war! . . . Among all the idiocies with which they stuff the heads of the poor people, there is none more incredible than that one. 'Depopulation' cannot have caused anything at all for the excellent reason that it doesn't exist! [. . .] or at least it didn't exist before the voluntary massacre of 10 million able-bodied men and the death, from sorrow, famine and epidemics of an almost equally great number of women and children."' "La question de la population et la guerre," *La Voix des femmes*, March 4, 1920.
32. According to an article in *La Fronde* (March 25, 1903), Nelly Roussel was a member of the loge mixte, Diderot.
33. "If women, even today, in the most developed countries, are treated by law as inferior and incapable, it is because all religions, *invented exclusively by men wishing to justify the supremacy of their sex, which they won thanks to brutal force,* have insulted and misunderstood ours."
34. "If we feminists still find so many adversaries and so many people who are indifferent . . . it is because Christian atavism is not quite dead yet . . . because the biblical legend, which makes the first woman responsible for all human evils and the instrument of man's damnation, has not yet lost its influence in the eyes of our contemporaries—even 'free-thinkers'."
35. "a noble scientific curiosity, an imperious *desire for knowledge*."
36. "Next to Adam, respectful of authority and accepting ignorance, Eve appears to us as the symbolic personification of conscious rebellion and of free thought!"
37. In *Le Mouvement féministe* 4 (September 15, 1913). Also published in *La Libre Pensée Internationale* (June 1, 1916), 4; *Au temps de l'anarchie, un théâtre de combat 1880–1914* (Paris: Séguier Archimbaud, 2001), 373–383.
38. Invitation to the meeting, Bibliothèque Marguerite Durand, Dossier Union Fraternelle des Femmes.
39. "I want something new, unknown, extraordinary."
40. "God, by giving us the intelligence to think, the reason to discuss, the language to express ourselves, God wanted our rebellion and prepared it himself. And I cannot allow myself to admit that I don't understand!"

41. "Go forth into this world that you wanted to know. You will find suffering, fear, hunger, cold, worry; you will eat bitter bread, paid for by your efforts, watered by your tears."

42. "EVE: I go without looking back, leaving nothing of me here but the heavy coat of boredom that has finally fallen from my shoulders, and the veil that, in covering my eyes, hid them from the true light. (*As Adam slowly gets up, she takes him by the hand and leads him away*). Come my friend, give me your hand. Let us enter without fear or regret into the immense unknown of the world. Come toward the painful struggles, the mind-altering conquests; come toward the fears that torture and the love that consoles. Come toward action and dreams; toward the darkness that is slowly becoming enlightened; come toward the eternal discovery and the ever-renewing mystery. Come toward the pain, all the hopes, all the pride. Come finally toward life, vast, tumultuous!"

43. "They love their religion *because they do not know it*, or at least, they do not know it well; because they only see the visible, attractive aspects, the lavish ceremonies and poetic legends."

44. "Let us show it as it is, without make-up and garlands. Let us rip off its hypocritical masque and brilliant accoutrements."

45. "If she could find the ardors and fervors of the Idea, the use of her energy, passion, desire to live and to be active, in interesting and enjoyable professional occupations, or else in study, in Science, in artistic or philosophical joys, or in propaganda, she would be saved."

46. "Politics, propaganda; well, that's not women's business."

47. "It must be pleasant to have philosophical discussions at home! . . . When a man goes home, he wants to eat his soup peacefully, without worrying about other things. That is how I understand family life."

48. "We must all, in addition to participating in events addressing the larger public, each in our own little sphere, *without imposing anything*, but by discussing, reasoning, and persuading, prepare for the triumph of the secular moral standards, the morality of the future, based on respect for human individuality, free to blossom. We must *interest all those who surround us* in our efforts, in our ideals, and make them sympathetic to them *by irreproachable personal behavior*."

49. "a radical form of political theater, emphasizing above all the goals of the struggle."

50. "Clearness of goal, brevity, textual concision, forceful language . . . are systematically sought in order to expose the social relationships, transpose the political or educational discourse into simple and understandable language."

51. In this sense, both Starkoff and Pelletier's plays discussed in chapters four and six are not strictly agitprop. Though their goal is to challenge the status quo and to incite the audience to action, they each develop a number of themes. Their effect on the audience is, therefore, more diffuse.

52. "Poverty of means is the general rule . . . The costumes are ordinary street clothes."

Chapter Four   Theater of a *Tolstoïenne*: Véra Starkoff

1. Her first name is sometimes written without an accent.

2. "We know little about this militant of Russian origin who was active in the Université Populaire movement."

3. Her last name is alternatively transliterated as Effront.

4. Archives d'Etat à Genève, AEG, Etrangers, Dj2, 91; State Archives of RF, fond N 102, 3rd dept. of Department of Police, 1884, file N 183. According to the archives at the University of Geneva, however, she was never officially enrolled as a student.

5. State Archives of RF, fond N 102, 3rd dept. of Department of Police, 1889, file N 129. For information on Gurari, see Marshall S. Shatz, *Jan Waclaw Machajski: A Radical Critic of the Russian Intelligentia.* (U of Pittsburg P, 1989), 131–132.

6. Private conversations with Sonia Peterson, née Efron (Jean's niece), Washington D.C., January 2001 and Gilles Effront (Jean's great-grandson), Paris, January 2001. Jean Effront (1854–1931)

emigrated first to Zurich where he completed his doctorate in chemistry in 1884, then to Belgium where he founded l'Institut Supérieur de Brasserie et de Distillerie de Gand.

7. In 1892, she married Léon Paul Nicod with whom she had at least two children: Thérèse and Jean Nicod. After her divorce from Nicod, she married Robert Schutz, an artist, whose portrait of Tolstoy illustrates her book *Le Vrai Tolstoï* published in 1911. Starkoff is buried in the Montparnasse Cemetery under the name Thérèse Schutz, née Effront.

8. Archives de la Préfecture de Police, BA 880 Agence Russe, Akim Effront.

9. One of her translations of Pushkin was published: Aleksandr Sergevitch Pouchkine, *Rouslane et Ludmile* (Paris: Librairie de l'art indépendant, 1898). Her translations of his plays, *Mozart et Salieri* and *Boris Godounov*, were performed in 1912.

10. For example, Nicolaï Gavrilovitch Tchernychevski, *La Jalousie* (Ed. de Floréal, 1923).

11. "Tolstoy's religion is the wisdom of human conscience, a morality based on goodness, a sociology of work . . . Tolstoy's religion is humanity."

12. "all the exploited people of the earth and those who suffer will glorify him as the greatest, the most engaging, the noblest defender of men."

13. "(1) To make women interested in all the issues that concern them and to make it easier for them to study these issues with the help of lectures, books, newspapers, documents, and communications of every type;
    (2) To work toward the improvement of the condition of women and to encourage women's evolution by efficient means."

14. "It is first of all a new conception of the family as the 'rock that supports the city' as opposed to the patriarchal family in which, by the way, the patriarch is currently missing; the family home nourished by the love of progress and not by war against humanity; it is also the perfect critique of the current laws on marriage that disorganize and corrupt the family; and above all, it is the affirmation, one might say the unique affirmation, by two great writers, of women's individuality, it is the both valuable and rare concern dedicated to giving women the means to put her heart and mind in harmony with the universal consciousness."

15. "Dear comrades,
    I dedicate my first play to you in witness of my profound gratitude. Your admirable efforts of thought and courage have strengthened my faith in Progress, shaken by the appalling bourgeois mentality. You carry the key to the future. Work will regenerate the world, according to the prophetic words of our great, late master, Emile Zola."

16. "Contemporary science and art have been taken over by capitalists who use them to exploit the human masses. Tolstoy fights against this exploitation."

17. "The false role that science and art play in our society results from the fact that so-called civilized people, led by intellectuals and artists, are a privileged caste like priests. And this caste has all the imperfections of any caste. [. . .] It weighs upon the masses, and moreover, deprives them of what it claims to propagate; and its greatest fault is the contradiction between the principles they profess and their actions."

18. "In addition to the demands of the stomach and the intellect, the working class needs to elevate its heart and to bring it in harmony with its ideas, its sentiments, and its actions, to elaborate, in a word, a social morality. This is the role of the people's theater."

19. "It is obviously not a question of the prejudices and superstitions taught by the Church and the Napoleonic laws, but rather of putting into practice the ideas of Justice and Truth, the improvement of the human condition. Theological thinkers see realism and morality as incompatible, for they consider natural phenomena as manifestations of the devil. On the contrary, the great playwrights . . . admire and reproduce nature in all its integrity with its shadows and its light. [. . .] Let us learn from their lessons. [. . .] It is not scholarly treatises that will elevate the moral standards of the masses, but rather spectacles of life observed faithfully. They contain valuable teachings, they awaken in the conscience of the audience the desire to fight against the errors, the vices, and the unjust laws that make men unhappy, they expose the human heart and make known the conditions of happiness."

20. "The *Université Populaire* is not a school made up of pupils who accept any lesson! It is cooperation, an exchange of ideas between the lecturer and the workers . . . It is the conscience, the bit of justice and of truth inside each of us that we try to bring out here, to develop through our common efforts. And the conscience of the lecturer, brought up in bourgeois conditions, is sometimes inferior to that of the worker, and in the meetings, he often receives more than he gives. He teaches us about science; we reveal justice to him!"

21. "We have a good time together, great, then we each go our own way, good night."

22. "Like dogs, huh? Just pleasure and no conscience, like animals."

23. "Let her deal with it."

24. "What do you want me to do about it?"

25. "Ha! Ha! Ha! So now it's the men who look after the kids . . . That's not a man's business to take care of kids."

26. "And why not? I love children. My daughter is so funny! She makes me laugh! And even if she didn't, she is both of ours, her mother's and mine. Why should my wife do all the work? We each do our bit."

27. "What do you mean she doesn't work hard? And who does the laundry? Who does the mending? Who makes the soup? Who washes and scrubs the whole house, from morning to night? I'd like to see you in her place, with the kids crying and getting in your way."

28. "And then, comrade, you forget the most important; women don't only feed the children, they bring them up, and if they are ignorant, they will bring them up badly, with false ideas, prejudices and devotion. Women need education like we do, and maybe even more than we do, since they hold the future in their hands. Our children, comrade, that is the future."

29. "No one cares if you're married or not."

30. Paternity suits were forbidden in France until 1912.

31. "I believe motherhood should be voluntary."

32. "Abolish the law that distinguishes illegitimate children, give all children an equal right to happiness, and you will do away with misery! And motherhood will no longer be a chain, but a title of glory, love—a blossoming of life."

33. "It is a disgrace that our children are taught by men with no sense of morality, for it is immoral, do you hear me, immoral to undermine paternal authority. The duty of a secular teacher is to instill in his pupils respect for the father and the laws."

34. "The father, the head of the family as you say, invested by his authority, instead of favoring the normal development of his children, paralyzes it; paternal authority, far from strengthening the family, disorganizes it! It brings into the home the terrible idea of oppression and banishes love and conscience from it."

35. "That's a bit much! So, for you, women and children are the same . . . As for the children, I can't do anything about it, the law gives you the authority over them . . . But as for saving my soul . . . That's another matter . . ."

36. "To sacrifice oneself is to give up the most important, one's conscience. The first duty of any human being is, on the contrary, to affirm one's conscience, not to sacrifice it!"

37. "What you say is beautiful; go on, I'm listening. Teach me!"

38. "ROUET: I have stated my wishes and I intend to be obeyed; I have an absolute authority over my children, damn it!

    LUCIE: (firmly) Excuse me! Until the age of 21, yes; I am 22, and I will prove to you that I am not a minor!"

39. "They are extremely poor . . . Everything is lacking in the house . . . . The children have no clothes and go around without shoes on the bare floors. It makes you cold just looking at them. Comrades, we are always talking about solidarity; why don't we buy shoes for the kids?"

40. "We can still always do something, since there are people even poorer than us."

41. "LUCIE: I am tired of searching in the dark, and I have finally found a way out that will lead me to the light.

    ROCHE: And what is this way out?

LUCIE: It is simple. You suggested it to me the other day without my realizing it; I remember your words: "Salvation is in work." Well, I have decided to work, to earn my living."

42. "My dear Lucie, I do not doubt your sincerity. I believe you are capable of the greatest acts of solidarity. Solidarity is an important and beautiful part of working-class life. In that way, you are one of us. But there is another, more difficult part that deters even the strongest souls. It is the everyday, mundane work of material life and even if it is secondary, we cannot have others do the work without falling into the age-old error, the error that divided humanity into masters and slaves, that still divides them today into bosses and servants. The workers today are disguised slaves! To rid work of all servitude, that is my goal in life . . ."

43. "You will live her life for a certain time, a beautiful and noble life, and if this lifestyle of poverty and work doesn't change your resolution, I need not tell you that I would be happy . . ."

44. "*Man has stupidly assumed a monopoly on the truth. He has taken away from women that which makes up the essence of life itself, thought and liberty! He has made a cadaver of her, and his living with a dead person precipitates both of them to their tomb! Man must help his companion rise up from the ground, so that he may remain standing.*"

45. This change showed a greater commitment to action and also eliminated the word "temperance," which was too closely associated with the English and American movements.

46. A distinction has traditionally been made in France between industrial distilled alcohol and the more natural and beneficial fermented wine.

47. In these restaurants, "alcohol" that is to say absinth and other industrial distilled drinks, were forbidden; they did however serve wine, "boisson noble" (Mercier 150). The general consensus at the time was that moderate consumption of wine (1 liter per day) was not harmful.

48. "For the worker, the employee and the peasant who haven't developed a taste for sound, wholesome reading, free time is both cheerless and dangerous, whereas it could be spent in pleasant and dignified ways, or even used for their physical, intellectual, and moral development, in other words for their social emancipation.

    As an alternative to the cabaret and café-concert, we propose to establish our Popular Universities."

49. "The comedy Le Petite Verre condemns the error that consists in believing that drunkenness causes pleasure when in reality it leads to brutality and to melancholia. In both cases, it destroys the family. Alcoholism is an obstacle to any social organization; it is the greatest enemy of unions and cooperatives."

50. "Absinth leads to a moronic state or insanity."

51. "A union would serve to prevent you from living like wolves, from seeing each other as enemies, and when a neighbor is in need, to help him out and rather than abandoning him to his poverty, letting him leave his fields to rot and go die in the city. When we are united, our work is made easier. A union allows you to buy tools wholesale, and thus cheaper . . . If we were unionized, you would have a brand new plow today, we would jointly own a threshing machine, horses, and carts . . . We would finish our work earlier and have a little free time to rest, or to participate in activities other than drinking. People who drink don't have fun, they are depressed or brutal. Alcohol is a poison."

52. "Paradise! If we could do the same here, we would relieve some of the torpor that dulls the brains and hearts of our peasants. And to think that they are engaged in the most healthy, the most useful, the most elevated profession; they are masters of their fields, their crops, their bread, their life in short, and they continue to bow down like dejected slaves [. . .] They never rest, they live like savages, they don't enjoy each other's company, they don't know conversation, reading, or walking. Their only pleasure is a drop of alcohol that destroys what remains of their consciousness."

53. "The misery of the workers makes the fortune of the church."

54. "As long as priests reign in the countryside, drunkenness is sure to prosper; it is the weakness that prevents man from seeing clearly."

55. "According to Catholicism, everything is allowed. Owning slaves . . . Amassing a fortune thanks to the work of oppressed brothers . . . Being rich amidst paupers like Lazarus crawling under

the tables of the feast . . . Defending one's fortune through violence against those in need . . . Spending one's youth in debauchery, and then calling one such debauchery marriage with the benediction of the Church . . . killing to punish . . . killing during war . . ."

56. "the wisdom of human conscience, a morality based on goodness, a sociology of work": "We must develop the divine in each of us, the love of all mankind, thanks to the exercise of solidarity. Feeling oneself closely united to the immense whole, to the universal consciousness, that is man's happiness, the goal of all religions. Religion is the pursuit of the link that unites us with the universe."

57. "it is high time we abolished it."

58. "She'll have to give me some, my bourgeoise . . . and if she doesn't want to, I'll make her . . . I've got strong arms . . . I want my money . . . I am the master in my home . . . if she is stubborn . . . good God . . . they'll both get it . . . mother and daughter . . ."

59. "Women are made to keep house . . . they're made to obey . . . they can't reason . . . they aren't strong . . . they're good for nothing . . . I want my money . . . *Cantin tries again to calm him down but he keeps going*: Women . . . they're made to serve men . . . that's their duty . . . she's hiding my money . . . I know how to find it . . . otherwise I'll break her bones . . . she has no right to hold on to what's mine . . . nothing in this house is hers . . . everything belongs to the husband . . . I am the master."

60. "Aren't you ashamed of yourself? you, the militant, who came here to do propaganda. Nice propaganda [. . .] Does a socially conscious man let himself get dragged down like that! . . . It's fine for those who don't know how to read, or reason, or live . . . Does a man who loves his wife and his children let himself become debauched?"

61. "Excessive cruelty and abuse."

62. "Aren't you afraid of what will happen to you when you get married? A brutal husband who will beat you, a brood of children who will prevent you from sleeping at night; and working like a servant from dawn to dusk."

63. Han Ryner, *Jusqu'à l'âme* (Paris: Editions de l'Hexagramme, 1910). This play was republished in 1925 by the anarchist press L'Idée Libre who published Madeleine Pelletier's plays.

64. "Would you do me the honor of being a member of the committee of the Théâtre d'Idées? [. . .] It is important to me to have renowned feminists on the committee, your place is self-evident." Bibliothèque Historique de la Ville de Paris, Fonds Bouglé, correspondance Céline Renooz-Hélène Slatoff.

65. "I read with bewilderment the prospectus of the Théâtre d'Idées with the name of Mme *Slatoff* as founder. On the pretext that I did not declare the title of the theater that *I founded*, she has appropriated it." Bibliothèque Marguerite Durand, Dossier Véra Starkoff.

66. Tolstoy was opposed to the principle of literary property. He believed that writers should create their works for the people. This may explain Starkoff's reluctance to join the Société des Gens de Lettres until this point.

67. See Eric Bentley, *The Playwright as Thinker* (New York: Reynal & Hitchcock, 1946).

68. Bibliothèque Marguerite Durand, dossier Starkoff.

69. "Trotsky shows himself to be a disciple of the 'great writer of the Russian land'. He puts into practice the means of enlightening the people of a belligerent land recommended by the cantor of human consciousness. This means is to expose the lies of a belligerent government and to refuse to adapt to its doctrine. The Russian people will not take up the murderous gauntlet. They throw down with disdain the arms that the Kaiser wished to force upon the world and his cruel methods of war borrowed from a primitive age. The Russian people do not want to fight the German militarists with their own arms. For Tolstoy taught them that the falsity of the militaristic doctrine is precisely in the arms; to take them up is to consent to the doctrine . . . Refusing to fight was the only way according to him to resist such violence."

70. Archives Nationales, F7 13489 (Notes Russes), anonymous report dated July 7, 1920; Archives Nationales, Fond Société des Gens de Lettres, Dossier Véra Starkoff, several letters from 1916.

71. Archives Nationales, Fond Société des Gens de Lettres, Dossier Véra Starkoff.

72. "in honor of the liberation of the Russian people."
73. Véra Starkoff was herself a Freemason. She may also have written works about the Freemasons that were read in the lodges (Jupeau-Réquillard 159).
74. Archives de la Préfecture de Police, BA 1709 (Russie), Liste des Révolutionnaires Russes soumis à examens 1918.
75. Archives Nationales, F7 13489 (Notes Russes), anonymous report dated July 7, 1920; Archives Nationale, F7 13506 Le Bolchevisme dans le monde, Russes émigrés, Dossier Franc-maçonnerie et bolchevisme, "Liste de Franc-maçons Russes établie par une Organisation Anti-Bolchéviste," May 18, 1922.
76. "It is interesting to show how a writer of the quality of Véra Starkoff, whose ideas are so very different from those of the Bolsheviks, endeavors to understand the great communist transformation and to explain it within the context of the social and political history of Russia."
77. "communal owning of land" . . . "the universe of the countryside, in other words all peasants who work together . . . a sort of rustic parliament that governs and judges the affaires of the whole village."
78. "In the word *soviet* (council), like in that of *Mir* and *Obstchine*, there is the gravity of common thought, the meditation of the collective consciousness of the earth. In public affairs, the religious preoccupation with human consciousness, as defender of a free land, is particularly Russian. And if it is true that to each people corresponds a universal idea, that of the Russian people seems to be the liberation of the land."
79. "We can suppose that their success is due to their putting into practice certain maxims that were dear to Tolstoy, originating from popular wisdom. The Bolsheviks endeavored to really cooperate with the people."
80. "The Red terror and revolutionary militarism are delaying the era of communism."
81. "the wisdom of human conscience, a morality based on goodness, a sociology of work."
82. "Women working outside of the home leads to the moral destruction of the family."

Chapter Five   Braving the Law: Madeleine Pelletier

1. For comprehensive studies of Madeleine Pelletier, see Gordon F., *The Integral Feminist: Madeleine Pelletier, 1874–1939* (U of Minnesota P, 1990); Sowerine C. and Maignien C., *Madeleine Pelletier, une féministe dans l'arène politique* (Editions Ouvrières, 1992); and *Madeleine Pelletier (1874–1939): Logique et infortune d'un combat pour l'égalité*, edited by Christine Bard (Côté-femmes, 1992).
2. "Without further ado, let's go to the laboratory to look more closely at your idea about stimulating the brain through the skull."
3. Other pacifist plays by women: Séverine, *À Sainte-Hélène* (Paris: Girard & Brière [Bibliothèque pacifiste internationale], 1904); Marie-Thérèse Baer, *La Haine* (Paris: Lib. du Parti Socialiste et de L'Humanité, 1919); Marie Lenéru, *La Paix* (Paris: Grasset, 1922); see discussion of *La Paix* in chapter six.
4. "Take my life, go ahead, it's not worth much; I'm 40 years old and I've got tuberculosis, as you know. What do a few years more or less matter? If I had been taken in this horrible war, I might be dead by now. I just have to imagine we're not in a laboratory, but in a battle. You aren't Professor Bernard, you are my military commander, you are Napoleon, you are certainly his equal in genius . . . and you trust me with a mission from which one cannot return. I would have gone and I would be dead like so many others . . . For what? . . . War is an idiocy . . . Here I am certain to die for a worthy cause."
5. "You spent two years at the front, you participated in charges with a bayonet; you aren't sentimental. One murder more or less, what difference can that make? For it's the same thing, killing at war or killing here, it's always killing."

6. "a first rate scientist, a man of genius."
7. "[. . .] in other words, there is no genius without a trace of madness. The boss is certainly a genius; he is inevitably a little mad."
8. "of superior intelligence also, though less brilliant. A great character."
9. "It is unfortunate that we must make animals suffer in order to carry out our experiments. You may make fun of me; but I never perform vivisection without revulsion. [. . .] I ignore my heart, I control my nerves; but I never open up animals unless absolutely necessary. Whenever possible I give them chloroform and I avoid killing them when I can."
10. "Of course, I work too; doctor of science, doctor of medicine, and I'm now preparing for an important competitive exam; but, I also have a life; my wife, my children . . ."
11. "WAGNER: I'll bet you don't have enough time left for love.
    DELAGE: I don't have enough for marriage. Marriage restricts life by encumbering it with material concerns. Whereas, when you're unmarried you can limit to a minimum these mundane preoccupations: at the restaurant, I read the newspaper; at night, when I'm not sleeping, I read historical memoirs."
12. "Thank God we don't depend on you and the boss to increase the population."
13. "The Middle Ages had monks who, relieved of the burden of material life, dedicated themselves entirely to praying and studying in their convents. We are like monks in a way, with the advantages of living freely, without having to submit to rules written for inferiors."
14. "And if we are found out, think about it boss: it would be a terrible scandal. A trial, prison, the guillotine. . . ."
15. "maybe an honest man: a father whose children and wife are waiting for him at home."
16. "sublime murder": "a man who brings together scientific genius, a great character, and magnificent audacity, thus placing him above the laws and humanity."
17. "The law, morality are for ordinary men and circumstances."
18. "I may be hardhearted but, you must not delude yourself. This material reality that impresses you so much will slip away from you. To make a name for yourself you have to do research alone, you aren't capable of that: you will remain a mirror scholar. [. . .] Here a brilliant career is waiting for you."
19. "Even without the results, it wasn't a great loss."
20. "Doctoresse Pelletier: Mémoires d'une féministe," autobiographical manuscript, Fonds Bouglé, Bibliothèque Historique de la Ville de Paris.
21. She describes several in her book *Mon Voyage aventureux en Russie Communiste*. For example, a 17-year-old living on his own and working for the party since he had been thrown out by his family for having participated in a communist demonstration (18); the self-taught *ex-ouvrier* who had become the head of the communist party in a German town (27).
22. "Oh! To go away, to go away, flee forever this milieu that is not mine; in which nobody understands me, in which everybody despises me and hates me, I am not exaggerating. How can I have been born here? For, truly, I have nothing . . . nothing in common with them."
23. "When the couple becomes two friends united by love, marriage will be eliminated, couples will unite and separate at will; the state will be responsible for the children. Women and men with common ideas and tastes will get together."
24. "a poor worker's room" . . . "an intellectual's space."
25. "*Monsieur* thinks he's better than his boss, better than us; than everybody. He reads his books and nobody can hold a candle to him."
26. "the foul bourgeois society"
27. "Politics don't interest me . . . A few mediocre and arrogant men with the gift of the gab who fool the masses in order to walk all over them."
28. "in the same garbage pail. You are a hundred times right about the little parliamentary - parties. The politicians only want to protect their dough; they don't care about the ideas, that's obvious."

29. In a letter to Arria Ly dated October 19, 1911, Pelletier complains of a similar problem in feminist circles: "Tous les jeunes gens qui veulent arriver sont féministes, repoussés dans les partis politiques encombrés; ils viennent chez nous espérant être accueillis et poussés, et quand on leur fait assez de réclame ils nous lâchent avec la plus grande désinvolture." ["All the young men who wish to succeed are feminists, driven away from the crowded political parties; they come to us hoping to be welcomed and promoted, and when we have given them enough publicity, they abandon us in the most offhand manner."] Yet, in fact, Pelletier herself used various political parties in a similar way; when she failed to promote her ideas within one party, she did not hesitate to join another. Her allegiance was clearly to her own ideas and career.

30. See W. Scott Haine, *The World of the Paris Café: Sociability among the French Working Class, 1789–1914* (Johns Hopkins UP, 1996).

31. "For the first time, in any country, socialism is going beyond ideology to become reality, I think it would be a crime not to help it."

32. "harmful man."

33. "DUVAL: People are wrong to think that individual acts don't do any good. The murder of a government that the working class hates can trigger the revolution, especially now that Russia has set the example."

34. "In times of agitation, [propaganda by the deed] can be of utmost importance by condemning, for example, a situation that couldn't be resolved otherwise. [. . .] In order to be effective, the attack must target a specific goal at a specific time; changing a situation by eliminating the man who is responsible for it; intensifying a strike, an insurrectional movement by making the rift between the rebels and the government irreparable."

35. "I am a revolutionary in theory, but in practice I can hardly kill a flea [. . .] and I let spiders live."

36. "To advocate [propaganda by the deed] is not enough. And I find it cowardly to advise others to risk their skin while remaining quietly at home by the fire."

37. Pelletier, M. "Le Droit à l'avortement," in *L'Education féministe des filles et autres textes*, C. Maignien, ed. (Paris: Syros, 1978), 123–140.

38. For the history of the neo-Malthusian movement prior to 1901, see chapter three. For more information see Guerrand R.-H., *La Libre Maternité: 1896–1969* (Casterman, 1971) and Ronsin, F., *La Grève des ventres: Propagande néo-malthusienne et baisse de la natalité en France, 19e et 20e siècles* (Aubier [col Historique], 1980).

39. "Today we can safely say that there is not one woman, besides those who are sterile or virgins, who has not had an abortion at least once in her life." Letter to Arria Ly, February 14, 1933.

40. "Come to my house tonight, we'll talk and you'll see that there's no reason to kill yourself."

41. "What could I do? . . . get married . . . like my mother . . . A man who gets you pregnant once a year and beats you up when he's drunk! Well, in short, I finally gave in."

42. "He was a brutal man" . . . "got her pregnant: You know, after a month, nothing . . ."

43. "Children! You are a fool, you poor little thing. I am a serious militant; and you should know that an anarchist doesn't have children. Besides, what would I do with my children? I only earn enough to support myself and by my honor I'm not going to ask anything from a man."

44. "Like you, I will never marry, and it is probable that I will never have a lover because under the current conditions sexual relations belittle women who are married and demean those who aren't." Letter to Arria Ly, June 1908.

45. "[This solution] is simply the consequence of the unjust situation that women are in." Letter to Arria Ly, June 1908.

46. "a combative stance." Letter to Arria Ly, November 13, 1911.

47. "On the subject of virginity, I have practiced it throughout my life, but I think that it is only advisable in today's society in which there is no choice besides virginity and slavery. In a society based on sexual equality, women could enjoy the pleasures of love." Letter to Arria Ly, June 4, 1932.

48. "A married woman is never a good militant." Letter to Arria Ly, June 3, 1913.
49. "You are the son of workers; you should work like your parents. It is in work that you will find happiness and stability in life. Get married and have lots of children; the fatherland needs them . . ."
50. "Oh! the society, the foul society! There's nothing to be done but destroy it."
51. "The profession of an Apache, on the contrary, is full of pleasant surprises. First, you have to prepare the attacks; then there's the emotion at the moment of action, the intense joy when you succeed without getting caught; finally, after a good attack you can take some time off to have some fun."
52. "It wouldn't be bad . . . if we had some Apaches with a political consciousness in our revolutionary army. [. . .] To prepare for the revolution, to encourage the skirmishes that make the revolutionary education of the masses, we need people who are not afraid of committing illegal acts."
53. "I am sending him to Russia where his great mind will contribute to building the new world."

Chapter Six   Theater of Ideas: Marie Lenéru

1. Ironically, Lenéru is better known today for her personal *Journal*, which was published after her death in 1922.
2. While Chandler mentions plays by several other women dramatists, Lenéru is the only one whose plays he considers important enough to merit analysis, albeit brief (Chandler 216–217).
3. In fact, she complains constantly in her journal of not having enough occupations: "je ne cesse pas de m'ennuyer" (*Journal* 159). ["I am always bored."]
4. "I can only see two futures for me: a seat in the choir of a Benedictine abbey or one of the great talents who earn the title and glory of peerage."
5. "I am a woman, and even a young lady, and even a young bourgeois lady and finally I wrote a play! In these deplorable conditions, Sir, will you consent to read it? I know that young writers send you their manuscripts; I pray you, do not let the prejudice of underestimation that I so dread stop you; I'm sure if I were you, I would stick to it."
6. "Mademoiselle, your work is extremely remarkable and, in places, infinitely beautiful, lofty, poignant. I am full of admiration and joy."
7. "It is not enough to write a play, one has to have it accepted, and then staged."
8. "Why, when there are so many women novelists, do we see so few women playwrights?"
9. "You ask, my dear colleague, why so few women are playwrights? You should ask rather why there are so few women *whose plays are performed*. Indeed, numerous are the women who have drawers full of manuscripts of plays that have been refused—or not even submitted because they were sure of not being read—and they would be more numerous if they had any hope of success."
10. "Perhaps we should understand women's abstention as a simple retreat when faced with the difficulties in being performed."
11. Régis-Leroi then gives credit to the exceptional women who have recently been successful as playwrights: "Quelques noms brillent cependant aux côtés de celui de Marie Lenéru: Karen Bramson, Colette, Jeanne Landre, Jehanne d'Orliac, Tonia Navar, H. Charasson, Germaine Acremant, Marguerite Duterme, etc. et plus récemment, Marcelle Maurette . . ." ("Souvenirs des heures laborieuses"). ["Several other names stand out along with Marie Lenéru [. . .] and more recently, Marcelle Maurette . . ."]
12. "There is no self-respect that survives such a trial."

13. "It's enough to make one give up a hundred times over."
14. "I am too old to bear the fatigue." For more information about women playwrights before the twentieth century, see Cecilia Beach, ed., *French Women Playwrights before the Twentieth Century: A Checklist* (Westport, CT: Greenwood, 1994).
15. "It is however true that the manner of putting on a play sometimes resembles the manner in which corporals and sergeants train the recruits. A woman who has written a play and wishes to see it performed, in order to impose her views, is disoriented and intimidated. Moreover, the actors obey her less readily than a man, perhaps out of habit. They obeyed Sarah. But that was Sarah. Others have more trouble, even directors and they say it . . . This is how women playwrights confront material obstacles, for the production of their plays, that their male competition doesn't face."
16. "A woman would never dare, unless she were used to the theater milieu since her childhood. She would run away, horrified. One can write a novel at home . . . But can you see a peaceful bourgeois woman, a young lady of the high society back stage? Can you imagine Mme de Noailles, whose poetry is splendid, giving orders to a stage hand or talking to a prompter? Really . . ."
17. "In the theater world, it is tiresome to have to deal with a woman. The negotiations happen in a café over a beer and a pipe, the collaborations, during which people argue often violently, the rehearsals where everyone says *tu* (uses the familiar form of speech), that is not the place for an honest woman. No matter what a good sport she is, her presence bothers and disconcerts you."
18. See Frazer Banks Lively, "Rachilde and the French Symbolist Theatre, 1890–1897," Diss., U of Pittsburgh, 1998; and Rachilde, *Madame la Mort and other plays*, Kiki Gounaridou and Frazer Lively, trans. and ed. (Baltimore: Johns Hopkins UP, 1998). On the other hand, Melanie Hawthorne's article on Rachilde in the *Feminist Encyclopedia of French Literature* (Connecticut: Greenwood, 1999) makes no mention of her work in the theater. Linda Stilman catergorizes her as "romancière, dramaturge, journaliste." ["novelist, playright, journalist"] in *Dictionnaire littéraire des femmes de langue française*, but does not discuss her plays at all.
19. Frazer Lively, "Introduction," Rachilde, *Madame la Mort and other Plays* (Baltimore: Johns Hopkins UP 1998), 3–53; see also Frantisek Deak, *Symbolist Theater, The Formation of an Avant-Garde* (Baltimore: Johns Hopkins UP, 1993).
20. One of Rachilde's own plays, *Le Char d'Apollon*, was produced at the Théâtre Antoine in 1913.
21. Laure Adler, *Secrets d'alcôve. Histoire du couple 1830–1930* (Paris: Hachette, 1983), 196; Theodore Zeldin, *Histoire des passions françaises 1848–1945. I. Ambition et amour* (Paris: Seuil, 1980), 417.
22. "The question of divorce is in vogue; it's in all the newspapers, the main law and sociological reviews; it is a theme for playwrights, and it continues to be the basis for the majority of the literary works of our time."
23. "For twenty years, they made us feel sorry for the fate of the poor spouses bound by their miserable chains, vainly yearning for deliverance . . . Given the celerity with which so many liberated spouses sought to take advantage of their new-found freedom, it became more and more difficult to complain about the limited number of divorces. The theater moralists had to look for a theme that was less obviously contrary to reality. Little by little they were converted. As divorce became acceptable, the theater turned against it, no longer seeing anything but its inconvenience, injustice and cruelty."
24. "You are not a Cistercian, you are free . . . I cannot offer you the career that you have requested."
25. Marie Lenéru herself read this novel in 1899 and wrote in her journal on March 15: "J'ai lu *Le Lys rouge*: 'votre courage élégant.' Soit! ni révolte, ni vertu, un redressement gracieux" (*Journal* 162).
26. "Oh! I would have forgiven anything, anything. That you love her, that you succumbed . . . But this, this closeness, this community . . . There is nothing left for me to do but go away, go away."

27. "to show the insufficiency of the old morality, the uselessness of its system of persuasion."
28. "a man with no moral conscience at all."
29. "Are we cowards or heroes?"
30. "The public demands a thesis."
31. "THE ABBESS: What have you been learning?

    MARIE: Everything . . . and my catechism.

    THE ABBESS: Ah! And what do you prefer, everything, or the catechism?

    MARIE, *interested*: The *Theodicy*.

    MARTHE, *interrupting*: But she hasn't been reading that! she doesn't know what she's saying, or what it is!

    MARIE: I don't learn about it during my lessons, but I read it.

    MARTHE, *interrupting again*: She's babbling, and you intimidate her!

    THE ABBESS *smiling at Marie who is staring at her.* No, you can see she was telling me a secret. (*Following the girl's gaze when she looks away after a sign from her mother*). At your age, I read *The Uplifting of the Soul on the Mysteries.*

    MARTHE, *with conviction*: Ah! But I hope she won't enter a convent.

    THE ABBESS: She will be a well-educated and spiritual woman like Marie de Rabutin.

    MARTHE: She will be a normal woman. We don't ask for more!

    PHILIPPE: Excuse me! I can't see anything wrong with her being distinguished.

    MARTHE: Does she need to be distinguished to be happy? Am I a distinguished woman? And don't you love me as I am?"
32. "A man cannot live on that alone."
33. "Those who are as intelligent, as active, as serious as us should live like we do. I don't care whether you are a man, a woman, married or single."
34. "As soon as people knew I was seeing Curel, they spread a rumor about marriage. As for Blum, some people—true, it was our enemies—said worse things."
35. "I can't forget that it was poor Mendès, who, the first, with Mme Rachilde, read the play and believed in it. He certainly was right to call it a masterpiece! It's been many years since we heard something as good at the theater. In saying this, I am not letting myself be swayed by a personal preference. It was the unanimous impression of the audience, the whole audience, even though the play demanded serious concentration. The curtain was dropped to the most enthusiastic ovations I have even heard. After the performance was over, the same feeling of admiration was expressed by writers of the most different genres and tastes."
36. According to Mary Duclaux in the preface of the 1927 edition of *La Maison sur le Roc*, Lenéru showed this play to François de Curel in February 1911. It was, however, first published in 1924 in *La Revue Hebdomadaire* and it was probably never performed.
37. "Divorce is deplorable, even for those who benefit from it . . . I can't allow you to enter into this inferior and illegitimate marriage, this deceitful form of free love."
38. MARCEL: Tell her that you respect the Church, that you appreciate the rules and the Christian discipline, but that you do not believe . . .

    If you had the courage to say to your daughter: Believe if you wish, but at your risk and peril, and moreover, believe alone because, do not mistake me, I do not believe in God. I possess in my learned mind the invincible proof of the emptiness of the promises . . . I know, I speak and I convert; I preach and I impose yokes; I call for submission and sacrifices; because, in order to develop the earth, to tame it and impose order and stability, I have found nothing stronger, nothing more efficient, than this discipline and this tradition."
39. "One mustn't joke around about faith."
40. "Do you blame me my child? I don't know. I don't know anything anymore."
41. "If my divorce is such a crime against society, against my children, if it distresses a man like my father so terribly, then I prefer to give it up."
42. MARCEL: It is the attitude of your father, isn't it? his return to Catholicism, that's the cause of your crisis of conscience.

ALEXANDRA: How can I remain indifferent to what a man like my father respects most in the world?"

43. "That wouldn't have been the same thing! It would have been her father's money, or her grandfather's . . . it would have been a man's money."

44. "One doesn't repudiate one's husband yet."

45. SORRÈZE: I admit it, Claude, at first I was moved by the rival. I understood immediately that I wouldn't be at peace unless I loved you: That one is as good as me, and it's a woman. She is everything I am and people will soon see it. She is equal to me, therefore she cancels me out . . . What can I do? She is a woman, a woman that a man will love. She shatters the glory from my hands, she is dangerous, and a man will love her, will hold her in the intimate and tender contempt of love. She must be humiliated by me, she will get on her knees for me, because she is a woman and, no matter how great she is, I alone can give her her whole destiny [. . .] In a normal love relationship, the man must prevail over the woman."

46. "SORRÈZE: Claude is not only a great writer, she is very nearly a great man.

CLAUDE, *surprised*: How so?

SORRÈZE: I mean that the woman in you, the woman with her weaknesses and her narrowness, doesn't exist. (*Claude reacts physically*) Firm and upright, intelligent and strong, you are a man, Claude, a man made to be esteemed and admired."

47. "DENISE: But there's not enough air for two women in this house. Do I exist here? Who looks at me, who loves me? I arrive in the world, which owes me happiness, and I have all the rights of youth, and yet, I arrive too late, my place is taken . . . a woman has spoiled it for me in advance, under her dangerous tutelage I have lost everything . . . My mother is my rival."

48. "BERSIER: There comes a moment, my dear friend, when one's duty is to be a little less charming and a little more self-effacing.

CLAUDE: I'm not sure I understand what you are trying to tell me.

BERSIER: I mean that the best mother is one nobody notices . . . That is what your daughter lacks . . . . The child has understood better than you, with all your intelligence, the law that governs the generations, the mother is a woman who has abdicated."

49. "Spent two hours yesterday with Curel and Mme Duclaux; neither of them likes *La Triomphatrice* and, if I dare say so, neither understands it. Mme D . . . calls her 'that tigress.' To which I reply: 'But Madame, it is she that is devoured.'

My poor *Triomphatrice* is judged by my most benevolent friends as a 'hypertrophy of the ego.' Whereas the criticism that should be directed at me is for having made her too good and magnanimous, this woman who despises glory so passionately and who, in all her lines throughout the play, only wants her daughter and her lover."

50. "The real signification of *La Triomphatrice*, what was interesting to me, the signification that I find in the spirit of every scene and in every line, is simply this: A woman needs to love above herself, to love with adoration; by lifting herself up, she gives to the man the amorous task of dominating from above . . . I remain persuaded that a woman who is equal in intelligence, but even more if she is equal professionally, will suffer, will be uncomfortable, disappointed in her love to the point of renouncing it perhaps, if she is not dominated, or at the very least, equalled by the man she loves."

51. "Obviously a work that is organized has many points of view."

52. "She asks me to explain my play, which she doesn't understand well and when I give her an interpretation she says: 'Oh, so, that's what it's supposed to mean.' No, it's not supposed to mean anything in particular! My play doesn't need to be interpreted that way. Even I, while writing it, didn't think that way. It is important that my play not contain definitions and explanations in itself . . . A profound work is not a problem to be solved . . ."

53. This confusion between pacifism and defeatism was developed in a play by Marie-Thérèse Baer (or Gil-Baer), *La Haine* (Paris: Librairie du Parti Socialiste et de *L'Humanité*, 1919). Baer, a feminist pacifist, was certainly inspired by the trial of Hélène Brion, a schoolteacher brought to trial for the crime of defeatism in 1918. In Baer's play, a schoolteacher is accused of defeatism by the mother and grandfather of one of her students. She explains that though both her husband and son were

killed by the Germans, she does not hate the enemy, only the war. Marie-Thérèse Baer wrote two other feminist plays: *Oh! La Musique* (Paris: A. Lesot, 1928) and *Le Nom* (performed in 1930).

54. "The truth is that there has not been one war in Europe in the past 500 years that could not have been prevented by a small amount of brainpower of a few people."

55. "I no longer wish to write about anything except against the war, for one can only have an effect upon opinion."

56. "To those who have died for the fatherland I want to dedicate my greatest effort, my greatest work, a play of which I know nothing yet, except that it will be called *Peace* and that I am drawn to it, that I am preparing myself religiously, like for a vocation, for it must have an effect. I do not want to exploit the catastrophe as an artist. I want to bring to the stage of the most important French theater, the most powerful literary machine that even served the cause of peace. Since I have had the heartbreak of not being able to do my job as a woman to soothe your agonies, I will make sure that they no longer massacre you, 'my son and my soldier.' "

57. "The actions of today are yesterday's words. If today we are part of this atrocious war, it is because, until now, we have spoken about peace badly and insufficiently."

58. "I believe like Wells that it is by a formidable 'campaign of opinion, led by all means at our disposal: the press, books, theater,' and not by asides at congresses and committees, that we will bring on results. It is always the same law of success and the same error committed by literature: You want to succeed? *Do not create anything in the margins*, neither minor revues, nor little theaters, but rather seize for yourselves the true fortresses of public opinion."

59. See Introduction, *War Plays by Women. An International Anthology*, Claire M. Tylee, Elaine Turner, and Agnès Cardinal, eds. (New York: Routledge, 1999), 1.

60. "Women are first of all, at the moment, mothers, sisters, wives of soldiers. They are also nurses and knitters and anything that the extraordinary misery of the times requires them to be. But they are also something else: struck in the trenches and on the front, in all their hopes and their reasons to live, women do not fight back and, no matter how united they are with those who are in combat, how passionately attached to the vital struggle that maintains their country, they are still neither actors, nor only victims, but witnesses of the drama."

61. "For the day will finally come when our duty will no longer be to accept and be silent, but to judge and rebel."

62. "They were so happy to leave! . . . I remember, when going to the train station . . . It was so beautiful."

63. "Peace is a utopia! . . . There have always been wars and there will always be more . . . As long as men shall live, we won't be able to prevent them from attacking one another."

64. "PERRINE: Children? . . . I don't want any! (*in reaction to Marguerite's surprise*) Children, I know what becomes of them later. Oh no! I've seen enough . . .
    MARGUERITE: You are not being a good Frenchwoman, my daughter.
    PERRINE: Alright, I'll tell you the truth. I have made the sacrifice of my happiness in this world. And so that God may not allow that other people's children be killed again as long as I am alive, I have made the vow not to have any of my own (*in reaction to Marguerite's silence*). You don't think that's good, Madame?
    MARGUERITE: My dear child, if it were enough to sacrifice oneself . . . which of us would not give her life?
    PERRINE: So, what must we do?
    MARGUERITE *hard*: Nothing."

65. The refusal to have children was also a theme developed by radical feminists and neo-Malthusians like Nelly Roussel. In her play *Par la révolte*, Roussel advocates *la grève des ventres* as a means of revolt against the oppression of women. Roussel does not ask women to give up having sex; she only advises them to take precautions not to have children (see chapter three of present volume). On the other hand, an earlier play by Marie Desprès, *La Grève des femmes* (Paris: Albert Savine, 1895) is a rewriting of Aristophanes's *Lysistrata* in which the women refuse to have sexual relations until the government officially grants them equal rights. Madeleine Pelletier also encourages women to practice celibacy in her play *Supérieur!* (Conflans-St. Honorine: Editions de l'Idée Libre, 1923).

Here, an anarchist militant explains that a woman *must* take the necessary steps to remain child-free in order to devote herself to the ideological cause (see chapter five of present volume).

66. For two other plays by women that deal with maternal pacifism see Séverine, *À Sainte-Hélène* (Paris: Girard & Brière [Bibliothèque pacifiste internationale], 1904) and Marie-Thérèse Baer, *La Haine* (Paris: Librairie du Parti Socialiste et de *L'Humanité*, 1919).

67. "It's enough already just to have wanted to do something."

68. "The great leader, the most powerful voice in France . . ."

69. "It is certain that in the abject materialism of modern societies, only war transfigures the people, awakens sleeping virtues, and revives times of ideals and of beauty on this earth."

70. "It is your feminine heart that must be wrested from the war and passionately bequeathed to life and to peace."

71. "What a powerful man's brain was hiding behind the stern forehead of Marie Lenéru. Her last play . . . never at any moment resembled a feminine work."

72. "truth of observation, philosophical import, [and] passion" . . . "confused and wild imaginings: Nothing is more declamatory, false, and empty."

73. "Much more than in 1910, today's audience likes theater that is easily understood, that demands no effort. . . The public has lost interest in great subjects and debates on stage." See Recueil Factice about *Les Affranchis* in Collection Rondel at the Bibliothèque de l'Arsenal (Rf. 64468).

74. "The evolution of the theater has not, especially since the end of the war, been favorable to works as full of thought and, we must say, as haughtily severe as *Les Affranchis*. The audience wants less and less to meditate and more and more to be pleasantly entertained."

75. Very early in her career, before her first play was performed, Marcelle Maurette went to visit Marie Lenéru's mother "en hommage à la mémoire de la fille dont elle s'indigne que la place ne soit pas plus grande" (Becdelièvre 23). ["to pay homage to the memory of the daughter who she feels should have had more glory."] The director Lugné-Poë complimented Marcelle Maurette in the mid-1930s, saying she was the most talented playwright he had met since Marie Lenéru (Becdelièvre 42).

76. *Modern Drama by Women, 1880s–1930s, an International Anthology*, Katherine E. Kelly, ed. (New York: Routledge, 1996); *War Plays by Women. An International Anthology*, Claire M. Tylee, Elaine Turner, Agnès Cardinal, eds. (New York: Routledge, 1999).

77. Becker, however, downplays the importance of Lenéru's theater and claims arguably that it is above all her *Journal* that deserves particular interest. Marcelle Maurette does not appear at all in the *Dictionnaire littéraire des femmes de langue française* although her 13 published plays certainly meet the authors' stated criteria of a minimum of two published books. Given Makward's demonstrated interest in drama, this is probably simply one of the *lacunes* that are inevitable in this type of monumental reference work, rather than a case of genre-based bias. On the other hand, the criteria based on *publications*, may be unintentionally prejudicial against dramatic works, given the great number of plays that have been performed but not published.

Chapter Seven   Conclusion and Epilogue

1. "[The theater] is, in a way, the supreme forum for propaganda through which the opinion of the audience is definitively oriented toward new social and moral ideas." Harlor (1871–1980), pseudonym of Jeanne-Fernande-Clothilde-Désirée Perrot, daughter of feminist activist Amélie Hammer. See "Harlor," *Feminisms of the Belle Epoque* 73–84.

2. See *Au temps de l'anarchie, un théâtre de combat, 1880–1914* (Paris: Séguier Archimbaud, 2001).

3. An exception is Marianne—note the symbolic name—in Pelletier's *Supérieur!* Yet, Marianne is not a main character in the play and only appears in one scene.

4. Clive Barker, "Alternative Theatre/Political Theatre," *The Politics of Theatre and Drama*, Graham Holderness, ed. (New York: St. Martin's Press, 1992), 18–43. See also McCreery and Stourac, *Theatre as a Weapon* (London: RKP, 1986).

5. "The theater is our arm and our combat."

6. "As Secretary of the Group, she took care of the accounting, the sets, the purchasing . . . She was responsible for managing the troupe. Among other things, she collected here and there written texts by Jacques Prévert, dialogues, spoken choruses, and the entire immense production of the Préverts, Tchimoukow, Decomble, and so on."

7. In their introduction to *Theatre as a Weapon. Workers' Theatre in the Soviet Union, Germany and Britain, 1917–1934*, Richard Stourac and Kathleen McCreery lament the lack of documentation on workers' theater. They claim that part of the reason may be overt censorship but that other more covert processes are at work: "often persecution is not necessary. Just as women have been ignored by historians, so revolutionary working-class artists are swept under the carpet by the chroniclers of culture. They are the members of the dominated class and subject to the cultural domination, however subtle, which expresses and reinforces the rule of capital" (xiii). In his preface to *Au temps de l'anarchie*, political playwright Alain Badiou similarly criticizes the dominant bourgeois culture for having obscured French anarchist theater from memory: "les bourgeois français exigent aussi que toute l'intelligence de ce qui les combattit soit, dans la mesure du possible, interdite aux générations à venir. Ils donnent de l'Histoire leur propre version, moralisée, linéaire, inerte" (8). ["The French bourgeois ensure that any knowledge of what fought against them be, as much as possible, hidden from future generations. They create their own moralizing, linear, and inert version of history."]

8. The notion of "communion" is also related to the idea that people's theater should be a substitute for religion. See Bradby and McCormick 15–44.

9. Neel Doff, Rose Combe, and Henriette Valet are the only women among the 29 authors listed in Paul Loffler's "Lexique des écrivains," *Chronique de la littérature prolétarienne française de 1930 à 1939* (Rodez: Eds. Subervie, 1967). Léon Moussinac's Théâtre d'Action International, founded in 1932, was one example of a political theater for the people. Influenced by Piscator, Moussinac associated popular theater with political theater. Moussinac's goal was to introduce the French to foreign revolutionary plays with the hope of inspiring French authors to produce a similar type of dramatic literature. The Théâtre d'Action International performed plays by Hans Chlumberg, Ysevolod Ivanov, and Friedrich Wolf at the Bouffes-du-Nord, a theater in a working-class neighborhood of Paris, where Maxime Lisbonne had staged Louise Michel's *Nadine* in 1882. His audience, like Michel's, was comprised of both the working class and the Parisian intelligentsia. Unfortunately, like so many of these enterprises, Moussinac's theater failed financially after the third production (Knowles 298–299).

10. "an overwhelming majority of women playwrights" . . . "the artisans of a theatrical renovation." In *Minerva*, June 4, 1939.

11. "We see women authors growing in number and in audacity, if not in genius, take possession of the theater in Paris." René Aubert, "Où l'on voit les femmes-auteurs croissant en nombre et en audace sinon en génie prendre possession des théâtres de Paris," *Paris-Spectacles*, May 24, 1939.

12. Marie Antoinette, Manon Lescaut, Marie Stuart, Christine de Suède, Jeanne d'Arc, Eugénie l'Impératrice, Thérèse Raquin, Anna Karenina, and the Russian princess, Anastasia.

13. An association founded by four theater directors: Baty, Dullin, Jouvet, and Pitoëff.

14. *Manon Lescaut*, an adaption of l'abbé Prévost's novel in 1939, a historical drama about *Marie Stuart* in 1941, and a play about *les montres sacrés* called *Neiges* in 1949.

15. Quoted in the full-page advertisement for the play in the *New York Times*, January 3, 1955. *Anastasia* was the play that gained Marcelle Maurette international renown. It was performed first in London by Lawrence Olivier and Vivian Leigh and, in the following year, at the Lyceum Theater on Broadway. Both productions were extremely successful: Marcelle Maurette was invited to appear before the Queen; the Broadway production was sold out six months in advance and continued much longer than its original engagement; and 20th Century Fox outbid both Warner and Metro-Goldwyn to buy the rights for the film version, which would feature Ingrid Bergman and Yul Brynner. More recently, her play was used as the base for the 1997 animated film *Anastasia* produced by Fox.

16. See Joseph Chiari, *The Contemporary French Theatre: The Flight from Naturalism* (London: Rockliff [ca. 1958]).

17. "Women take the stage to talk about themselves, their lives, their daily work, to come out of the confinement and silence in which they have been shut up for so long. They want to communicate with each other, have men hear a new discourse, break taboos, and attempt to express the unsaid that has been repressed for so long."

18. "The urgency of showing, saying what each woman thought to herself or repressed into the depths of her subconscious: the weariness of being shut away, the daily sexism, her dependence on others, the learned lack of power, the constant waiting, the trap of maternity, the dread of time passing and leaving her empty-handed, the guilt that sets in when she follows her desires, the painful alternative between being normal and letting loose the imaginary that can lead to madness. The urgency of condemning the incomprehension and the egoism of her companion, the fear of solitude, but also of talking about friendship, solidarity between women, change, talking about tomorrow in a language that is simple, without sounding triumphant, of preparing subversion in everyday life."

19. "A theater of intervention in the profound sense of the term, for it incites each of us not to submit, but to dare to imagine life otherwise."

Bibliography

A. Plays Cited

Baer, Marie-Thérèse. *La Haine*. Paris: Librairie du Parti Socialiste et de *L'Humanité*, 1919.

———. *Oh! La Musique*. Paris: A. Lesot, 1928.

Deraismes, Maria. *Le Père coupable*. Paris: Amyot, 1862.

———. *A bon chat bon rat*. Paris: Amyot, 1862.

Desprès, Marie. *La Grève des femmes*. Paris: Albert Savine, 1895.

Lenéru, Marie. *Les Affranchis*. Paris: Hachette, 1910; *Modern Drama by Women, 1880s–1930s, An International Anthology*. Ed. Katherine E. Kelly. Trans. Melanie C. Hawthorne. New York: Routledge, 1996. 147–150.

———. *Le Bonheur des autres*. Paris: Bloud & Gay, 1925.

———. *La Maison sur le roc*. Paris: Plon, 1927.

———. "La Paix." *Annales Politiques et Littéraires* 1973 (April 17, 1921): 323–326; 1974 (April 24, 1921): 337–341; 1975 (May 1, 1921): 369–373; 1976 (May 8, 1921): 389–391. Paris: Grasset, 1922; *War Plays by Women. An International Anthology*. Ed. Claire M. Tylee, Elaine Turner, Agnès Cardinal. Trans. Claire Tylee. New York: Routledge, 1999. 46–80.

———. *Pièces de Théâtre*. Contains "Les Lutteurs" and "La Triomphatrice." Paris: Figuière, 1928.

———. *Le Redoutable*. Paris: Hachette, 1912.

Maurette, Marcelle. *Anastasia*. Paris: Buchet-Chastel, 1957.

———. *Madame Capet*. Paris: Albin Michel, 1938.

———. *Manon Lescaut*. Paris: Fayard, 1919.

Michel, Louise. *Le Coq rouge*. Paris: Edinger, 1888; *Au temps de l'anarchie, un théâtre de combat 1880–1914*. Vol. II. Paris: Séguier Archimbaud, 2001. 85–136; Ms. International Institute of Social History, Coll. Descaves, pf. 62, Comm. 7.

———. "La Grève." *Au temps de l'anarchie, un théâtre de combat 1880–1914*. Vol. II. Paris: Séguier Archimbaud, 2001. 137–195; Ms. F^{18}1321, Archives Nationales, Paris.

———. "Nadine." *Au temps de l'anarchie, un théâtre de combat 1880–1914*. Vol. II. Paris: Séguier Archimbaud, 2001. 11–84; Ms. F^{18}1167^A, Archives Nationales, Paris.

Neis, Jeanne. "La Lame Sourde." *La Grande Revue* 119 (January 1926) 394–407 (February 1926): 582–592; 120 (March 1926): 91–104.

Pelletier, Madeleine. *In anima vili, ou un crime scientifique*. Conflans-St.-Honorine: Editions de l'Idée Libre, 1920.

———. *Supérieur!* Conflans-St.-Honorine: Editions de l'Idée Libre, 1923.

Rachilde. "Le Char d'Apollon." *Comœdia* December 11, 1913: 2.

———. *Madame la Mort and Other Plays*. Trans and ed. Kiki Gounaridou and Frazer Lively. Baltimore: Johns Hopkins UP, 1998.

Roussel, Nelly. "La Faute d'Eve." *Le Mouvement féministe* 4 (September 15, 1913): 21–22; *La Libre Pensée Internationale* (June 1, 1916) 4; *Au temps de l'anarchie, un théâtre de combat 1880–1914*. Vol. I. Paris: Séguier Archimbaud, 2001. 373–383.

———. *Par la révolte*. Paris: Impr. L. et A. Cresson, n.d.; *Au temps de l'anarchie, un théâtre de combat 1880–1914*. Vol. I. Paris: Séguier Archimbaud, 2001. 345–358.

———. *Pourquoi elles vont à l'église*. Paris: N. Roussel [ca. 1910]; *La Libre Pensée Internationale* January 1, 1916; *Au temps de l'anarchie, un théâtre de combat 1880–1914*. Vol. I. Paris: Séguier Archimbaud, 2001. 359–372.

Reynolds, Berthe. *Les Moutons noirs*. Paris: E. Figuière, 1911.

Séverine. *À Sainte-Hélène*. Paris: Girard & Brière (Bibliothèque pacifiste internationale), 1904.

Starkoff, Véra. *L'Amour libre*. Paris: P.V. Stock, 1902; *Au temps de l'anarchie, un théâtre de combat 1880–1914*. Vol. I. Paris: Séguier Archimbaud, 2001. 289–312.

———. *L'Issue*. Paris: P.V. Stock, 1903; *Au temps de l'anarchie, un théâtre de combat 1880–1914*. Vol. I. Paris: Séguier Archimbaud, 2001. 313–340.

———. *Le Petit Verre*. Paris: P.V. Stock, 1904.

B. Historical Background

Adler, Laure. *Secrets d'alcôve. Histoire du couple 1830–1930*. Paris: Hachette, 1983.

Albistur, Maïté and Daniel Armogathe. *Histoire du féminisme français*. Paris: des femmes, 1977.

Ariès, Philippe. *Histoire des populations françaises*. Paris: Seuil, 1971.

Bard, Christine. *Les Filles de Marianne. Histoire des féminismes 1914–1940*. Paris: Fayard, 1995.

Bernard, Philippe. *La Fin du monde: 1914–1929*. Paris: Seuil, 1975.

Burnet-Vigniel, Marie-Claude. *Femmes russes dans le combat révolutionnaire*. Paris: Institut d'études slaves, 1990.

Cerf, Marcel. *Le d'Artagnan de la Commune (Le Colonel Maxime Lisbonne)*. Bienne Suisse: Ed. du Panorama, 1967.

Dépinay, J. *Le Divorce—le sort des enfants*. Paris: Marchal et Billard, 1903.

Dubief, Henri. *Le Déclin de la IIIe République: 1929–1938*. Paris: Seuil, 1976.

Duby, Georges and Michelle Perrot, eds. *Histoire des femmes*. 4 vols. Paris: Plon, 1992.

Edie, James M., James P. Scanlan, Mary-Barbara Zeldin, eds. *Russian Philosophy*. Chicago: Quadrangle Books, 1965.

Gautier, Xavier. *Naissance d'une liberté. Contraception, avortement: le grand combat des femmes au XXe siècle*. Paris: Robert Laffont, 2002.

Grave, Jean. *La Société Future*. Paris: Stock, 1895.

Guerrand, Roger-Henri. *La Libre Maternité: 1896–1969*. Paris: Casterman, 1971.

Haine, W. Scott. *The World of the Paris Café: Sociability among the French Working Class, 1789–1914*. Baltimore: Johns Hopkins UP, 1996.

Hillyar, Anna and Jane McDermid. *Revolutionary Women in Russia 1870–1917*. Manchester: Manchester UP, 2000.

"Historique de l'émigration." Ms. Archives Nationales. Dossier "Les Réfugiés révolutionnaires russes à Paris." F7 12894 (1907).

Horne, Alistair. *The Fall of Paris: The Siege and the Commune 1870–1871*. London: Papermac, 1997.

Jupeau-Réquillard, Françoise. *L'Initiation des femmes*. Paris: Editions du Rocher, 2000.

Kelly, Aileen. *Mikhail Bakunin: A Study in the Psychology and Politics of Utopianism.* Oxford: Clarendon P, 1982.

Kropotkin, P. *Memoirs of a Revolutionist.* Boston: Houghton Mifflin, 1899.

Lalouette, Jacqueline. *La Libre pensée en France, 1848–1940.* Paris: Albin Michel, 1997.

Maitron, Jean, ed. *Dictionnaire Biographique du Mouvement ouvrier français.* Paris: Ed. Ouvrières, 1992.

Maitron, Jean. *Le Mouvement anarchiste en France.* Paris: F. Maspero, 1975.

Malato, Charles. *Les Joyeusetés de l'exil.* Paris: Stock, 1897.

Mercier, Lucien. "Les Universités populaires en France et le mouvement ouvrier, 1899–1914." Diss. U de Paris I, 1979.

———. *Les Université Populaires: 1899–1914. Education populaire et mouvement ouvrier au début du siècle.* Paris: Ed. Ouvrières, 1986.

Nahoum-Grappe, Véronique. "France." *International Handbook on Alcohol and Culture.* Ed. Dwight B. Heath. Westport, CT: Greenwood, 1995. 75–87.

Naimark, Norman M. *Terrorists and Social Democrats. The Russian Revolutionary Movement Under Alexander III.* Cambridge: Harvard UP, 1983.

Nataf, André. *La Vie quotidienne des anarchistes en France: 1880–1910.* Paris: Hachette, 1986.

Patsouras, Louis. *Jean Grave and the Anarchist Tradition in France.* Middletown NJ: Caslon Co., 1995.

Prestwich, Patricia E. *Drink and the Politics of Social Reform: Antialcoholism in France since 1870.* Palo Alto, CA: The Society for the Promotion of Science and Scholarship, 1988.

Quail, John. *The Slow Burning Fuse.* London: Paladin, 1978.

Ronsin, Francis. *La Grève des ventres: Propagande néo-malthusienne et baisse de la natalité en France, 19e et 20e siècles.* Paris: Aubier (col. Historique), 1980.

Roulleau-Berger, Laurence. "Les Intellectuels dans un mouvement social et culturel: Les Universités Populaires (1880–1914)." Diss. Université de Lyon II, 1982.

Shatz, Marshall S. *Jan Waclaw Machajski: A Radical Critic of the Russian Intelligentia.* U of Pittsburg P, 1989.

Sonn, Richard D. *Anarchism.* New York: Twayne, 1992.

———. *Anarchism and Cultural Politics in Fin de Siècle France.* Lincoln: U of Nebraska P, 1989.

Sowerine, Charles. *Les Femmes et le socialisme.* Paris: Presses de la Fondation nationale des Sciences politiques: 1978.

"Union Fraternelle des Femmes." *La Française* February 11, 1912.

Université Populaire. Bulletin de la Fédération Nationale des Universités Populaires. August 1910.

Varias, Alexander. *Paris and the Anarchists: Aesthetes and Subversives during the Fin de Siècle.* New York: St. Martin's P, 1996.

Waelti-Walters, Jennifer and Steven C. Hause, eds. *Feminisms of the Belle Epoque. A Historical and Literary Anthology.* Lincoln: U of Nebraska P, 1994.

Wandycz, Piotr S. *The Lands of Partitioned Poland, 1795–1918.* Seattle: U of Washington P, 1974.

Weir, David. *Anarchy and Culture: The Aesthetic Politics of Modernism.* Amherst: U Mass P, 1997.

Zeldin, Theodore. *Histoire des passions françaises 1848–1945. I. Ambition et amour.* Paris: Seuil, 1980.

Zimmerman, Judith E. *Mid-Passage: Alexander Herzen and European Revolution, 1847–1852.* Pittsburgh: U of Pittsburgh P, 1989.

C. History of Theater

Alla, M. "Projet de Théâtre populaire." *Revue d'Art dramatique* Tome XI (1901): 348–353, 438–439, 501–503, 548–551.

L'Almanach féministe. Paris: E. Cornély, 1899–1900.

"L'Art Social." *L'Art Social* November 1891: 1.

Asholt, Wolfgang. "*Les Mauvais Bergers* et le théâtre anarchiste des années 1890." *Octave Mirbeau: Actes du colloque international d'Angers, 19–22 sept. 1991.* Angers: Presses Universitaires d'Angers, 1992.

Barker, Clive. "Alternative Theatre/Political Theatre." *The Politics of Theatre and Drama.* Ed. Graham Holderness. New York: St. Martin's P, 1992. 18–43.

Bentley, Eric. *The Playwright as Thinker.* New York: Reynal & Hitchcock, 1946.

Bernard, Lucien. "Le théâtre populaire en 1900." *Revue d'Art dramatique,* Tome XI (January 1901): 26–28.

Berny, E. "Théâtre Populaire de Belleville." *Revue d'Art dramatique,* Tome XIII (June 1902): 200–203.

Blanchard, Paul. *Firmin Gémier.* Paris: L'Arche, 1954.

Bourgin, Georges and Gabriel Henriot, eds. *Procès-verbaux de la Commune de Paris.* Paris: Lahure, 1945.

Bracco, Pierre-Paul. "Le théâtre populaire en 1900: étude du théâtre populaire en France de 1895 à 1905." Diss. U de Nice, 1979.

Bradby, David. *Le Théâtre Français Contemporain: 1940–1980.* Cambridge: Cambridge UP, 1984. Trad. Georges and Françoise Dottin. Lille: Presses Universitaires de Lille, 1990.

Bradby, David, Louise James, and Bernard Sharrat, eds. *Performance and Politics in Popular Drama.* Cambridge: Cambridge UP, 1980.

Bradby, David and John McCormick. *People's Theatre.* London: Croom Helm, 1978.

Brustein, Robert. *The Theatre of Revolt.* Boston: Little Brown, 1962.

Bulletin des Universités Populaires 1 (March 15, 1900).

Chandler, Frank Wadleigh. *The Contemporary Drama of France.* Boston: Little, Brown and Co., 1920.

Chiari, Joseph. *The Contemporary French Theatre: The Flight from Naturalism.* London: Rockliff [ca. 1958].

Congrès des U.P. mai 1904. Paris: Cahiers de la Quinzaine, 1904.

Correspondance. Octave Mirbeau-Jean Grave. Ed. Pierre Michel. Paris: Ed. du Fourneau, 1994.

Corvin, Michel. *Dictionnaire encyclopédique du théâtre.* Paris: Bordas, 1991.

Dargel, Henri. "Le théâtre du peuple à la Coopération des Idées." *Revue d'art dramatique* (April 1903): 114–130.

Deak, Frantisek. *Symbolist Theater. The Formation of an Avant-Garde.* Baltimore: Johns Hopkins UP, 1993.

Doumic, René. *Le Théâtre nouveau.* Pairs: Perrin et Cie, 1908.

Durand, Xavier. "L'Art social au théâtre: deux expériences (1893, 1897)." *Le Mouvement Social* (April–June 1975): 13–33.

Ebstein, Jonny, John Hughes, Philippe Ivernel, Monique Surel-Tupin, eds. *Le Théâtre de contestation sociale autour de 1900.* Paris: Publisud, 1991.

Ebstein, Jonny, Philippe Ivernel, Monique Surel-Tupin, and Sylvie Thomas, eds. *Au temps de l'anarchie, un théâtre de combat, 1880–1914.* Paris: Séguier Archimbaud, 2001.

Esslin, Martin. *Brecht. The Man and His Work.* New York: Doubleday, 1971.

Faure, Sébastien. "La Fête de 'l'Action.' " *L'Action* August 23, 1905.

Figes, Eva. *Tragedy and Social Evolution.* New York: Persea Books, 1976.

Goldman, Emma. *The Social Significance of Modern Drama.* New York: Applause Theatre Book Publishers, 1987 (first published in 1914).

Gray, Ronald. *Brecht: The Dramatist.* Cambridge: Cambridge UP, 1976.

Hamilo, Ludovic. "Le théâtre d'Art Social." *L'Art Social* (April 1893): 129–132.

Hemmings, F. W. J. *Theatre and State in France, 1760–1905.* Cambridge: Cambridge UP, 1994.

Holderness, Graham, ed. *The Politics of Theatre and Drama.* New York: St. Martin's P, 1992.

Jomaron, Jacqueline de, ed. *Le Théâtre en France.* 2 vols. Paris: Armand Colin, 1989.

Kahn, Maurice. "Causerie sur 'Liberté.' " *Cahiers de la quinzaine,* vol. 27 (September 13, 1904): 140–147.

Knapp, Bettina. *Louis Jouvet, Man of the Theater*. New York: Columbia UP, 1957.

Knowles, Dorothy. *French Drama of the Inter-War Years 1918–39*. New York: Barnes and Noble, 1967.

Krakovitch, Odile. "Preface." *Ce que veulent les femmes: Articles et discours et de 1869 à 1894* by Maria Deraismes. Paris: Syros, 1980.

————. *Hugo censuré: La Liberté au théâtre au XIXe siècle*. Paris: Calmann-Lévy, 1985.

Labarthe, Gustave. *Le Théâtre pendant les Jours du Siège et de la Commune*. Paris: Fischbacher, 1910.

Linert, August. "Le Socialisme au théâtre: Notes de critique de d'art." *L'Art Social* (January 1892): 59–62.

Loffler, Paul A. *Chronique de la littérature prolétarienne française de 1930 à 1939*. Rodez: Edictions Subervie, 1967.

————. *Chronique de l'association des écrivains et des artistes révolutionnaires (Le mouvement littéraire progressiste en France) 1930–1939*. Rodez: Editions Subervie, 1971.

Lumet, Louis. "Le Théâtre Civique." *Revue d'Art dramatique*, Tome V (October–December 1898): 118–121.

Michelet, Jules. *L'Etudiant. Cours de 1847–1848*. Paris: Calmann Lévy, 1977.

Miller, Judith Graves. *Theater and Revolution in France since 1968*. Lexington Kentucky: French Forum, 1977.

Morel, Eugène. "Discours pour l'ouverture d'un théâtre populaire." *Revue d'Art dramatique*, Tome XIII (October 1903): 277–287.

————. "Projet de Théâtres populaires." *Revue d'Art dramatique*, Tome X (December 1900): 1114–1188.

Pottecher, Maurice. "Le Théâtre populaire à Paris." *Revue d'Art dramatique*, Tome VII (September 1899): 401–423.

Poulet, Jacques. "Introduction au théâtre populaire." *La Nouvelle Critique* no. 65 (June–July 1973): 25–34.

Reszler, André. *L'Esthétique anarchiste*. Paris: Presses Universitaires de France, 1973.

Rolland, Romain. *Le Théâtre du Peuple*. Paris: Hachette, 1913.

Rothen, Edouard. "Théâtre." *Encyclopédie anarchiste*, vol. 4. Paris: Librairie internationale, [1934]: 2757–2769.

Slonim, Marc. *Russian Theater from the Empire to the Soviets*. New York: The World Publishing Company, 1961.

Spitzer, Susan Jane. *Jacques Prévert and the Groupe Octobre (1932–1936)*. Diss. Brown U, 1975.

Stourac, Richard and Kathleen McCreery. *Theatre as a Weapon. Workers' Theatre in the Soviet Union, Germany and Britain, 1917–1934*. London and New York: Routledge & Kegan Paul, 1986.

Szanto, George H. *Theater and Propaganda*. Austin: U of Texas P, 1978.

Taylor, Diana. *Theatre of Crisis: Drama and Politics in Latin America*. U of Kentucky P, 1991.

"Universités Populaires." *Comœdia* December 24, 1907: 5.

D. Women's Theater/Feminist Theater

Albert-Dulac, Germaine. "Figures d'aujourd'hui et d'autrefois: Madame Marya Cheliga." *La Française* August 4, 1907: 1–2.

Aubert, René. "Où l'on voit les femmes-auteurs croissant en nombre et en audace sinon en génie prendre possession des théâtres de Paris." *Paris-Spectacles* May 24, 1939: 1.

Barlow, Judith E., ed. and intro. *Plays by American Women, 1900–1930*. New York: Applause, 1985.

Beach, Cecilia. "De la maternité au matriciel: la représentation du maternel dans les œuvres modernes de femmes dramaturges françaises." Diss. New York U, 1993.

————, comp. *French Women Playwrights before the Twentieth century: A Checklist.* Connecticut: Greenwood P, 1994.

————, comp. *French Women Playwrights of the Twentieth Century: A Checklist.* Connecticut: Greenwood P, 1996.

Blum, Léon. "Le Féminisme au théâtre." *Comœdia* January 29, 1913: 2.

Cheliga, Marya. "Le Théâtre féministe." *Revue d'Art dramatique,* Tome XI (October 1901): 650–658.

Chevalley, Sylvie. "Les femmes auteurs dramatiques de la Comédie-française." *Europe* n. 427/428 (November–December 1964): 41–47.

Grey, Germaine. "Quand les femmes se jettent dans la mêlée théâtrale." *Minerva* June 4, 1939.

Harlor. "La Femme dans le théâtre de demain." *Revue d'Art dramatique,* Tome XI (October 1901): 682–688.

Kelly, Katherine E., ed. *Modern Drama by Women, 1880s–1930s, An International Anthology.* New York: Routledge, 1996.

Lamar, Celita. *Our Voices, Ourselves. Women Writing for the French Theater.* New York: Peter Lang, 1991.

Lively, Frazer. Introduction. *Madame la Mort and Other Plays* by Rachilde. Baltimore: Johns Hopkins UP, 1998. 3–53.

————. "Rachilde and the French Symbolist Theatre, 1890–1897." Diss. U of Pittsburgh, 1998.

Makward, Christiane and Madeleine Cottenet-Hage, eds. *Dictionnaire littéraire des femmes de langue française.* Paris: Karthala, 1996.

Makward, Christiane P. and Judith Miller, eds. and trans. *Plays by French and Francophone Women: A Critical Anthology.* Ann Arbor: U of Michigan P, 1994.

Marnière, J. "Les Premières: La Bodinière, Théâtre Féministe International." *La Fronde* February 4, 1898: 3.

————. "Les premières: Théâtre Féministe." *La Fronde* January 10, 1898: 2–3.

Mille, Pierre. "Pourquoi les femmes-auteurs n'ont-elles jamais réussi au théâtre?" n.p. July 21, 1924. Bibliothèque Marguerite Durand, Dossier Femmes dramaturges.

Millstone, Amy Blythe. "Feminist Theatre in France: 1870–1914." Diss. U of Wisconsin-Madison, 1977.

Montmartre, Jean de. "Le Droit du mari." n.p. (February 2, 1896). Bibliothèque Marguerite Durand. Dossier Marya Cheliga.

Moss, Jane. "Women's Theater in France." *Signs,* 12.3 (1987): 548–67.

Noonan, Mary. "Voicing the Feminine: French Women Playwrights of the Twentieth Century." *A History of Women's Writing in France.* Ed. Sonya Stephens. Cambridge: Cambridge UP, 2000. 220–235.

"Notre enquête." *Le Cri de Paris.* September 7, 1924: 10; September 14, 1924: 10; September 21, 1924: 9; September 28, 1924: 10.

Plays by Women: An International Anthology. 3 vols. New York: UBU Repertory Theater Publications, 1988–1996.

Sartori, Eva Martin, ed. *Feminist Encyclopedia of French Literature.* Westport, CT: Greenwood P, 1999.

Séché, Alphonse and J. Bertaut. "Les Femmes auteurs dramatiques." *Revue Politique et Littéraire (Revue Bleue),* II (1904): 413–416, 445–448.

Sullivan, Victoria and James Hatch, eds. *Plays by and about Women.* New York: Vintage Books, 1973.

Surel-Tupin, Monique. "Les Femmes et le théâtre d'intervention depuis 1980." *Théâtre/Public,* 61 (1985): 32–33.

————. "La Prise de parole des femmes au théâtre." *Théâtre Recherche—Le théâtre d'intervention depuis 1968,* Tome II. Lausanne: L'Âge d'homme, 1983. 56–78.

Tylee, Claire M., Elaine Turner and Agnès Cardinal, eds. *War Plays by Women. An International Anthology.* New York: Routledge, 1999.

1. Louise Michel

Gullickson, Gay L. *Unruly Women of Paris: Images of the Commune.* Ithaca: Cornell UP, 1996.

"The International School." Prospectus. British Library: 8305.f.27 (4).

La Fournière, Xavier de. *Louise Michel: matricule 2182.* Paris: Perrin, 1986.

Michel, Louise. *Matricule 2182. "Souvenirs de ma vie" par Louise Michel (extraits).* Paris: Dauphin, 1981.

———. *Mémoires.* Arles: Sulliver, 1997.

———. *Souvenirs et aventures de ma vie.* Ed. Daniel Armogathe. Paris: La Découverte/Maspero, 1983.

Mullany, Marie Marmo. "The Female Revolutionary, the Woman Question, and European Socialism: 1871–1921." Diss. Rutgers, 1980.

———. "Sexual Politics in the Career and Legend of Louise Michel." *Signs,* 15.2 (Winter 1990): 300–322.

Sizaire, Anne. *Louise Michel: L'Absolu de la générosité.* Paris: Desclée de Brouwer, 1995.

Stivale, Charles J. "Louise Michel's Poetry of Existence and Revolt." *Tulsa Studies on Women's Literature,* 5.1 (Spring 1986): 41–61.

Suvin, Darko. "Politics, Performance and The Organisational Mediation: The Paris Commune Theatre Law." *To Brecht and Beyond. Soundings in Modern Dramaturgy.* Sussex: Harvester Press Limited, 1984. 83–111.

Thomas, Edith. *Les "Pétroleuses."* Paris: Gallimard, 1963.

a. Reviews of Performances of Louise Michel's Plays

Nadine

Benjamin, Edmond. "Les Premières de la semaine." *Revue Théâtrale* 14: 17 (1882) 2.

Fauchery. "Les Premières." *L'Intransigeant* May 1, 1882: 2.

Philinte. "Courrier des théâtres." *Le Drapeau National* May 9, 1882: 4.

Richepin, Jean. "Les Premières." *Le Gaulois* April 30, 1882: 3.

Sarcey, Francisque. "Chronique théâtrale." *Le Temps* May 1, 1882: 2–3.

"Spectacles et concerts." *Le Temps* June 8, 1882: 3.

Un Monsieur de l'Orchestre. "La Soirée Théâtrale. La Première de Mlle Louise Michel" *Le Figaro* April 30, 1882: 3.

Wolff, Albert. "Courrier de Paris." *Le Figaro* May 4, 1882: 1

Le Coq Rouge

Chincholle, Charles. "Le Coq rouge." *Le Figaro* May 20, 1888: 3.

" 'Le Coq Rouge': Conversation avec Mlle Louise Michel." n.p. September 17, 1888. Archives de la Préfecture de Police, BA 1187.

Fauchery. "Premières représentations." *L'Intransigeant* May 21, 1888: 2.

Le Voltaire. May 21, 1888.

Martel, Charles. "La Soirée d'hier." *La Justice* May 20, 1888: 3.

La Grève

Larcher, Claude. "Une première au Théâtre de la Villette." *Le Gaulois* December 6, 1890: 3.

Pouget, Emile. "Au théâtre!" *Le Père Peinard* December 14, 1890: 15.

2. Nelly Roussel

Bodin, Louise. "Une école de propagandistes pour les femmes." *L'Humanité* December 23, 1920: 1.

"Conférences de Mme Nelly-Roussel." *Le Petit Méridional* April 3, 1904: 3.

"Dans la 19ᵉ arrondissement." *Le Rappel* October 13, 1903.

"La Fête de l''Action'." *L'Action* August 23, 1905: 1.

Flammèche. "Dénouements." *L'Action* September 9, 1905: 1.

Godet, Henri. "Nelly Roussel, Souvenirs." *La Mère Educatrice* 6ᵉ année, no. 11 (November 1923): 147–148.

Maignien, Claude and Magda Safwan. "Deux Féministes: Nelly-Roussel, Madeleine Pelletier, 1900–1925." Mémoire de Maîtrise, Université de Paris VII, 1975.

Marbel (ps. Marguerite Belmant). "L'Apothéose de la femme, Nelly Roussel." *Le Féminisme intégral* 1: 9 (December 1913): 2; *La Mère Educatrice* 6ᵉ année, no. 11 (November 1923): 153.

———. "Les femmes d'aujourd'hui: Nelly Roussel." Ms. Bibliothèque Marguerite Durand, Dossier Nelly Roussel.

"Nelly Roussel." Special issue of *La Mère Educatrice* 6ᵉ année, no. 11 (November 1923).

Roussel, Nelly. "Eclaircissements." *L'Action* September 16, 1905: 1.

———. Notebook. Bibliothèque Marguerite Durand, Fond Nelly Roussel.

———. "La Question de la population et la guerre." *La Voix des femmes* March 4, 1920.

———. *Trois conférences de Nelly Roussel.* Paris: Marcel Giard, 1930.

3. Véra Starkoff

Delecraz, Antoine. "Le Théâtre d'Idées." *Comœdia* March 22, 1909: 2.

Effront, Gilles. Personal interview. Paris, January 2001.

Le Senne, Camille. "Revue Théâtrale." *Le Siècle* March 29, 1909: 1.

P. "Le Théâtre d'Idées." *La Française* June 23, 1912: 3.

Peterson, Sonia. Personal interview. Washington D.C., January 2001.

Starkoff, Véra. *Le Bolchevisme.* Paris: Ed. du Fauconnier, 1922.

———. "C'est Tolstoï qui triomphe." *Journal du peuple* February 15, 1918: 2.

———. "Le Crime rituel et le ghetto." *Les Droits de l'homme* 143 (December 13–20, 1913): 2.

———. "Les Décadents Russes." *La Revue* April 1, 1908: 327–331.

———. "Les 'Ennemis' de Maxime Gorky." *La Revue* February 1907: 391–394.

———. *Jalousie* by Tchernichevsky. Translation. [Paris]: Ed. de Floréal, 1923.

———. "Les Origines profondes du communisme russe." *Le Populaire* April 6, 1919: 3.

———. *Rouslane et Ludmile* by Alexandr Sergevitch Pouchkine. Translation. Librairie de l'art indépendante, 1898.

———. *La Sibérie.* Paris: Plon, 1899.

———. "Tchernichevsky." *Portraits d'hier* 30 (June 1, 1910): 163–191.

———. *Le Vrai Tolstoï.* Paris: Eugène Figuière, 1911.

Une Féministe. "Les Réunions féministes." *La Fronde* May 5, 1903: 2.

"Union Fraternelle des Femmes." *La Française* March 15, 1913: 3.

"Véra Starkoff." *L'Ere Nouvelle* March 23, 1923: 3.

Yarin, Jim. "Efron genealogy." Email to the author. December 16, 2000.

Zenkovsky, V. V. *A History of Russian Philosophy.* New York: Columbia UP, 1953.

4. Madeleine Pelletier

Bard, Christine, ed. *Madeleine Pelletier (1874–1939): Logique et infortune d'un combat pour l'égalité.* Paris: Côté-femmes, 1992.

Gordon, Felicia. *The Integral Feminist: Madeleine Pelletier, 1874–193: Feminism, Socialism and Medicine.* Minneapolis: U of Minnesota P, 1990.

Pelletier, Madeleine. "Doctoresse Pelletier: Mémoires d'une féministe." Autobiographical manuscript. Fonds Bouglé, Bibliothèque Historique de la Ville de Paris.

Pelletier, Madeleine. *L'Education féministe des filles*. Paris: Syros, 1978.

———. "Etre Apache." *La Guerre Sociale* June 9–15, 1909: 3.

———. *La Femme vierge*. Paris: Indigo & Côté-femmes, 1996.

———. *Mon Voyage aventureux en Russie Communiste*. Paris: Indigo & Côté-femmes, 1996.

———. "La Tactique de l'attentat." *La Guerre Sociale* July 14–20, 1909: 3.

Pelletier, Madeleine and N. Vaschide. "Les Signes physiques de l'intelligence." *Revue de Philosophie* October 1, 1903: 796–831; February 1, 1904: 168–195.

Sowerine, Charles and Claude Maignien. *Madeleine Pelletier, une féministe dans l'arène politique*. Paris: Editions Ouvrières, 1992.

5. Marie Lenéru

Antoine, André. "Les Affranchis." *Information* October 24, 1927.

Beauplan, Robert de. "*Les Affranchis* à la Comédie-Française." *La Petite Illustration* 358 (November 19, 1927): 23–24.

Blum, Léon. "Les Affranchis." *Comœdia* December 10, 1910: 1.

———. "La Triomphatrice." *Comœdia* June 27, 1922: 1.

Dorgeles, Roland. "Au théâtre." *Lanterne* February 13, 1921: 3.

Forestier, Monique. "Des femmes dans le sillage de Molière et de Shakespeare." *Minerva* December 26, 1937: 7.

Lavaud, Suzanne. *Marie Lenéru: sa vie—son journal—son théâtre*. Paris: Société française d'édition littéraire, 1932.

Lenéru, Marie. *Journal*. Paris: Grasset, 1945.

———. "Le Témoin." *The Book of France*. Ed. Winifred Stephens. London: MacMillan, 1915.

Mondadon, Louis de. "Marie Lenéru." *Les Etudes* September 20 and October 20, 1922 (206–213).

Régis-Leroi. "Souvenirs des heures laborieuses." *Minerva* November 13, 1932: 6.

———. "Les femmes auteurs dramatiques." *Minerva* February 12, 1933: 15.

———. "Lorsque les femmes deviennent auteurs dramatiques: De Marie Lenéru à Anne Mariel, elles abordent tous les genres." *Minerva* June 27, 1937.

"Les Théâtres. Les Premières. À la Comédie-française." *Le Cri de Paris* October 23, 1927: 12.

E. Archives consulted

Archives d'Etat de la République de Canton de Genève:

- AEG, Etrangers, Dj2, 91.

Archives de la Préfecture de Police:

- BA 73–80 Anarchists
- BA 880 Agence Russe (Akim Effront)
- BA 1184–1187 Louise Michel
- BA 1709–1710 Russie

Archives Nationales

- F7 12894 à 12896—Révolutionnaires russes en France (1907–1918)
- F7 13489 Notes Russes
- F7 13506 Le Bolchevisme dans le monde, Russes émigrés
- Fond Société des Gens de Lettres, Dossier Véra Starkoff

Bibliothèque Historique de la Ville de Paris, Fond Bouglé, Dossier Féminisme, Série 83

- Correspondance Céline Renooz-Hélène Slatoff.
- Correspondance Arria Ly-Madeleine Pelletier.
- "Doctoresse Pelletier: Mémoires d'une féministe" (autobiographical manuscript).

Bibliothèque Marguerite Durand

- Dossiers Marya Cheliga, Maria Deraismes, Marie Lenéru, Louise Michel, Madeleine Pelletier, Nelly Roussel, Véra Starkoff, Théâtre-Auteurs, Union Fraternelle des Femmes
- Fond Nelly Roussel

Bibliothèque de l'Arsenal, Collection Rondel

- Recueil Factice about *Les Affranchis* (Rf. 64468).
- Théâtre Féministe International

State Archives of RF (Russian Dept. of Police)
Hoover Institution, Okhrana (files of the Imperial Russian secret police)
Archives of the Université de Genève, Faculté de Lettres, 1884–1901.

Index